Social Change in Migration Globalization

ABOUT THE AUTHOR

Prof.Menon Shroff, is an Ecologist and Environmental Specialist with more than 28 years of academic and consulting experience. He holds a Ph.D in geography from the Univeristy of Birmingham,UK and wrote the Ph.D and Master Academic Programs of Environmental Sciences for the Universidad de Guayana, Venezuela.

ABOUT THE BOOK

Social change as a sociological term is defined as, alterations in basic structures of a social group or society. Social change is an ever present phenomenon in social life, but has become especially intense in the modern era. The origins of modern sociology can be traced to attempts to understand the dramatic changes shattering the modern world and promoting new forms of social order. An example of this is globalization. Migration is a process of social change where an individual, alone or accompanied by others, because of one or more reasons of economic betterment, political upheaval, education or other purposes, leaves one geographical area for prolonged stay or permanent settlement in another geographical area. It must be emphasized that migration is not only a trans-national process but can also be rural–urban. Any such process involves not only leaving social networks behind (which may or may not be well established) but also includes experiencing at first a sense of loss, dislocation, alienation and isolation, which will lead to processes of acculturation. Migration was almost exclusively male, short-term and seasonal, mostly between one and six months at a time. Since then migration has if anything increased further (respondents uniformly reported this), with a greater diversity of migration destinations and durations, and some move towards longer-term migration, especially to urban areas. But there is still very little permanent migration, in the sense of definitive departure of households from the village. The book is expected to be useful for the students of sociology and others who are interested in the studies of social change.

Social Change in Migration Globalization

Prof.Menon Shroff

AMIGA PRESS. INC
Delhi -110051

AMIGA PRESS. INC
H.O :- 28-A, Indra Park, Chander Nagar
Delhi :- 110051 (India)
Tel :- 011-22504028, +91-98736-57000
Email :- info@amigapress.co.in
amigapub@gmail.com
Website :- www.amigapress@co.in

This edition is published by Amiga Press.Inc

ISBN : 978-93-87295-18-6

First Published 2019

Printed and bound in India by Replika Press Pvt. Ltd.

Preface

Social change (or Social development) is a general term which refers to change in the nature, the social institutions, the social behaviour or the social relations of a society, community of people, or other social structures; any event or action that affects a group of individuals that have shared values or characteristics; acts of advocacy for the cause of changing society in a normative way. Social change is a topic in sociology and social work, but also involves political science, economics, history, anthropology, and many other social sciences. Among many forms of creating social change are direct action, protesting, advocacy, community organizing, community practice, revolution, and political activism.

Migration was almost exclusively male, short-term and seasonal, mostly between one and six months at a time. Since then migration has if anything increased further (respondents uniformly reported this), with a greater diversity of migration destinations and durations, and some move towards longer-term migration, especially to urban areas. But there is still very little permanent migration, in the sense of definitive departure of households from the village. The original reason for the growth of migration was lack of employment in the village. This reason continues to be cited by respondents, but nowadays cultivators in the village complain of labour shortage, so lack of local employment may no longer be the main factor. Migration has become a way of life in these two villages, as it has in many parts of Bihar. In 1999, there were already migrants to northwestern India from the majority of households, especially poorer households.

Migration is a process of social change where an individual, alone or accompanied by others, because of one or more reasons of economic betterment, political upheaval, education or other purposes, leaves one geographical area for prolonged stay or permanent settlement in another geographical area. It must be emphasized that migration is not only a trans-national process but can also be rural–urban. Any such process involves not only leaving social networks behind (which may or may not be well established) but also includes experiencing at first a sense of loss, dislocation, alienation and isolation, which will lead to processes of acculturation.

Although few scholars would deny the direct contribution of migration and remittances to the livelihoods and survival of families left behind, the extent to which migration and remittances can bring about sustained human development and economic growth in migrant-sending areas and countries is quite a different question. This issue has been the subject of heated debate over the past four decades, and it is possible to distinguish four periods in the post–Second World War thinking on migration and development. While "developmentalist" optimism dominated in the 1950s and 1960s, large-scale pessimism prevailed in the 1970s and 1980s. This changed with the emergence of more nuanced views in the 1990s and the current rediscovery of remittances, and the concomitant resurgence of optimism on migration and development in recent years. In the developmentalist era of the 1950s and 1960s, it was widely assumed that, through a policy of large-scale capital transfer and industrialization, poor countries would be able to jump on the bandwagon of rapid economic development and modernization.

Recent research on migration, gender and remittances show distinct and disparate behaviours and practices that raise a number of questions and suggest the need for a more complete theory of migration that incorporates notions of cultural dynamics as they relate to behaviour and societal outcomes. For example, migrants to the U.S. from the Dominican Republic show distinct savings and remittance behaviours. Men save to take money home and women do not, instead investing in their new local environs and purchasing durable items. Rural-urban migrants in Thailand also show distinct remittance behaviour. Although men and women are equally likely to migrate, women remit wages and gifts to their parents' home at a significantly higher rate, and are expected to do so. However, more recently there is some evidence that gendered remittance patterns are changing, where men are possibly remitting almost as much as women.

This is a reference book. All the matter is just compiled and edited in nature, taken from the various sources which are in public domain.

The book is expected to be useful for the students of sociology and others who are interested in the studies of social change.

—*Editor*

Contents

1

Modernization of Social Progress

Modernization theory and history have been explicitly used as guides for countries eager to develop rapidly, such as China. Indeed, modernization has been proposed as the most useful framework for World history in China, because as one of the developing countries that started late, "China's modernization has to be based on the experiences and lessons of other countries.".

Theory

According to theories of modernization, each society can in theory develop from traditionalism to modernity, and that those which have made the transition have followed similar paths. The more modern states are wealthier and more powerful, and their citizens freer and having a higher standard of living. According to the Social theorist Peter Wagner, modernization can be seen as processes, and as offensives. The former view is commonly projected by politicians and the media, and suggests that it is developments, such as new data technology or need to update traditional methods, which make modernization necessary or preferable. This view makes critique of modernization difficult, since it implies that it is these developments which control the limits of human interaction, and not vice versa.

The view of modernization as offensives argues that both the developments and the altered opportunities made available by these developments are shaped and controlled by human agents. The view of modernization as offensives therefore sees it as a product of human planning and action, an active process capable of being both changed and criticized.

Modernization emerged in the late 19th century and was especially popular among scholars in the mid-20th century. One foremost advocate was Harvard sociologist Talcott Parsons. The theory stressed the importance of societies being open to change and saw reactionary forces as restricting development.

Maintaining tradition for tradition's sake was thought to be harmful to progress and development. Proponents of modernization lie in two camps, optimists and pessimist. The former view what a modernizer would see as a setback to the theory (events such as the Iranian Revolution or the troubles in Lebanon) as temporary setbacks, with the ability to attain "modernism" still existing. Pessimists would argue that such non-modern areas are incapable of becoming modern.

IDEA OF PROGRESS

In historiography, the Idea of Progress is the theory that advances in technology, science, and social organization inevitably produce an improvement in the human condition.

That is, people can become happier in terms of quality of life (social progress) through economic development (modernization), and the application of science and technology (scientific progress). The assumption is that the process will happen once people apply their reason and skills, for it is not divinely foreordained. The role of the expert is to identify hindrances that slow or neutralize progress.

Historian J. B. Bury wrote in 1920:

> *"To the minds of most people the desirable outcome of human development would be a condition of society in which all the inhabitants of the planet would enjoy a perfectly happy existence....It cannot be proved that the unknown destination towards which man is advancing is desirable. The movement may be Progress, or it may be in an undesirable direction and therefore not Progress..... The Progress of humanity belongs to the same order of ideas as Providence or personal immortality. It is true or it is false, and like them it cannot be proved either true or false. Belief in it is an act of faith."*

Sociologist Robert Nisbet finds that "No single idea has been more important than...the Idea of Progress in Western civilization for three thousand years.", and defines five "crucial premises" of Idea of Progress:

1. value of the past
2. nobility of Western civilization
3. worth of economic/technological growth
4. faith in reason and scientific/scholarly knowledge obtained through reason
5. intrinsic importance and worth of life on earth.

The Idea of Progress emerged primarily in the Enlightenment in the 18th century, although some scholars like Nisbet (1980) have traced it to ancient Christian notions. The theory of evolution in the nineteenth century made progress a necessary law of nature and gave the doctrine its first conscious scientific form. The idea was challenged by the 20th century realization that destruction, as in the two world wars, could grow out of technical progress.

Antiquity

Historian J. B. Bury argued that thought in ancient Greece was dominated by the theory of world-cycles or the doctrine of eternal return, and was steeped in a belief parallel to the Judaic "fall of man," but rather from a preceding "Golden Age" of innocence and simplicity. Time was generally regarded as the enemy of humanity which depreciates the value of the world. He credits the Epicureans with having had a potential for leading to the foundation of a theory of Progress through their materialistic acceptance of the atomism of Democritus as the explanation for a world without an intervening Deity. "For them, the earliest condition of men resembled that of the beasts, and from this primitive and miserable condition they laboriously reached the existing state of civilisation, not by external guidance or as a consequence of some initial design, but simply by the exercise of human intelligence throughout a long period."

Robert Nisbet and Gertrude Himmelfarb have attributed a notion of progress to other Greeks. Xenophanes said "The gods did not reveal to men all things in the beginning, but men through their own search find in the course of time that which is better."

Plato's Book III of *The Laws* depicts humanity's progress from a state of nature to the higher levels of culture, economy, and polity. Plato's *The Statesman* also outlines a historical account of the progress of mankind. The Roman philosopher Seneca recognized the progress of knowledge, but he did not expect from it any improvement in the world, because any advance in the arts and inventions promotes deterioration by ministering to luxury and vice.

Enlightenment

The scientific advances of the 16th and 17th centuries provided a basis for the optimistic outlook of Bacon's 'New Atlantis.' In the 17th century Bernard le Bovier de Fontenelle argued in favour of progress with respect to arts and the sciences, saying that each age has the advantage of not having to rediscover what was accomplished in preceding ages. The epistemology of John Locke provided further support and was popularized by the Encyclopedists Diderot, Holbach, and Condorcet.

Locke had a powerful influence on the American Founding Fathers

In the Enlightenment, French historian and philosopher Voltaire (1694-1778) was a major proponent. At first Voltaire's thought was informed by the Idea of Progress coupled with rationalism. His subsequent notion of the historical Idea of Progress saw science and reason as the driving forces behind societal advancement. The first complete statement of progress is that of Turgot, in his "A Philosophical Review of the Successive Advances of the Human Mind"

(1750). For Turgot progress covers not simply the arts and sciences but, on their base, the whole of culture—manner, mores, institutions, legal codes, economy, and society. [{Condorcet]] pre-dicted the disappearance of slavery, the rise of literacy, the lessening of inequalities between the sexes, reforms of prison harsh prisons and the decline of poverty.

Immanuel Kant (1724-1804) argued that progress is neither automatic nor continuous and does not measure knowledge or wealth, but is a painful and largely inadvertent passage from barbarism through civilization toward enlightened culture and the abolition of war. Kant called for education, with the education of humankind seen as a slow process whereby world history propels mankind toward peace through war, international commerce, and enlightened self-interest.

Scottish theorist Adam Ferguson (1723-1816) defined human progress as the working out of a divine plan, though he rejected predestination. The difficulties and dangers of life provided the necessary stimuli for human development, while the uniquely human ability to evaluate led to ambition and the conscious striving for excellence. But he never adequately analysed the competitive and aggressive consequences stemming from his emphasis on ambition even though he envisioned man's lot as a perpetual striving with no earthly culmination. Man found his happiness only in effort.

American Revolution

The intellectual leaders of the American Revolution—such as Benjamin Franklin, Tom Paine, Thomas Jefferson and John Adams, were immersed in Enlightenment thought and believed the Idea of Progress meant that they could reorganize the political system to the benefit of the human condition—for Americans and also, as Jefferson put it, for an "Empire of Liberty" that would benefit all mankind. Thus was born the idea of inevitable American future progress. What gave the American Revolution its widespread appeal and linked it to all subsequent political revolutions was its association with the Idea of Progress. The most original 'New World' contribution to historical thought was the idea that history is not exhausted but that man may begin again in a new world. Besides rejecting the lessons of the past, the Jeffersonians Americanized the Idea of Progress by democratizing and vulgarizing it to include the welfare of the common man as a form of republicanism.

As Romantics deeply concerned with the past, collecting source materials and founding historical societies, the Founding Fathers were animated by clear principles. They saw man in control of his destiny, saw virtue as a distinguishing characteristic of a republic, and were concerned with happiness, progress, and prosperity. Thomas Paine, combining the spirit of rationalism and romanticism, pictured a time when America's innocence would sound like a romance, and concluded that the fall of America could mark the end of 'the noblest work of human wisdom.'

That human liberty was put on the agenda of fundamental concerns of the modern world was recognized by the revolutionaries as well as by many British commentators. Yet, within two years after the adoption of the Constitution, the American Revolution had to share the spotlight with the French Revolution. The American Revolution was eclipsed, and, in the 20th century, lost its appeal even for subject peoples involved in similar movements for self-determination. Thus, its life as a model for political revolutions was relatively short. The reason for this development lies in the fact that its concerns and preoccupations were overwhelmingly political; economic demands and social unrest remained largely peripheral. After the middle of the 19th century, all political revolutions would ultimately have to involve themselves with social questions and become revolutions of modernization.

But the American Colonies in the 1770s, in contrast to all other colonies, had been modern from the beginning. The American patriots were protecting the modernity and liberty they had already achieved, while later revolutions were fighting to obtain liberty for the first time. However, since so few modern revolutions have evinced much concern for the preservation and extension of human freedom, the American model may still come to provide a lesson for the future.

The notion that America is a highly favourable place for people seeking progress in their own lives comprises the American Dream.

SOCIAL PROGRESS

Social progress is the idea that societies can or do improve in terms of their social, political, and economic structures. The concept of social progress was introduced in the early 19th century social theories, especially those of social evolutionists like Auguste Comte and Herbert Spencer. It was present in the Enlightenment's philosophies of history.

Enlightenment

The big breakthrough to a new idea in Europe Enlightenment, when social commentators and philosophers began to realize that people *themselves* could change society and change their way of life. Instead of being made completely by gods, there was increasing room for the idea that people themselves *made their own society*-and not only that, as Giambattista Vico argued, *because* people practically made their own society, they could also fully comprehend it. This gave rise to new sciences, or proto-sciences, which claimed to provide new scientific knowledge about what society was like, and how one may change it for the better. In turn, this gave rise to progressive opinion, in contrast with conservational opinion.

The social conservationists were skeptical about panaceas for social ills. According to conservatives, attempts to radically remake society normally make things worse. Edmund Burke was the leading exponent of this, although later-day liberals like Hayek have espoused similar views. They argue that society changes organically and naturally, and that grand plans for the remaking of society, like the French Revolution, National Socialism and Communism hurt society by removing the traditional constraints on the exercise of power.

The Notion of Freedom

This new idea implied a new concept of human freedom, i.e. people independently making their own lives using their own judgment. Initially, this concept appeared rather paradoxical; thus, Jean-Jacques Rousseau wrote, "People are born free, but are everywhere in chains". A big breakthrough was the French Revolution of 1789, which inspired a lot of new philosophical thought. In the philosophy of the German thinker Hegel, history radically recasts itself as the continual development of humanity towards ever-greater freedom, continually extending the limits of freedom.

This philosophy is still religious and mystical however, insofar as Hegel sees history as culminating in the unity of God with the world, but at the same time, Hegel also affirmed and imputed a Logos or teleology to human history, and fully recognized that both evolutionary and revolutionary transformations took place in history. This was a hopeful philosophy, which in a rational way sees real progress occurring in history.

It was possible to detect human advances, as well as human regressions to an earlier state. In Hegel's view, if something existed, it was rational. If it passed out of existence, that was because it had become irrational. This contained a very important idea, however poorly expressed, namely that history was not a fluke of fate (a kismet) but that it could be *rationally understood*, at least in principle.

Marxism

Marx developed a theory of historical materialism. He describes the mid-19th century condition in the Communist Manifesto as follows:

> *"The bourgeoisie cannot exist without constantly revolutionizing the instruments of production, and thereby the relations of production, and with them the whole relations of society. Conservation of the old modes of production in unaltered form, was, on the contrary, the first condition of existence for all earlier industrial classes. Constant revolutionizing of production, uninterrupted disturbance of all social conditions, everlasting uncertainty, and agitation distinguish the*

bourgeois epoch from all earlier ones. All fixed, fast frozen relations, with their train of ancient and venerable prejudices and opinions, are swept away, all new-formed ones become antiquated before they can ossify. All that is solid melts into air, all which is holy is profaned, and man is at last compelled to face with sober senses his real condition of life and his relations with his kind."

The capitalism is thought by Marx as a process of continual change, in which the growth of markets dissolve all fixities in human life. This is an almost absolute rejection of the conservative ethos, according to which nothing really changes in human life. Marxism further states that capitalism, in its quest for higher profits and new markets, will inevitably sow the seeds of its own destruction. Marxists believe that, in the future, capitalism will be replaced by socialism and eventually communism.

Modernism

"The reasonable man adapts himself to the world. The unreasonable man persists in trying to adapt the world to himself. Therefore, all progress depends on the unreasonable man."—George Bernard Shaw.

Many advocates of capitalism such as Schumpeter agreed with Marx's analysis of capitalism as a process of continual change through creative destruction, but, unlike Marx, believed and hoped that capitalism could essentially go on forever.

Thus, by the beginning of the 20th century, two opposing schools of thought-Marxism and liberalism-believed in the possibility and the desirability of continual change and improvement. Marxists strongly opposed capitalism and the liberals strongly supported it, but the one concept they could both agree on was modernism.

Modernism is a trend of thought which affirms the power of human beings to make, improve and reshape their society, with the aid of scientific knowledge, technology and practical experimentation. It reaches its extreme limits with the Russian Revolution and the third Chinese revolution, inspired by Marxist ideology.

Here, people claimed such confidence in the ability to change their world for the better, which they thought that, in a relatively short time, largely illiterate peasants could begin to build a just, egalitarian and socialist order in a conscious way, armed with science and technology.

Postmodernism

"As it will be in the future, it was at the birth of Man.

There are only four things certain since Social Progress began.

That the Dog returns to his Vomit and the Sow returns to her Mire." —Rudyard Kipling.

In the postmodernist thought steadily gaining ground from the 1980s, the grandiose claims of the modernizers are steadily eroded, and the very concept of social progress is again questioned and scrutinized. In the new vision, radical modernizers like Stalin and Mao appear as totalitarian despots, whose vision of social progress is held to be totally deformed.

Postmodernists question the validity of 19th century and 20th century notions of progress-both on the capitalist and the Marxist side of the spectrum. They argue that both capitalism and Marxism over-emphasize technological achievements and material prosperity while ignoring the value of inner happiness and peace of mind.

Postmodernism posits that both dystopia and utopia are one and the same, over arching grand narratives with impossible conclusions. The romanticism of our past due to present discontent has set western society into a state of nostalgia where modernism is feared. Here the past is re-presented as solution to our current problems.

Contemporary Trends

In the present time, this trend of thought about social progress leads to four main kinds of responses:

- Neo-conservatism, which returns to the old idea that nothing ever truly changes in the human condition, and the eternal values of religion. The ability of people to change anything other than themselves is vastly overrated. Here, the emphasis is on honouring a traditional way of life which proved itself as superior in the past, to which we should adhere.
- Neo-liberalism, which affirms the power and potential of change, but only on a personal, individual level. The idea that the state should be an instrument of social betterment in society as a whole is totally rejected; only free choices made in markets can hold any promise of social progress.
- Socialism, which argues that state direction of social progress could have very important positive results; at the simplest level, would be able to help the poor by taking from the rich. This leads to the defence of public services and assets, and the case for heavy regulation of market activity.
- Various strands of new radicalism, which begin to question again the objective criteria by which we could measure human social progress. For example, labour productivity might be a criterion of social progress, but how about infant mortality? This kind of thinking rejects the political traditions of the past, and argues that a variety of criteria must be applied to assess social progress. In some cases, this leads to new charters for the moral criteria to which a society should aspire; in other cases,

authentic lived experience in society with all its complexities is emphasized.

PURITY AND POLLUTION

Many status differences in Indian society are expressed in terms of ritual purity and pollution. Notions of purity and pollution are extremely complex and vary greatly among different castes, religious groups, and regions. However, broadly speaking, high status is associated with purity and low status with pollution. Some kinds of purity are inherent, or inborn; for example, gold is purer than copper by its very nature, and, similarly, a member of a high-ranking Brahman, or priestly, caste is born with more inherent purity than a member of a low-ranking Sweeper (Mehtar, in Hindi) caste. Unless the Brahman defiles himself in some extraordinary way, throughout his life he will always be purer than a Sweeper. Other kinds of purity are more transitory—a Brahman who has just taken a bath is more ritually pure than a Brahman who has not bathed for a day. This situation could easily reverse itself temporarily, depending on bath schedules, participation in polluting activities, or contact with temporarily polluting substances.

Purity is associated with ritual cleanliness—daily bathing in flowing water, dressing in properly laundered clothes of approved materials, eating only the foods appropriate for one's caste, refraining from physical contact with people of lower rank, and avoiding involvement with ritually impure substances. The latter include body wastes and excretions, most especially those of another adult person. Contact with the products of death or violence are typically polluting and threatening to ritual purity.

During her menstrual period, a woman is considered polluted and refrains from cooking, worshiping, or touching anyone older than an infant. In much of the south, a woman spends this time "sitting outside," resting in an isolated room or shed. During her period, a Muslim woman does not touch the Quran. At the end of the period, purity is restored with a complete bath. Pollution also attaches to birth, both for the mother and the infant's close kin, and to death, for close relatives of the deceased.

Members of the highest priestly castes, the Brahmans, are generally vegetarians (although some Bengali and Maharashtrian Brahmans eat fish) and avoid eating meat, the product of violence and death. High-ranking Warrior castes (Kshatriyas), however, typically consume nonvegetarian diets, considered appropriate for their traditions of valour and physical strength. A Brahman born of proper Brahman parents retains his inherent purity if he bathes and dresses himself properly, adheres to a vegetarian diet, eats meals prepared only by persons of appropriate rank, and keeps his person away from the bodily exuviae of others (except for necessary contact with the secretions of family infants and small children).

If a Brahman happens to come into bodily contact with a polluting substance, he can remove this pollution by bathing and changing his clothing. However, if he were to eat meat or commit other transgressions of the rigid dietary codes of his particular caste, he would be considered more deeply polluted and would have to undergo various purifying rites and payment of fines imposed by his caste council in order to restore his inherent purity.

In sharp contrast to the purity of a Brahman, a Sweeper born of Sweeper parents is considered to be born inherently polluted. The touch of his body is polluting to those higher on the caste hierarchy than he, and they will shrink from his touch, whether or not he has bathed recently. Sweepers are associated with the traditional occupation of cleaning human feces from latrines and sweeping public lanes of all kinds of dirt. Traditionally, Sweepers remove these polluting materials in baskets carried atop the head and dumped out in a garbage pile at the edge of the village or neighbourhood. The involvement of Sweepers with such filth accords with their low-status position at the bottom of the Hindu caste hierarchy, even as their services allow high-status people, such as Brahmans, to maintain their ritual purity.

Members of the Leatherworker (Chamar) caste are ascribed a very low status consonant with their association with the caste occupation of skinning dead animals and tanning the leather. Butchers (Khatiks, in Hindi), who kill and cut up the bodies of animals, also rank low on the caste hierarchy because of their association with violence and death. However, castes associated with ruling and warfare—and the killing and deaths of human beings—are typically accorded high rank on the caste hierarchy. In these instances, political power and wealth outrank association with violence as the key determinant of caste rank.

Maintenance of purity is associated with the intake of food and drink, not only in terms of the nature of the food itself, but also in terms of who has prepared it or touched it. This requirement is especially true for Hindus, but other religious groups hold to these principles to varying degrees. Generally, a person risks pollution—and lowering his own status—if he accepts beverages or cooked foods from the hands of people of lower caste status than his own. His status will remain intact if he accepts food or beverages from people of higher caste rank. Usually, for an observant Hindu of any but the very lowest castes to accept cooked food from a Muslim or Christian is regarded as highly polluting. In a clear example of pollution associated with dining, a Brahman who consumed a drink of water and a meal of wheat bread with boiled vegetables from the hands of a Sweeper would immediately become polluted and could expect social rejection by his caste fellows. From that moment, fellow

Brahmans following traditional pollution rules would refuse food touched by him and would abstain from the usual social interaction with him. He would not be welcome inside Brahman homes—most especially in the ritually pure kitchens—nor would he or his close relatives be considered eligible marriage partners for other Brahmans.

Generally, the acceptance of water and ordinary foods cooked in water from members of lower-ranking castes incurs the greatest pollution. In North India, such foods are known as *kaccha khana*, as contrasted with fine foods cooked in butter or oils, which are known as *pakka khana* . Fine foods can be accepted from members of a few castes slightly lower than one's own. Local hierarchies differ on the specific details of these rules. Completely raw foods, such as uncooked grains, fresh unpeeled bananas, mangoes, and uncooked vegetables can be accepted by anyone from anyone else, regardless of relative status. Toasted or parched foods, such as roasted peanuts, can also be accepted from anyone without ritual or social repercussions. (Thus, a Brahman may accept gifts of grain from lower-caste patrons for eventual preparation by members of his own caste, or he may purchase and consume roasted peanuts or tangerines from street vendors of unknown caste without worry.)

Water served from an earthen pot may be accepted only from the hands of someone of higher or equal caste ranking, but water served from a brass pot may be accepted even from someone slightly lower on the caste scale. Exceptions to this rule are members of the Waterbearer (Bhoi, in Hindi) caste, who are employed to carry water from wells to the homes of the prosperous and from whose hands members of all castes may drink water without becoming polluted, even though Waterbearers are not ranked high on the caste scale.

These and a great many other traditional rules pertaining to purity and pollution constantly impinge upon interaction between people of different castes and ranks in India. Although to the non-Indian these rules may seem irrational and bizarre, to most of the people of India they are a ubiquitous and accepted part of life. Thinking about and following purity and pollution rules make it necessary for people to be constantly aware of differences in status. With every drink of water, with every meal, and with every contact with another person, people must ratify the social hierarchy of which they are a part and within which their every act is carried out. The fact that expressions of social status are intricately bound up with events that happen to everyone every day—eating, drinking, bathing, touching, talking—and that transgressions of these rules, whether deliberate or accidental, are seen as having immediately polluting effects on the person of the transgressor, means that every ordinary act of human life serves as a constant reminder of the importance of hierarchy in Indian society.

There are many Indians, particularly among the educated urban elite, who do not follow traditional purity and pollution practices. Dining in each others' homes and in restaurants is common among well-educated people of diverse backgrounds, particularly when they belong to the same economic class. For these people, guarding the family's earthen water pot from inadvertent touch by a low-ranking servant is not the concern it is for a more traditional villager. However, even among those people whose words and actions denigrate traditional purity rules, there is often a reluctance to completely abolish consciousness of purity and pollution from their thinking. It is surely rare for a Sweeper, however well-educated, to invite a Brahman to dinner in his home and have his invitation unself-consciously accepted. It is less rare, however, for educated urban colleagues of vastly different caste and religious heritage to enjoy a cup of tea together. Some high-caste liberals pride themselves on being free of "casteism" and seek to accept food from the hands of very low-caste people, or even deliberately set out to marry someone from a significantly lower caste or a different religion. Thus, even as they deny it, these progressives affirm the continuing significance of traditional rules of purity, pollution, and hierarchy in Indian society.

SOCIAL INTERDEPENDENCE

One of the great themes pervading Indian life is social interdependence. People are born into groups—families, clans, subcastes, castes, and religious communities—and live with a constant sense of being part of and inseparable from these groups. A corollary is the notion that everything a person does properly involves interaction with other people. A person's greatest dread, perhaps, is the possibility of being left alone, without social support, to face the necessary challenges of life. This sense of interdependence is extended into the theological realm: the very shape of a person's life is seen as being greatly influenced by divine beings with whom an ongoing relationship must be maintained.

Social interaction is regarded as being of the highest priority, and social bonds are expected to be long lasting. Even economic activities that might in Western culture involve impersonal interactions are in India deeply imbedded in a social nexus. All social interaction involves constant attention to hierarchy, respect, honour, the feelings of others, rights and obligations, hospitality, and gifts of food, clothing, and other desirable items. Finely tuned rules of etiquette help facilitate each individual's many social relationships.

Western visitors to India are sometimes startled to find that important government and business officials have left their posts—often for many days at a time—to attend a cousin's wedding or participate in religious activities in a distant part of the country. "He is out of station and will be back in a week or two," the absent official's officemates blandly explain to the frustrated visitor. What is going on is not laziness or hedonistic recreation, but is the official's proper recognition of his need to continually maintain his social ties with relatives, caste fellows, other associates, and God. Without being enmeshed in such ties throughout life, a person cannot hope to maintain long-term efficacy in either economic or social endeavours. Social bonds with relatives must be reinforced at family events or at rites crucial to the religious community. If this is not done, people who could offer vital support in many phases of life would be alienated.

In every activity, there is an assumption that social ties can help a person and that their absence can bring failure. Seldom do people carry out even the simplest task on their own. From birth onward, a child learns that his "fate" has been "written" by divine forces and that his life will be shaped by a plan decided by more powerful beings. When a small child eats, his mother puts the mouthfuls of food into his mouth with her own hand. When a boy climbs a tree to pluck mangoes, another stands below with a basket to receive them. When a girl fetches water from the well in pots on her head, someone at her home helps her unload the pots. When a farmer stacks sheaves of grain onto his bullock cart, he stands atop the cart, catching the sheaves tossed up to him by his son.

A student applying to a college hopes that he has an influential relative or family friend who can put in a good word for him with the director of admissions. At the age of marriage, a young person expects that parents will take care of finding the appropriate bride or groom and arranging all the formalities. At the birth of a child, the new mother is assured that the child's kin will help her attend to the infant's needs. A businessman seeking to arrange a contract relies not only on his own abilities but also on the assistance of well-connected friends and relatives to help finalize the deal. And finally, when facing death, a person is confident that offspring and other relatives will carry out the appropriate funeral rites, including a commemorative feast when, through gifts of clothing and food, continuing social ties are reaffirmed by all in attendance.

SCIENTIFIC PROGRESS

Scientific progress is the idea that science increases its problem solving ability through the application of some scientific method.

Discontinuous Model of Scientific Progress

Several Philosophers of Science have supported arguments that the progress of science is discontinuous. In that case, progress is not a continuous accumulation, but rather a revolutionary process where brand new ideas are adopted and old ideas become abandoned. Thomas Kuhn was a major proponent of this model of scientific progress, as explained in his book The Structure of Scientific Revolutions. This is especially supported by studying the incommensurability of theories. For example, consider Newtonian mechanics and relativistic mechanics. From a strict vantagepoint, in newtonian mechanics mass and energy are always conserved, where in relativistic mechanics energy and mass are always interchangeable. (Note the difference between the strict vantagepoint, and the layperson's vantagepoint that Newton's theory is applicable at low energies and low velocities relative to the velocity of light.) Because the theories are completely incompatible, scientists using one paradigm will not be able to discuss meaningfully with scientists from the other paradigm.

A discontinuous model of scientific progress may disagree with a realist's construction in the philosophy of science. This is because the intrinsic nature of the objects referred to may change wildly.

History of Science as a Model of Scientific Progress

Another model of Scientific Progress, as put forward by Richard Boyd, and others, is History of Science as a model of scientific progress. In short, methods in science are produced which are used to produce scientific theories, which then are used to produce more methods, which are then used to produce more theories and so on. Note that this does not conflict with a continuous or discontinuous model of scientific progress. This model supports realism in that scientists are always working within the same universe; their theories must be referring to real objects, because they create theories that refer to actual objects that are used later in methods to produce new theories.

A good example supporting realism is the case of the electron. It is hard to prove the existence of an electron because it is so small. However, any microscopist will tell you that he knows an electron exists, because he uses it in his electron microscope.

Origins of the Concept

Early technological and religious traditions did not concern themselves with gaining knowledge in any systematic way, and thus the concept of scientific progress would have been largely alien to them. Societies deeply invested in tradition were primarily occupied with the verbatim passing of thoughts and practises to the next generation, and did not engage in the scientific method. Even if some esoteric traditions may have involved themselves with a rudimentary experimental method as the nucleus of their initiation, they did not overtly separate exploration from instruction. Some classical Greeks like

Hippocrates did systematically gather evidence, but as a *concept* incremental increase of knowledge is first formulated in connection with the art of warfare.

Quotes on Scientific Progress

Dr. Terry Halwes wrote:

"What is required for scientific progress is mainly ordinary curiosity, ordinary awareness, ordinary learning, ordinary reasoning, and fairly ordinary communication. Of course scientists work hard to develop and use precise technical terms for many of the things they talk about, but so do lawyers and golfers and cooks."

Sir Karl Popper wrote in *The Logic of Scientific Discovery*:

The wrong view of science betrays itself in the craving to be right; for it is not his possession of knowledge, of irrefutable truth, that makes the man of science, but his persistent and recklessly critical quest for truth.

The Science Hobbyist says:

Lots of important science comes NOT from proposing hypotheses or even from performing experiments, but instead comes from unguided observation and curiosity-driven exploration: from sniffing about while learning to see what nobody else can see. Scientific discovery comes from something resembling "informed messing around," or unguided play.

PHILOSOPHICAL PROGRESS

A prominent question in metaphilosophy is the that of whether or not philosophical progress occurs, and more so, whether such progress in philosophy is even possible. It has even been disputed, most notably by Ludwig Wittgenstein, whether genuine philosophical problems actually exist. The opposite has also been claimed, most notably by Karl Popper, who held that such problems do exist, that they are solvable, and that he had actually found definite solutions to some of them.

Overview

Some philosophers believe that, unlike scientific or mathematical problems, no philosophical problem is truly solvable in the conventional sense, but rather problems in philosophy are often refined rather than solved. For example Bertrand Russell, in his 1912 book *The Problems of Philosophy* says: "Philosophy is to be studied not for the sake of any definite answers to its questions, since no definite answers can, as a rule, be known to be true, but rather for the sake of the questions themselves."

However, this is not universally accepted amongst philosophers. For example Martin Cohen, in his 1999 iconoclastic account of philosophy, *101 Philosophy Problems*, offers as the penultimate problem, the question of whether or not 'The problem with philosophy problems is that they don't have proper solutions'. He goes on to argue that there is a fundamental divide in philosophy between those who think philosophy is about *clarification* and those who think it is about recognising *complexity*.

According to Cohen, Etienne Bonnot de Condillac and Moritz Schlick illustrate this divide in views of the 'purpose of philosophy'. The former, writing in the eighteenth century, describes someone waking up from a deep sleep to find that they are in the middle of labyrinth together with some other people who are arguing over the general strategy and principles for trying to find the way out. What could appear more ridiculous says Etienne, yet that, he says, is what philosophers are doing, concluding: "It is more important to find ourselves merely where we were at first than to believe prematurely that we are out of the labyrinth."

Cohen contrasts this with the approach of the Logical Positivist movement in the interwar years of the Twentieth Century who, in the spirit of David Hume, wished to consign unanswerable questions 'to the flames'. As the 'hub' of the Logical Positivist circle, Moritz Schlick put it in an article entitled 'Unanswerable Questions' for the journal The Philosopher:

"It is very easy to ask questions the answers to which, we have the strongest reasons to believe, will never be known to any Human being. What did Plato do at eight o'clock in the morning of his fiftieth birthday? How much did Homer weigh when he wrote the first line of the Iliad? Is there a piece of silver to be found on the other side of the moon, three inches long and shaped like a fish? Obviously, men will never know the answers to these questions, however hard they may try.

But at the same time, we know that they would never try very hard. These problems, they will say, are of no importance, no philosopher would worry about them, and no historian or naturalist would care whether he knew the answers or not."

Argument for Progress in Philosophy

If it is conceded that philosophical claims are a function of the sophistication of conceptual distinctions, arguments, and logical tools, and if it is conceded that there has been progress in making conceptual distinctions, progress in our sophistication about the nature of philosophical arguments, and progress in logic, then clearly there is progress in philosophy.

Those who deny progress because of lack of agreement must take stock of the fact that agreements must be relativized to those who are taking part in the discussion. And, of course, there will be degrees of sophistication. For example, someone who lacks sophistication in symbolic logic is not in a position to discuss an argument presented in symbolic form. Or, suppose that one person accuses the other of "begging the question," and the other responds: "So what?" What is the significance of lack of consensus in this instance?

Argument for Lack of Progress in Philosophy

It is often complained that philosophy has developed more slowly than the special sciences, and has not enjoyed the same sort of remarkable and definitive progress seen in chemistry or physics. It is nearly universally agreed (a remarkable feat, amongst philosophers) that this has something to do with the peculiar methods of philosophical inquiry. In particular, philosophy seems to lack the sort of developments that Thomas Kuhn called *paradigms*—achievements which, by their success, clearly determine which sort of questions are to be asked and what sort of considerations count as evidence for or against answers to those questions. However, even if it is common to hear that, there is no consensus on the issue—some philosophers, such as Marx, Sartre, and Barthes, do consider that philosophy is *historical,* i.e. in step with society, a superstructure of it. This amounts to a consideration of the contribution of philosophers of the past as obsolete, or inadequate with respect to synchronic concerns.

Optimism, Pessimism, and Paradigms

But this is where the agreement ends; philosophers differ widely over the exact diagnosis of the situation, and the lesson to be taken from it. They differ, for example, over whether the lack of paradigms is an *accidental* or an *essential* feature of philosophy. We might call the former *optimists* about philosophical progress and the latter *pessimists.*

The optimists (such as the early modern philosophers George Berkeley and David Hume) typically argue that philosophy has not made much progress because philosophers have historically used methods that are unsystematic, obscure, confused, or otherwise unsuccessful; but, citing the example of the revolutionary achievements in the natural sciences during the scientific revolution, they argue that philosophers could enjoy the same sort of progress, rather than endlessly recapitulating the same obscure debates, if only philosophers can find an appropriate paradigm and a clear method for their work. The introduction to David Hume's Treatise of Human Nature is a *locus classicus* of this view; Hume subtitled his book "Being An Attempt To Introduce the Experimental Method of Reasoning Into Moral Subjects."

Pessimists, on the other hand, take the lack of progress to be an *essential* feature—arguing that philosophy *must* remain without paradigms as long as it is remains philosophy rather than something else. One way of putting the worry might be this: for something to count as a paradigm *just is* for it to be the sort of achievement that cuts off certain sorts of foundational worries about the essential nature of the subject-matter and the validity of particular methods for studying it; but these sorts of foundational worries are quintessentially *philosophical* worries. In Kant's words, human reason can say nothing about noumena, things in themselves, but only about phenomena, how things appears to us. Human understanding and thus science doesn't concern itself with the foundations of science, but only of its workings. However, in Kant's mind, this only separated dogmatism from *critique* philosophy: neither sciences nor philosophy must answer questions about noumenons, since this superate their innate capacities. That doesn't mean that it is never worthwhile to set such questions to one side—you can't make any serious progress in *physics,* for example, while you are still arguing over whether it is coherent to talk about laws of nature. But it *does* mean that whatever it is you are doing, you are, in an important respect, *ceasing* to do philosophy. If this is correct, then there is no chance of achieving progress in philosophy by adopting a paradigm—adopting a paradigm can achieve progress in *something else,* but only by making it cease to be philosophy.

Pessimists may also make a historical point about the emergence of the various natural sciences from philosophy. In the ancient and medieval world, nearly all fields of study were considered to be parts of the discipline of philosophy. (This historical reality is still reflected in the institutions of the University, where the highest degree awarded in most academic fields is still the Ph.D., or Doctor of Philosophy.) The clearest point at which the natural sciences diverged from philosophy proper just was when they adopted paradigms for research—especially the work of Galileo and Newton in mechanics. The critical step here is for the pessimist to argue that the natural sciences separated from philosophy *precisely because* they adopted a paradigm—that it was *in virtue of* that change in their direction that they began engaging in scientific rather than philosophical studies.

There seems to be a persuasive case to be made for *that* point, but even if there is the consideration is not necessarily decisive. An optimist might very well accept everything that the pessimist says about the emergence of the natural sciences—and *still* disagree with the conclusion. The argument would go something like this: it might very well be that *natural scientists* stopped doing philosophy in virtue of their adoption of a paradigm during the Scientific Revolution. But that's because they adopted *scientific* paradigms—the achievements that set the course of their research programmes were*experimental* achievements. That doesn't mean that there cannot *also* be paradigms which are specifically *philosophical* achievements. (That is, an achievement which decisively settles *certain* foundational philosophical questions for the purposes of a research programme, but which leaves other *distinctively philosophical* questions open for further inquiry, and which addresses them through *distinctively philosophical* methods.) They might even point to historical examples of seminal philosophical works which have, to some degree or another, played a similar role to paradigm achievements in the natural sciences—landmark, tradition-establishing works such as those of Plato, or Immanuel Kant's three Critiques, or the ground-breaking Analytic works of Bertrand Russell and G. E. Moore.

It seems historically unquestionable that these works have played at least *some* of the roles that Kuhn attributed to paradigms. They did create coherent traditions of research—whether Platonist, Kantian, or Analytic. It also seems that (like scientific paradigms) they achieved this by (1) convincing enough philosophers that the work had decisively settled certain philosophical problems, and (2) redirecting subsequent philosophy into energetic work on a set of specialized questions that the seminal work had left open. Kant's Critical philosophy, for example, was widely understood to put a more or less final end to the debate between rationalism and empiricism by demonstrating that the debate was based on a false alternative. A great deal of post-Kantian philosophy abandoned such debates and redirected its focus toward specific concerns that arise from within the Critiques, such as the foundations of mathematics or the possibility of an intellectual intuition.

On the other hand, it is another question whether works such as these actually live up—and whether they *could ever* live up—to *everything* that Kuhn says about scientific paradigms. Kuhn argues that the history of science is a sort of punctuated equilibrium: when a long period of "normal science" eventually stagnates, and an established paradigm can no longer hold together a coherent tradition of research, progress depends on the establishment of a new paradigm, and a scientific revolution based on this paradigm shift. Once the old paradigm breaks down and the new one is established, there seems to be no going back: the old scientific paradigm is *decisively* repudiated, and simply becomes obsolete. But does such a picture capture the history of philosophy as well as the history of science? The waxing and waning of philosophical traditions seems to be far less decisive and far more cyclical; if this doesn't cast doubt on the notion of philosophical progress *simpliciter,* it does at least tend to suggest that *lasting* progress may be an illusory goal. Similarly, although the works pointed to by optimists have had remarkable impacts in setting research programmes, it's far from clear that the specialized inquiry they inspired plays quite the same role that "normal science" plays in Kuhn's understanding of scientific progress. J. G. Fichte and Arthur Schopenhauer, for example, are sharply differing writers who focused on questions raised by Kant; but Schopenhauer's doctrine of the will or Fichte's dialectical spin on transcendental idealism could hardly be seen as examples of inquiries that close off *fundamental* questions in order to consider technical problems of *application.* At most it seems that Kant's work encouraged these later philosophers to do fundamental work in *different* areas from those that he was taken to have shown fruitless.

Would it have been Worth it, After all?

An answer to the question of whether philosophical practice is *possible,* however, is not the end of the story: it may still leave open the question of whether it is *desirable.* Those who are *optimists* about the prospect for philosophical progress have a pretty clear answer: it is, they could argue, just part of what we *mean* by "progress," that you ought to pursue it if you can get it. But the issue is somewhat trickier for pessimists. If philosophical progress is *not* possible, then there are two different lessons that could be, and have been, taken from that.

Philosophy as Worthless

On the one hand, a pessimist might take the impossibility of scientific progress in philosophy to be a sign that philosophy is a dead-end job—thus, a pessimist about philosophical progress might also be a pessimist about philosophy. The argument goes something like this: scientific progress is what makes an intellectual effort worthwhile; but there is no hope for scientific progress in philosophy; therefore there is no hope for philosophy to be worthwhile. On this view, philosophy is regarded as a sort of pseudoscience which *aspires* to scientific progress, but which (by its very nature) can never *achieve* it; and so it is best abandoned in favour of empirical scientific inquiry. Needless to say, this is not a view that most professional philosophers are particularly fond of or comfortable with, but it does seem to have been the consensus of the Vienna Circle positivists towards more or less all traditional philosophical inquiry, although not necessarily to the use of *philosophical method* to get clear on the logical structure of *empirical* questions. It is, perhaps, much more popular with professional scientists (as some of the Vienna positivists were themselves), who are inclined to think of philosophy as airy speculation that retards the serious empirical work of science.

Philosophy as Intrinsically Worthy

However, this critique of metaphysics, carried on by the first Wittgenstein, in his 1921 *Tractatus Logico-Philosophicus*, for example, has been in return criticized by philosophers, such as Heidegger in his 1927 *Being and Time*, as a form of positivism or, worse, scientism, which is accused of having decided to abandon the most important questions about humanity and the Being, under the pretext that no definitive answer can be brought to them.

Marxist Georg Lukacs would also criticize, in his book *History and Class Consciousness* (1923), the Kantian abandon of knowledge of the *concrete totality*:

according to Lukacs, Kant's distinction between noumenons and phenomena lead to the abandon of the knowledge of the historical process, which could be only apprehended, in his eyes, by dialectical materialism. As marxism is essentially concerned with the historical process and the possibility of a revolution, that is of superating capitalism, marxist philosophy, from Marx and Engels to Althusser passing by Lukacs, etc., has discussed at lengths the problems of possible historical progress of philosophy and what would that mean.

Althusser, for example, considered the "epistemological break" (separating protosciences from sciences) to apply itself to philosophy itself: the discovery by Marx of a new "continent" of knowledge, History, provided the epistemological break between ancient metaphysics and modern dialectical materialism. However, if dialectical materialism was considered by Althusser as a "scientific theory", this does not mean it was permanently assured of its truth: it is a science, not a prophecy! In effect, Althusser stressed that the epistemological break was not an *event*, which could be chronologically located (in this or that book of Marx) and thus definitively separated science from ideology.

Instead, this epistemological break was a *process* that had to be endlessly renewed, thus explaining revisionist tentatives to break away from this progress and renew with the old protoscientifical (and "bourgeois") theory, which ignored the social and historical conditions which made human society what it is. Althusser's theory is interesting insofar as, contrary to Kuhn, it does not considers various paradigms to be incommensurable between themselves. In Kuhn's eyes, Ancient's sciences simply can't be compared to modern science, and they have nothing in common.

Althusser argues that this amounts to deny progress between modern sciences and ancient sciences, since the cumulative aspect of progress is ignored. However, the cumulative aspect of progress, both in philosophy and science, is not considers by Althusser as obtained "once for all": it is always a political struggle against ideology, which endlessly penetrates science and philosophy. This explains his famous word about the existence of "class struggle inside the theory" itself. Although Althusser's marxist philosophy may repels many people today, his criticisms of the notion of a "neutral science", which followed the Frankfurt School's criticisms of scientifical and technical progress, and his conception of a cumulative although discontinuous "progress" of philosophy represents one of the toughest attempt to think a cumulative progress of sciences and philosophy (both subsumed under the term of "theory") without falling into a plain scientist optimism about a "continuous and linear necessary progress". As in any marxist theory, ultimately theory is dependent on human *praxis*, and only the rebellion and continuous struggle against the dominant ideology that allows theory, whether scientific or philosophical, to be truly an objective theory.

Henceforth, one might draw the conclusion that pessimism about philosophical progress allows for a sort of *liberation* from the expectations for scientific progress, and thus for a *reasoned optimism* about philosophy. Philosophers in this camp argue that once we recognize that it makes no sense for philosophy to *make* scientific-technical progress, we ought to also realize that it makes no sense for philosophy to *aspire* to it either. In other words, philosophy is not science, and shouldn't imitate sciences. Rather than expect philosophy to prove its worth with scientific-technical progress, and then judge it worthless when it fails to, these philosophers argue that philosophical inquiry must be worthy *in its own right.*

The perceived need for philosophy to prove itself in terms of some sort of scientific-technical progress is often diagnosed as a sort of creeping scientism, and repudiated as a drastic oversimplification of our intellectual life. This *may* have been the position of Wittgenstein against the Vienna positivists—although if Wittgenstein saw any intrinsic value in philosophical inquiry he certainly didn't think that most people could profit from it. In any case, it was certainly the position of latter Wittgensteinians such as Peter Winch, as well as other contemporary philosophers such as Heidegger. The view also, its proponents argue, represents a "return" to the conception of philosophy and its value found in ancient philosophers such as Plato and Aristotle.

In *What Is Philosophy?* (1991), Deleuze and Guattari would argue that while science creates percepts and art affects, philosophy creates concepts. These concepts are *not* answers to existential questions, but a specific way of conceiving the *problem*. In other words, the accent is not, as in science, put on the answer or explanation given to a specific phenomenon, but on the way the problem itself is posed.

An illustration of this may be given by Marx's critique of political economy: *bourgeois* political economy is denounced as concerning itself with only how the capitalism system works day-to-day, but doesn't poses the problem of *how* capitalism first appeared, what are the conditions of possibility of this appearance of capitalism and, finally, what are the conditions of its dissolving. Hence, while ordinary political economy is concerned by the so-called "laws of economics", presented as universal (i.e. valid in all times and places), marxism attempts to demonstrate that these principles are only historical products of human history. A historian such as Fernand Braudel, for example, would be more interested in trying to answer the question of why capitalism appeared in Europe and not in China, exploring the historical conditions which made capitalism possible, than describing the "laws of economics".

Philosophy as Instrumentally Worthy

Nor do these alternatives exhaust the possibilities: one might agree with the optimists that philosophical inquiry *has* value, but agree with the pessimists that philosophical inquiry must justify itself in terms of scientific-technical progress to have any value. This may seem to conflict with the shared premise between progress-pessimists that there is no progress in philosophy, but the trick here is to argue that *philosophical* progress is not the only sort of progress to which philosophical inquiry might contribute. Philosophy is seen as being justified by progress—but not by progress in *philosophy*, but rather in providing *useful tools* for making progress in *other fields*.

Since this view values philosophy as a means to an end rather than as an end in itself, we might call it "instrumental optimism" about philosophy, as opposed to the "intrinsic optimism" already discussed. On this view, philosophy is seen neither as a sort of pseudoscience, nor as something *radically distinct* from the sciences, but rather as a sort of *incubator for new sciences* — protosciences. While the intrinsic optimists draw on Plato and Aristotle's writings on the value of philosophical inquiry, the instrumental optimists can draw on another aspect of the ancients' work: specifically, Aristotle was concerned both about "physics" (and biology) and "metaphysics". He didn't really make any distinction between these two fields. Actually, the name "meta-physics" was given by later scholars who meant by this word: what is "beyond" or "after" the study of "nature" (*phusis*-physics).

Thus, "philosophy" ("love of wisdom" in Greek) at that time included both "physics" and "metaphysics". Instrumental optimists thus argue this non-distinction between physics and metaphysics, and point out the historical role that the Ancient's philosophical works played in the development of the natural sciences, and then later the social sciences. From this history instrumental optimists might urge that speculative philosophy can have value as a place for proposing new sciences and new research programmes within the sciences, as well as a critical location for exposing and clearing away confusions that obstruct progress in the natural sciences. Philosophy, then, is seen as a sort of midwife: she does not give birth to any progress of her own, but proves her worth by making it possible for others to bring *their* progress into the world. Thus, whereas the value of mechanics or biology or psychology is taken to be *internal* to the practice (i.e., judged in terms of the progress of *mechanical, biological,* or *psychological* achievements), the value of *philosophy* is taken to be *external* (i.e., judged in terms of its effects on achievements in other fields, such as mechanics, biology, and psychology). This view is congenial to the conception of philosophy, most famously propounded by John Locke, as a sort of intellectual "underlabourer" to the sciences. It is also a view endorsed in various articles by Hilary Putnam, and may be the most popular view amongst contemporary Analytic philosophers—especially those with a naturalistic bent.

Instrumental optimism is, of course, not without its own difficulties. For example, there's hardly any reason to deny the truth of what the instrumental optimists say about the historical relationship between what some philosophers did and what natural scientists do today. But that doesn't necessarily mean that the ancients philosophers were doing *philosophy* when they did work that contributed to natural science. Of course, they might have *called* what they were doing "philosophy." But if so, that just means that they meant something more expansive by the word than what we mean by it today, and we might think that there are perfectly good reasons for sticking to the narrower conception of philosophical method. Moreover, whatever the status of their works that eventually contributed to natural science, and whatever the value of those contributions it's very difficult to make a case that the *philosophical* value is best captured by its contribution to scientific posterity. (Is the lasting value of Aristotle's work better exhibited by his Physics or by his Metaphysics? By his reflections on horse's teeth or on the good life for rational beings?)

Critics of this conception of philosophy as being essentially an epistemology (or philosophy of science) dedicated to exploring psychic or ideological blocks which prevent scientifics from making specific hypothesis (such as in Gaston Bachelard's theory) argue that this only reverse the hierarchy between philosophy and science. Instead of philosophy being located on top of the pyramid of knowledge, as in Hegel's *Phenomenology of Spirit*, it becomes a simple tool for rationalism and sciences.

This view has been criticized by certain philosophers, such as Deleuze or Michel Foucault, who declared that Thought couldn't be identified to rationalism, and that irrationalism wasn't to be considered as the contrary of thought (i.e. as madness, which, as Foucault demonstrated, is the product of a historical conception and disciplinary technologies of power). Deleuze, for example, argued that thought, which could take the form of philosophy, arts or sciences, basically *created* new possibilities of thought and life, and therefore new modes of existence.

This liberty of thought was, in the eyes of these French philosophers, the only real "use" of philosophy-although Deleuze mocked the utilitarian view which would assigned to philosophy a specific "use", which could, in his mind, only be ideologically assigned. This joins a critique of science often made, first of all by the Frankfurt School: scientific research only tries to resolve certain problems and exclude others. For example, tropical diseases are not subject to much research, as it is not considerated profitable by the pharmaceutical industry. On the other side, fat or sex-issues are considered much more important, thus allowing for the huge investments necessary to the invention of Viagra. Henceforth, saying something is "useful" only extends the problem to the criteria of this "usefulness": science is often said "useful" because it has "practical effects", which "philosophy" doesn't seems to have. However, is science that ignores tropical diseases in order to concentrate itself on Viagra really is useful? Does it helps to have, as in Aristotle's views, a "good life"? This explains why Deleuze rejected the definition of philosophy as something "useful", and preferred it to be an "opening of possibles", something which made new possible worlds possible.

Nor, of course, does accepting the instrumental value of philosophy for other fields require one to abandon the view that philosophy *also* has *intrinsic* worth, nor the view that its intrinsic worth should be the primary reason to pursue philosophical inquiry. Some things are valued both for themselves and for their consequences; if the instrumental optimist wants (as some of them surely *do*) to insist not only on accepting the instrumental worth of philosophy, but also of accepting *nothing but* its instrumental worth, then she must *support* the stronger claim that philosophy could *only* have value in virtue of its contribution to scientific-technical progress in *some* field or another. But, if philosophy is like a mother-lode for the nascent sciences, so too like a godmother, philosophy has traditions which can guide her godchildren past ethical and moral quagmires, into which they might stray, to the detriment of their progress.

THEMES IN INDIAN SOCIETY

India is a hierarchical society. Within Indian culture, whether in the north or the south, Hindu or Muslim, urban or village, virtually all things, people, and groups of people are ranked according to various essential qualities. If one is attuned to the theme of hierarchy in India, one can discern it everywhere. Although India is a political democracy, in daily life there is little advocacy of or adherence to notions of equality.

Castes and castelike groups—those quintessential groups with which almost all Indians are associated—are ranked. Within most villages or towns, everyone knows the relative rankings of each locally represented caste, and people's behaviour toward one another is constantly shaped by this knowledge. Between the extremes of the very high and very low castes, however, there is sometimes disagreement on the exact relative ranking of castes clustered in the middle.

Castes are primarily associated with Hinduism but also exist among other Indian religious groups. Muslims sometimes expressly deny that they have castes—they state that all Muslims are brothers under God—but observation of Muslim life in various parts of India reveals the existence of castelike groups and clear concern with social hierarchy. Among Indian Christians, too, differences in caste are acknowledged and maintained.

Throughout India, individuals are also ranked according to their wealth and power. For example, there are "big men" (*bare admi,* in Hindi) and "little men" (*chhote admi*) everywhere. "Big men" sit confidently on chairs, while "little men" come before them to make requests, either standing or crouching down on their haunches, certainly not presuming to sit beside a man of high status as an equal. Even men of nearly equal status who might share a string cot to sit on take their places carefully—the higher-ranking man at the head of the cot, the lower-ranking man at the foot.

Within families and kinship groupings, there are many distinctions of hierarchy. Men outrank women of the same or similar age, and senior relatives outrank junior relatives. Several other kinship relations involve formal respect. For example, in northern India, a daughter-in-law of a household shows deference to a daughter of a household. Even among young siblings in a household, there is constant acknowledgment of age differences: younger siblings never address an older sibling by name, but rather by respectful terms for elder brother or elder sister. However, an older sibling may address the younger by name.

Even in a business or academic setting, where colleagues may not openly espouse traditional observance of caste or class ranking behaviour, they may set up fictive kinship relations, addressing one another by kinship terms reflecting family or village-style hierarchy. For example, a younger colleague might respectfully address an older colleague as *chachaji* (respected father's younger brother), gracefully acknowledging the superior position of the older colleague.

2

Migration and Cultural Identity

In this section, the focus is on cultural identity among black and ethnic minority groups in the UK. However, it is essential that we are clear about the definitions of ethnicity being applied. Ethnic identity depends upon the cultural or physical criteria which set the group apart. An ethnic *group* may set itself apart using superiority or inferiority on the basis of real or alleged physical characteristics and/or placed on cultural criteria, which set the group apart. Ethnicity is a common heritage shared by a particular group and will include history, language, rituals, preference for music and food. Although there may be an overlap between race and ethnicity each has a different social meaning.

Racial identity refers to a sense of group or collective identity based on the perception that the individual shares a common racial heritage with a particular racial group. With racial identity, individuals are seen as inside or outside a particular biological group. This differentiation between ethnic and racial group is helpful to a degree but can also be criticized for helping to create stereotypes and over generalizations, thereby further compounding the complexity of the problem. In practice, the concepts of ethnic, racial and cultural identities are often not easily distinguishable. Berry recommends using the term *ethnocultural identity*. When studying migrants, and their health and health behaviour, acculturation (the adoption of the values and behaviours of the surrounding culture) and cultural identity have to be studied at both individual and group levels.

MIGRATION AND ACCULTURATION

When individuals migrate they do not leave their beliefs or idioms of distress behind, no matter what the circumstances of their migration. Their beliefs influence their idioms of distress, which influence how they express symptoms and their help-seeking behaviour. For example, a study of Punjabi women who had been in the UK for a number of years found that they maintained the belief that depression was not a medical condition. Although they recognized its symptoms and also identified various aetiological and perpetuating factors, their method of help-seeking was related to their explanatory models—which led them to seek help from religious practitioners and by reading scriptures rather than seeking medical help from statutory services because they believed that this stigmatizes them and their families. They saw depression as a part of life's ups and downs and there was nothing that doctors could do about it.

When two cultures come in contact, then a number of events may occur. Berry suggests that the process of acculturation is akin to the psychological models of moving towards, moving against and moving away from a stimulus. This change will correspond to adaptation or simulation, rejection and deculturation. The process of acculturation requires two cultures to come into contact and both cultures may experience some change. In reality, however, one cultural group will often dominate the other group.

Acculturation has been defined as a 'phenomenon' which results when groups of individuals from different cultures come into continuous first hand contact with subsequent changes in the original culture patterns of either one or both groups. For clinicians, it is helpful to have a notion of acculturation so that the individual's psychological distress can be understood in the context of what is happening to them and their cultural changes in identity.

Berry has identified assimilation (where cultural differences disappear), although others have argued that assimilation and acculturation are similar. Gordon differentiates between structural, identification and behavioural assimilation. Berry recommends looking at the exposure between two cultures in terms of rejection (the individual or the group withdraws from the larger society) and deculturation (loss of cultural identity, alienation and acculturative stress). In rejection, the extreme outcome may be apartheid or segregation and in deculturation, the outcome may lead to ethnocide. The individual and group identities may well respond in different ways at different levels.

At an individual level in terms of behaviour, six domains have been identified which can be linked with acculturation. These include language, religion, entertainment, food and shopping habits. Other areas, which may be more difficult to identify and measure, include cognitive styles, behavioural patterns and attitudes.

These elements of the concept of acculturation are very closely linked with self-esteem and identity of the self as culture and personality are inter-linked. In a study of Puerto Ricans in the USA, Cortes found that feelings of nostalgia and disillusionment were linked with beliefs about depression. Childhood or early experiences and socialization may also play a role; child rearing differences across cultures too will contribute to this. Clinicians must remember that none of these acculturative processes are static and these acts keep occurring and the individual keeps responding to these acts.

With acculturation, some aspects of identity are likely to change, including the concept of self, and this will be dependent upon the cultural context. A person's identity is defined as the totality of one's self—formed by how one construes oneself in the present, how one construed oneself in the past and how one construes oneself as one aspires to be in the future. Two points need to be emphasized here. Firstly that racial, ethnic and cultural identities form part of one's identity, and secondly, the development of identity and the resulting changes owing to migration and acculturation will change the construction of identity. Gender, familial and socio-economic factors also contribute to identity.

Acculturation can occur at the psychological level as well as at the cultural level. There are a number of reasons why understanding the process of acculturation is important for those who may be concerned with the health of migrants. Persistent problems in cultural adaptation are associated with a higher risk for long-term mental health problems.

Many factors play a role in the process of acculturation: the effects of pre-migration trauma, post-migration factors such as loss of social roles, confidants, attitudes, *etc.*, socio-demographic factors such as age, sex, education and economic status, and the effects of cultural orientation, *e.g.* assimilation (becoming a part of the majority culture), separation (becoming alienated), biculturalism (feeling reasonably comfortable in both the cultures) and marginalization (becoming withdrawn and isolated from both the cultures) and acceptance from the host society. The role of spirituality and religiosity also has to be understood. Assessing the relationship between acculturation and mental health thus poses important theoretical and empirical challenges. Many mental health measures have been developed for American and European groups but are frequently used for minorities without any adaptation. This raises questions as to the validity of such measures when used in this way.

However, a further important point is that of Hofstede's descriptions of cultures, as individualistic and collectivist. *Individualism* refers to a society where the ties between individuals are loose and everyone is expected to look after himself/herself and his/her immediate family. *Collectivism* refers to a society in which people from birth onwards are cohesively integrated and which throughout their lifetime continues to protect them from aggression from outsiders in exchange for unquestioning loyalty. Hofstede suggests that individualistic societies emphasize 'I' consciousness: autonomy, emotional independence, individual initiative, the right to privacy, pleasure seeking, financial security and the need for specific friendship and universalism.

Collective societies stress 'we' consciousness: collective identity, emotional inter-dependence, group solidarity, sharing, duties and obligations, the need for stable and predetermined friendships, group decisions and particularism. These are paralleled at the individual psychological level by *idiocentrism* and *allocentrism*, respectively.

Individualistic societies support the basic tenets of liberalism whereas those of collectivist societies support traditionalism. The former assumes that individuals are rational and able to use reason to make personal choices and therefore they should be given individual rights to choose freely and to define their own goals. At the interpersonal level, the individuals are seen as discreet, autonomous, self-sufficient and respectful to the rights of others. From a societal point of view, these individuals are abstract and universal and their status and role defined by their achievement (*e.g.* occupational, economic and educational status).

The individual members' interaction with others is based on equality, equity, non-interference and detachability. Collectivist societies, therefore, prioritize common good and social harmony over individual interests.

Individuals are bound by relationships, which emphasize a common fate. Individuals are encouraged to put other people and the group's interest before their own. Concession and compromise are essential ingredients in promoting role-based and virtue-based conceptions of justice, and institutions are seen as an extension of the family—and paternalism and legal moralism reign supreme. Triandis differentiates between the individualistic self—'I am kind, my strengths are...' and the collectivist self—'my family expects me to be kind', 'my co-workers believe that my strengths are...'

Individualism has been shown to be related to high levels of GNP but extreme individualism can lead to several forms of social pathology such as high crime, suicide, divorce, child abuse, emotional stress and physical and mental illness. Allocentric persons tend to have happy marriages and are more likely to receive social support that acts as a buffer for life change stresses. Allocentric individual defines self in terms of in-group relationships and knows more about others than selves.

In-group goals have primacy over personal goals and cognitions are context-dependent. The way people think for example for procreation and partnerships is influenced by cultural norms.

The attitudes of allocentric individuals reflect interdependence and their values are that of security, obedience, and duty, in group harmony, hierarchy and personalized relationships. A major calamity for this group is ostracization by others. Their values are of pleasure, achievement, competition, freedom, autonomy and fair exchange.

Thus, it is likely that allocentric individuals from a collectivist society will face different types of stresses if they migrate to an individualistic society and their social links are with idiocentric individuals. Similarly idiocentric individuals from collectivist society who migrate to individualistic societies and come across idiocentric individuals may have different experiences. Schwartz further described mastery, hierarchy, conservatism, harmony, autonomy-intellectual or affective and egalitarian commitment. In order to understand the impact of migration on an individual, the characters of their group and the groups they originate from have to be studied with respect to these concepts. Not surprisingly, the People's Republic of China scored high on mastery and hierarchy and other Western nations such as France, Israel, Portugal and Switzerland scored highly on autonomy, conservatism and egalitarian commitment. Hofstede, demonstrates that such cultural concepts can be unpackaged into a set of interpretable etic (an outsider's understanding of another culture) dimensions on which specific nations and cultures can be compared. It is worth using the same concepts for understanding both the aetiology and management of psychiatric problems in different migrant groups; interaction with acculturation comes into play as well.

ETHNIC DIVERSITY *VERSUS* ETHNIC IDENTITY: A NEW HYPOTHESIS

As discussed at the beginning of this chapter, it is clear that the rates of schizophrenia amongst African–Caribbeans are elevated. Although it has been argued that all migrant groups to the UK have higher-than-expected rates, this has not been a consistent finding. It has been suggested that South Asians in the UK are more likely to be living in high-density areas where there are other Asians with possibly more social contact and traditional (collectivist) views which may explain low rates of schizophrenia in this group.

Boydell *et al* reported that low ethnic density of black individuals in an electoral ward may contribute to an increase in the incidence rates of schizophrenia. These rates nearly doubled if the population density of ethnic minorities fell to one-third of the base population in particular electoral wards. Rosenberg described the context of dissonant religions in high schools in New York. After stratifying the populations of public schools, the students were given three questionnaires. Respondents were asked about the religious affiliations of the neighbourhood they had lived in the longest and found that the experience of living in the context of a dissonant religion had certain psychic consequences for the individual. In every case, Rosenberg found the students who had been raised in a dissonant context were more likely than those who had been reared in a consonant or mixed religious environment to manifest psychic or emotional disturbance.

MIGRATION, REMITTANCES AND DEVELOPMENT

Although few scholars would deny the direct contribution of migration and remittances to the livelihoods and survival of families left behind, the extent to which migration and remittances can bring about sustained human development and economic growth in migrant-sending areas and countries is quite a different question. This issue has been the subject of heated debate over the past four decades, and it is possible to distinguish four periods in the post–Second World War thinking on migration and development. While "developmentalist" optimism dominated in the 1950s and 1960s, large-scale pessimism prevailed in the 1970s and 1980s. This changed with the emergence of more nuanced views in the 1990s and the current rediscovery of remittances, and the concomitant resurgence of optimism on migration and development in recent years.

Developmentalist and Neoclassical Views

In the developmentalist era of the 1950s and 1960s, it was widely assumed that, through a policy of large-scale capital transfer and industrialization, poor countries would be able to jump on the bandwagon of rapid economic development and modernization. In the same period, large-scale labour migration from developing to developed countries began to gain momentum. Many developing countries (such as the source countries of "guest workers" in the Mediterranean) became involved in the migration process amidst these expectations of the "dawning of a new era" (Papademetriou 1985:212). Governments of developing countries started to actively encourage emigration since they considered it as one of the principal instruments to promote national development.

Developmentalist "migration optimists" tend to think that migration leads to a North-South transfer of investment capital and accelerates the exposure of traditional communities to liberal, rational and democratic ideas, modern knowledge and education. From this perspective, (return) migrants are perceived as important agents of change, innovators and investors. The general expectation was that the flow of remittances—as well as the experience, skills and knowledge that migrants would acquire abroad before returning—would greatly help developing countries in their economic take-off. Return migrants were expected to invest large sums of money in enterprises in the country of origin. Interestingly, this optimistic view has recently experienced a renaissance, although it is now linked to (neo)liberal, rather than the state-centrist, visions of development policy that predominated in the 1950s and 1960s. Neoclassical economists also tend to see migration in a positive light. However, it is important to note that neoclassical migration theory has no place for remittances (Taylor

1999:65). Neoclassical advocates of the theoretical model of balanced growth perceive migration as a process that contributes to the optimal allocation of production factors for the benefit of all, in which the process of factor price equalization will lead to migration ceasing once wage levels are equal at both the origin and destination. From this perspective, the re-allocation of labour from rural, agricultural areas (within and across national boundaries) to urban, industrial sectors is considered as an essential prerequisite for economic growth and, hence, as an integral component of the whole development process (Todaro 1969:139). The free movement of labour—in an unconstrained market environment—is eventually expected to lead to the increasing scarcity of labour, which will then lead to a higher marginal productivity of labour and increasing wage levels in migrant-sending societies. Capital flows are expected to go in exactly the opposite direction as labour migration.

So, in a strictly neoclassical world, the developmental role of migration is entirely realized through this process of factor price equalization. Until recently, this neoclassical view of migration and development was dominant in international financial institutions. For instance, the "Policies toward migration" section of the *Globalization, Growth, and Poverty* report of the World Bank (2002) saw the benefits of migration for receiving countries uniquely in terms of factor price equalization, and did not mention remittances at all. This is in contrast with Ratha's (2003) chapter entitled "Workers' remittances: An important and stable source of external development finance" in the World Bank's *Global Development Finance* only one year later, and which played a major role in the sudden resurgence in the interest for remittances.

Historical Structural and Dependency Views

The 1973 oil crisis heralded a period of worldwide economic downturn, industrial restructuring and increasing unemployment. It was also thought that the great age of international migration had ended. This more or less coincided with a turning point in thinking on migration and development. As of the late 1960s, optimistic views on migration and development in sending areas were increasingly challenged due to the combined influence of a paradigm shift in social sciences toward (historical) structuralist views and an increasing number of empirical studies that often did not support optimistic views on migration and development.

An increasing number of academic studies seemed to support the hypothesis that migration sustains or even reinforces problems of underdevelopment instead of the reverse. These "migration pessimists" have argued that migration provokes the withdrawal of human capital and the breakdown of traditional, stable village communities and their economies. This would then lead to the development of passive, non-productive and remittance-dependent communities. Besides the "brain drain" (Adams 1969), a "brawn drain" (Penninx 1982)—the massive departure of young, able-bodied men and women from rural areas (Lewis 1986)—is typically blamed for causing a critical shortage of agricultural and other labour, depriving areas of their most valuable work force. Because it is generally not the poorest who migrate the most, migration and remittances were also believed to increase inequality in communities of origin (Lipton 1980).

Migration pessimists have also argued that remittances were mainly spent on conspicuous consumption and "consumptive" investments (such as houses), and rarely invested in productive enterprises. Scepticism about the use of migrant remittances for productive investments became the common thread of the migration and development debate. Besides weakening local economies and increasing dependency, increased consumption and land purchases by migrants were also reported to provoke inflationary pressures (Russell 1992) and soaring land prices.

Also, in a sociocultural respect, the effects of migration and remittances were increasingly seen as detrimental. Exposure to the wealth of migrants was assumed to contribute to a change in rural tastes (Lipton 1980) that would increase the demands for imported urban or foreignproduced goods and food. This would further reinforce the cycle of increasing dependency. Migration has often been held responsible for the loss of community solidarity and undermining the sociocultural integrity of migrant-sending communities (Hayes 1991). Moreover, the main "positive" effect of migration, the increase in family welfare for migrants and their families, was considered to be artificial and dangerous, because remittances were supposed to be an unstable and temporary source of revenue.

From this perspective, South-North migration was perceived as discouraging instead of encouraging the autonomous economic growth of migrant-sending countries. Such views conform to the historical-structuralist paradigm on development that perceives migration as one among many other expressions of the developing world's increasing dependency on the global political-economic systems dominated by the powerful (Western) states. As a natural outgrowth of capitalist penetration, migration was seen as having ruined traditional peasant societies by undermining their economies and uprooting their populations.

In particular, the dependency school of development thinking viewed capitalist penetration and its concomitant phenomena such as migration not only as detrimental to the economies of underdeveloped countries, but also as the very *causes* of the "development of underdevelopment" (Frank 1966). In a process known as cumulative causation (Myrdal 1957), increasing prosperity in the economic core areas of the Western world was causally linked to the draining of capital and labour from peripheral areas. In fact, these approaches turned the argument of neoclassical and developmentalist approaches upside down: migration does not decrease, but instead reinforces spatial and interpersonal disparities in development.

In neo-Marxist terms, migration and remittances reproduce and reinforce the capitalist system based on inequality. Although these pessimistic views have been increasingly contested in recent years, they have remained prevalent in some recent studies. Dependency and structuralist perspectives are not alone in making the point that migration can exacerbate international inequalities and can lead to a concentration of qualified human resources in a few recipient countries. New research, partly based on endogenous growth theories with increasing returns, also predicts this result (Solimano forthcoming).

New Economics of Labour Migration and Livelihood Approaches

In the 1980s and 1990s, the new economics of labour migration (NELM) emerged mainly within the American research context as a response to developmentalist and neoclassical theories (the migration optimists) and structuralist theory (the migration pessimists). Such approaches seemed too rigid and determinist to deal with the complex realities of the migration and development interactions. NELM offered a much more subtle view of migration and development, which links causes and consequences of migration more explicitly, and in which both positive and negative development responses are possible.

Stark (1978, 1991), in particular, revitalized academic thinking on migration from the developing world by placing the behaviour of individual migrants within a wider societal context and considering the *household*—rather than the individual—as the most appropriate decision-making unit (Taylor 1999). This new approach models migration as the risk-sharing behaviour of households. Better than individuals, households seem able to diversify resources such as labour in order to minimize income risks. This approach integrates motives other than individual income maximization that play a role in migration decision making. Migration is perceived as a household response to income risks since migrant remittances serve as income insurance for households of origin. This can theoretically explain why people migrate even in the absence of substantial income differentials. In addition to its contribution to more stable and secure household livelihoods, NELM scholars argue that migration plays a vital role in providing a potential source of investment capital, which is especially important in the context of the imperfect credit (capital) and risk (insurance) markets that prevail in most developing countries. Such markets are often weakly developed and inaccessible to non-elite groups. Hence, migration can be considered as a livelihood strategy to overcome various market constraints, potentially enabling households to invest in productive activities and improve their livelihoods. This went along with fundamental criticism on the weak methodological foundations, poor analytical quality or empiricist character of much prior research, which often failed to take into account the complex, often indirect, positive impacts of migration and remittances on migrant-sending communities as a whole, including non-migrant households.

NELM has striking—though as yet unobserved—conceptual parallels with the *livelihood approaches* that evolved as of the late 1970s among geographers, anthropologists and sociologists conducting microresearch in developing countries. On the basis of their research, they argued that poor people cannot be seen only as passive victims of global capitalist forces (as neo-Marxist and dependency approaches tended to do), but also as trying to actively improve their livelihoods within the constraining conditions in which they live. This view points to the fundamental role of *human agency*. From this perspective, migration is seen as one of the main elements of strategies to diversify, secure and improve livelihoods. This conception comes rather close to the premises of NELM, and both approaches can be integrated if migration is seen as part of a broader *household livelihood strategy* to diversify income sources and overcome social, economic and institutional development constraints in places of origin.

These shifts in thinking on migration and development seem deeply influenced by the paradigm shift in social theory in which social scientists, sometimes inspired by Giddens' (1984) structuration theory, sought to harmonize actor-and structure-oriented approaches. Recognition of the interaction between structure and agency seems essential for the migration and development debate, as this also enables a clearer understanding of the heterogeneity of migration impacts. In "pluralist" views on migration and development such as NELM and the livelihoods approach, the results of the structure-actor interactions allow for a greater variety of outcome than would have been allowed from either the aggregation of individual decision making or from the unidirectional imperatives of structure. The fundamental question is, therefore, not whether migration has either positive or negative developmental impacts, but why migration has contributed to development in some communities and much less, or even negatively, in others and what factors explain this differentiation. Furthermore, impacts often change with the different stages of the migration process. Hence, we need to better understand the geographically differentiated and socially disparate nature of migration and remittance impacts as well as how these impacts change over time.

The sparse amount of pertinent micro-level data has long constrained the field of research on migration, remittances and development. Fortunately, there has been a considerable increase in the number of empirical studies over the past decade. The remainder of this paper not only reviews the empirical literature on the impacts of remittances and migration on social development, but also addresses the theoretical implications of these empirical findings.

CURRENT INSIGHTS INTO REMITTANCE IMPACTS

In line with NELM and livelihood approaches, most recent empirical research supports the view that labour migration, rather than being a response to destitution or absolute poverty (Hampshire 2002), is a livelihood strategy pursued by social groups (typically households) in reaction to relative deprivation in order to spread livelihood risks, secure and increase income and acquire investment capital. Remittances are central elements of such household strategies to overcome local development constraints. Although this seems to contradict structuralist and dependency views in pointing to human agency, the extent to which households succeed in achieving these goals critically depends on the specific circumstances under which such migration occurs. After all, these circumstances determine the destination, selectivity and the returns to migration. For instance, recent studies conducted in Burkina Faso and Morocco suggest that internal and international migration *within* the African continent should primarily be seen as a means to enhance livelihood security through income diversification because the welfare gains, if any, are relatively small. In both countries, it was mainly migration to Europe that allowed households to accumulate substantially more wealth. In these cases, intracontinental migration is difficult to explain from a neoclassical viewpoint, and instead seems to corroborate the risk-spreading argument put forward by NELM and livelihood approaches.

The rather extensive literature on motivations to remit provides additional insight into this issue. Generally, the literature distinguishes two main motives for remitting money: altruism, on the one hand, and self-interest to secure inheritance and to invest in home assets in the expectation of a return, on the other. Findings from empirical studies are often conflicting, with some finding support for altruism and others for self-interest (Agunias 2006:21). However, Lucas and Stark (1985:904) argued that the motives of altruism and self-interest are often inextricable, and that, in the end, one cannot probe whether the true motive is one of caring or more selfishly wishing to enhance prestige by being perceived as caring.

Therefore, they argued that instead of opposing these two motivations, one could develop a far richer model of "tempered altruism or enlightened self-interest in which remittances are one element in a selfenforcing arrangement between migrant and home". In such a model, remittances can simultaneously be seen as the return to household investments in migration, as part of a household risk diversification strategy (co-insurance through risk spreading, securing inheritance claims) and as a source of investment capital that can be used for entrepreneurial activities, education or to facilitate the migration of other household members.

This view is supported by micro-level empirical research indicating that a mixture of individualistic and familial motives explains the likelihood and size of remittances. At first sight, this evidence provides mixed support for neoclassical and NELM theory. Analysing survey data on Mexico–United States remittances, Amuedo-Dorantes and Pozo (2006) concluded that income increases in migrant receiving countries significantly raises both the propensity and the proportion of labour earnings sent home for family-provided insurance as well as for self-insurance.

A growing number of studies indicate that economic and currency crises in origin countries tend to increase remittance transfers. Such evidence further corroborates the risk-spreading and co-insurance hypotheses. An analysis of household data collected in the North-West Frontier Province in rural Pakistan indicated that the ability to cope with negative income shocks is lower for households that do not regularly receive remittances (Kurosaki 2006). Similarly, a recent study of Turkish remittances concluded that consumption smoothing is an important short-run motive for sending remittances to Turkey. Lindley (2006) equally found that migrants in Hargeisa, Somalia, tend to send more remittances from abroad when the family experiences a decline in fortunes and, therefore, concluded that people receiving regular remittances are better protected from exchange-rate fluctuations and have an improved ability to assist relatives in rural areas in times of crisis. Such evidence corroborates the NELM hypothesis that remittances function as income insurance and protect people from income shocks caused by economic downturns, political conflicts or climatic vagaries. Besides protecting against income shocks, a range of empirical studies has indicated the often positive contribution of international remittances to household welfare, nutrition, food, health and living conditions in places and regions of origin.

For instance, half of the households surveyed by Lindley (2006) in Hargeisa were entirely reliant on remittances. In the Moroccan Todgha valley, 40 per cent of all surveyed households received international remittances, which doubled their income in comparison to other households. Internal and international remittances accounted for 10 per cent and 33 per cent, respectively, of the cash income of all surveyed households, and 53–59 per cent of the income of households involved in international migration (de Haas 2006). Agunias (2006:17) cited evidence from Latin America indicating that remittances accounted for a significant proportion of the average recipient's annual income. This share ranged from 18 per cent in Ecuador to 43 per cent in Brazil. Another study in Bangladesh and Nepal found that remittances may account for at least half of total household income in some areas (Seddon 2004, cited in Agunias 2006). A study in southeast Nigeria concluded that the contribution of those who migrate outside of the African continent may be up to 50 per cent of household expenditure (Nwajiuba 2005).

Macro Impacts

Also, on the national level, there is substantial evidence that remittances are an increasingly important and relatively stable source of external finance that often play a critical social insurance role in countries afflicted by economic and political crises (Kapur 2003). Remittances have proved to be less volatile, less pro-cyclical and, therefore, a more reliable source of foreign currency than other capital flows to developing countries such as foreign direct investment and development aid. It is claimed that remittances are nearly three times the value of the official development assistance provided to low-income countries, and that they comprise the secondlargest source of external funding for developing countries after foreign direct investment.

Because many remittances are sent through informal channels, the actual importance of remittances is even higher than official figures show. A recent review concluded that the economies of countries such as Fiji, Somalia and Surinam are in a much better state than official figures would imply thanks to highly developed informal remittance systems (Pieke et al. 2005). In the case of Somalia, for instance, it has been argued that remittances have been far more important for livelihood and survival in the country than development and humanitarian aid put together (Gundel 2002). Remittances often cover an important part of developing countries' trade deficits. Besides their importance as a source of foreign currency, remittances can also improve a country's creditworthiness for external borrowing, and they can expand access to capital and lower borrowing costs. At first sight, such evidence seems to corroborate developmentalist and neo developmentalist views on remittances.

From dependency and structuralist viewpoints, remittances have been commonly seen as an unreliable source of external revenue for families, communities and states. This view was based on the assumption that remittances would rapidly decline with the settlement or return of migrants. Combined with the idea that remittances are rarely spent productively, it has often been thought that remittances would create an artificial and temporary improvement in livelihoods and establish a dangerous dependency on external revenues. Bonds to the sending country would weaken and remittances would decline rapidly after migrants settle and integrate at the destination. This remittance decay hypothesis is linked to the common notion that young, married, lowskilled and temporary male migrants remit the most, and that integrated, highly educated, wellpaid migrants invest more in host countries

(Ghosh 2006:23). In migration policy debates, this remittance decay is often taken for granted. Recent pleas for temporary migration programmes have been advocated based on the argument that temporary migrants would remit more money and would, therefore, be more beneficial to the development of origin countries.

Ultimately, the remittance decay hypothesis is based on the assumption that remittances are primarily sent either to pay back migration debts or for altruistic reasons. It is also based on the assimilationist model of immigrant integration, which assumes a gradual weakening of transnational ties over time. Theoretically, this model conflicts with NELM and other household approaches that see migration and remittances as co-insurance and investment capitalgenerating strategies for households and families. It also conflicts with theories on migrant transnationalism that criticize traditional assimilationist models based on evidence that social ties with origin societies can be sustained and renewed over many generations. However, Stark (1991:223) already argued that it is difficult to predict future remittances, because migrants are part of larger social units such as families and households. The inclination to remit strongly depends on contractual arrangements and bargaining power within the family. Therefore, it is far from certain that remittances would rapidly decline over time. Poirine (2006) argued that even from an altruistic point of view there is no necessary tendency for remittance effort to rise or fall over time.

Hypothesis-testing empirical research on the issue of remittance decay is scarce and often conflicting at first sight. Whereas some studies show declining remittances over time (Agunias 2006:12), others show much more stable or even increasing patterns. Yet, it is possible to integrate such apparently conflicting findings by conceiving of a more dynamic model in which the relationship between the duration of stay, social and economic integration and remittances is not linear. Integration indicators such as employment and income tend to have a positive effect on migrants' capability to remit. This effect might partly or entirely counterbalance the remittance-decreasing effect of the weakening of ties with home countries over time. Even this weakening of transnational ties over time cannot be taken for granted, as such ties can often be sustained over very long periods. This evidence casts doubts on the proposition that temporary migrants would be better and more reliable remitters than integrated and settled migrants. As observed by de Haas and Plug (2006), bilateral per (migrant) capita remittance flows from destination countries to Morocco only started to stagnate or decline after two decades from the onset of large-scale migration. Other survey-based studies suggest that migrant remittances sent by individuals tend to reach a peak approximately 15–20 years after migration. There is also evidence that remittances increase with wages, though apparently only up to a certain point (Taylor 1999). A survey conducted in Egypt, Morocco and Turkey concluded that employed migrants remit four times more money than unemployed migrants (Fokkema and Groenewold 2003). This seems to complement macroevidence that the level and cyclical fluctuations in economic activities in destination countries explain most of the variations in remittance flows.

Sustained migration and the often higher than previously expected durability of transnational bonds explain why declines in remittances often occur in a much more delayed fashion, and are less steep, than once expected. Although evidence is still limited and scattered, there is generally no clear support for remittance decay as an automatic mechanism. Although declines may occur some decades after migration ceases, remittances seem to be a more stable and sustainable source of income than more volatile sources of foreign exchange for states, while they protect people from the destabilizing effects of absent or ill-functioning markets, failing state policies and a lack of state-provided social security.

REMITTANCES, POVERTY AND INEQUALITY

Because of the important contribution of remittances to welfare, it has been argued that remittances are a safety net for relatively poor areas (Jones 1998a). This "private" foreign aid seems to flow directly to the people who really need it, does not require a costly bureaucracy on the sending side and "far less of it is likely to be siphoned off into the pockets of corrupt government officials" (Kapur 2003:10). Jones (1998b), therefore, stated that there is probably no other more "bottom-up" way of redistributing and enhancing welfare among populations in developing countries. While there is certainly an element of truth to this logic, there is also a clear danger of unrestrained optimism concerning the potential of remittances to reduce poverty and inequality.

First, there is a tendency to overestimate the magnitude of migration and remittances. In fact, international migrants comprise only about 3 per cent of the world's population and, in 2001, remittances represented only 1.3 per cent of total gross domestic product (GDP) of all developing countries. These figures are enough to put the argument that remittances alone can generate take-off development into a more realistic perspective. Second, the observation that remittances significantly contribute to income stability and welfare in developing countries does not necessarily imply that they contribute to poverty alleviation. This issue is related to the selectivity of migration. Because of the costs and risks associated with migration, it is generally not the poorest who migrate the most, and certainly not internationally. As migration is a selective process, most direct benefits of remittances are also selective and tend not to flow to the poorest members of communities nor to the poorest countries.The main beneficiaries of remittances are lower or middle-income countries, which receive nearly half of all remittances worldwide. The shares of remittances to GDP tend to be rather high in typical emigration countries such as Mexico, Morocco or the Philippines, and even higher in some small countries, especially island economies in the Caribbean, the Pacific or the Atlantic. Although middle-income countries receive most remittances, in relative terms they tend to be more important to small and sometimes very poor countries, which often receive more than 10 per cent of their GDP in remittances. In other poor countries, such as Somalia, official remittance figures are not available, but are likely to be very high relative to GDP.

Although most international remittances do not flow directly to the poorest people, remittances often make up an important share of the income of poor people and poor communities. Moreover, non-migrant poor might be affected indirectly (positively or negatively) through the economy-wide effects of remittance expenditure on wages, prices and employment in migrantsending communities. Furthermore, it is important to realize that the specific patterns of migrant selectivity fundamentally affect poverty impacts. High-skilled or international migration is often more selective than low-skilled or internal migration, and migration occurring under liberal immigration regimes is likely to be less selective than migration under restrictive immigration regimes. For instance, guest workers who were actively recruited in the 1950s and 1960s by Northern and Western European countries in the Mediterranean were often low skilled and *relatively* poor (de Haas 2003).

Equally, guest worker schemes with Gulf countries have enabled relatively poor Egyptian peasants to migrate. Most studies conclude that international remittances have reduced poverty either directly or indirectly. On the basis of an analysis of a data set covering 71 developing countries, Adams and Page (2005) concluded that international migration and remittances significantly reduce the level, depth and severity of poverty in the developing world. Their results suggest that, on average, and after controlling for the possible endogeneity of international remittances, a 10 per cent increase in per capita international remittances leads to a 3.5 per cent decline in the share of people living on less than $1.00 per person per day. Teto (2001) estimated that 1.17 million (out of 30 million) Moroccans would fall back into absolute poverty without international remittances, and the proportion living below the poverty line would increase from 19.0 to 23.2 per cent. Another analysis of Egyptian and Ghanaian survey data equally indicates that migration enables poor people to move out of poverty. However, it also found that the largest determinant of current poverty status for all groups was their past poverty situation, highlighting the existence of poverty traps.

Although internal migration is generally associated with lower overall income gains, relatively poor people often migrate internally. This also implies that the positive role of *internal* migration in income redistribution should not be overlooked (Deshingkar 2006). In a separate study in Guatemala, Adams (2004) found that the poverty-reducing effect of internal and international remittances was particularly large in relation to the severity of poverty (measured by the squared poverty gap, which considers number, distance and distribution of poor households beneath the poverty line), because households in the lowest decile group receive a large share (between 50 and 60 per cent) of their total household income from (internal) remittances. An analysis of Chinese household data found that having an (internal) migrant increases a household's income per capita by 8.5–13.1 per cent, but that the overall impact on poverty is modest because most poor people do not migrate, not even internally (Du et al. 2005).

Migration and Inequality in a Spatio-temporal Perspective

One of the "truths" put forward by structuralist and dependency perspectives has been that migration and remittances have a negative effect on income inequality within migrant-sending communities as well as between peripheral and central regions. In turn, this increased inequality would further stimulate out-migration, setting in motion a cycle of "cumulative causation" of migration—deepening inequalities—and more migration. However, recent research has provided enough evidence to reject this as a general hypothesis. Although inequality-increasing effects have been found in various studies at the regional (Adams 1989) and national (Mishra 2007) levels, this mechanism is not inevitable. It is more correct to say that the impacts of migration on income inequality in migrant-sending communities vary for different types of migration and for different periods in a community's migration history. First, non-migrants can benefit indirectly from consumption and investments by remittance-receiving migrant households through employment creation and income multipliers. Second, there are other arguments to contradict blanket claims that migration leads to more inequality, which are related to the spatio-temporal dimensions of migration.

As with impacts on poverty, the effect of remittances on income distribution and other aspects of wealth is primarily a function of migration selectivity. If migrants mainly originate from relatively wealthy households, migration is more likely to imply greater inequality in the community of origin, while the reverse seems likely if migrants come from relatively poor households. Pioneer migrants tend to be from relatively wealthy households, as early migration—analogous to the adoption and diffusion of a new technology through space and populations—often entails high costs and risks. Although (pioneer) migrants tend to be relatively wealthy and educated, this is not always the case. The initial pattern of migration selectivity differs according to destination (for example, international versus internal migration), type of work (for example, low skilled or high skilled, legal or undocumented) and mode of job acquisition (for example, formal recruitment or family-based forms of "self-help"). Second, migration selectivity tends to change over time. During the first stages of the evolution of a migration system—defined as spatially clustered flows and counterflows of people, goods and remittances between a particular community of origin and a particular destination— selectivity tends to decrease rapidly. Through the development of social networks between migrants and people staying behind, which diminish the risks and costs of migration (Bauer and Zimmermann 1998:5), and the flow back of information (Korner 1987), less wealthy households tend to gain increasingly easy access to international migration. As a consequence of this diffusion process, the initially negative effect of remittances on income equality might, therefore, be dampened or even reversed in the long term. However, Jones (1998b) demonstrated that inequality may again increase at the "late adopters" stage of migration, when selectivity of migration, other things being equal, tends to increase again.

Thus, the impacts of migration on village income distribution clearly vary for different types of migration and for different periods in a community's migration history. Kanbur and Rapoport (2005) demonstrated that increased migration from poorer to richer areas may in fact coexist with increasing or decreasing spatial inequalities, and that the question of whether divergence or convergence occurs critically depends on specific patterns of migration selectivity and agglomeration effects arising from migrant networks.

Third, differences in spatial scales of analysis may account for contradictory conclusions concerning the effect of migration on income distribution. For instance, one might conclude that migration has contributed to increasing interhousehold income inequality within a certain community or region. However, when comparing this migrant-sending region as a whole with other more wealthy and centrally located regions in the same country (or between countries), one may find that inequality between the regions has actually *decreased* as a consequence of the developmental effects of migration and remittances. The choice for either of the two scales is not obvious, and might partly reflect value judgements.

Spatial and temporal scales of analysis also matter when identifying whether so-called extraregional *leakage* of migrant remittances to central regions and cities occurs, which, according to dependency and centre-periphery theory, would lead to a deepening of spatial development inequalities. For the result of such analysis, it matters whether or not the village or the wider region in which it is located is identified as "origin". In the first case, all investments made outside the village are thought to deepen spatial inequalities. In the second case, the analysis will tend to be far more on the positive side. In Morocco, for instance, many migrants do not necessarily invest their money in houses or businesses in the village of origin, but often do so in small-to medium-sized regional towns, which has given rise to a process of microurbanization *within* migrant-sending regions (Berriane 1997).

Such evidence indicates that migration and remittances do not automatically lead to increased inequalities between the developed "core" and the underdeveloped "periphery", as predicted by dependency and structuralist views. However, the neoclassical assumption that migration leads to factor price equalization certainly should not also be taken as axiomatic.

Value Judgements, Ancient and New Forms of Inequality

Structuralist views on migration and development see migration as a process that has destabilized and uprooted traditional peasant communities. However, the idea that migration has uprooted peasants from their stable communities for the first time reflects a romanticized, and fundamentally flawed, sedentary view of traditional peasant life (Skeldon 1997:32). Assumptions of the negative impact of migration and remittances on inequality and community cohesion or solidarity are often based on the implicit, romantic idea that "traditional" communities were more egalitarian. This often ignores ancient inequalities between ethnic and class groups. Migration and remittances can have profound consequences for class and ethnic hierarchies. Traditional social hierarchies may be fundamentally upset if lower-or middle-status groups manage to migrate internationally and obtain access to international remittances. However, whether to judge such changes as "positive" or "negative" strongly depends on whether we adopt the viewpoints of the relative winners or losers of such community transformations. While older elites might view migration as a devastating process, lower-or middle-class groups may have a more mixed or positive opinion. In San Pedro Pinula (Guatemala), for instance, the migration and return of Mayan residents has permitted them to slowly challenge ethnic roles that have developed over the last five centuries.

In southern Moroccan oases, migration and remittances have been an important avenue for upward socioeconomic mobility for the *haratin*, a low-status social group mainly consisting of black sharecroppers. In this case, *new* forms of inequality, which are to a considerable extent based on access to international remittances, have been partly superimposed upon the traditional, castelike forms of hereditary inequality based on kinship, skin colour and land ownership (de Haas 2006). There are no objective, scientific standards for determining which form of inequality was worse. However, it is important not to ignore the fact that traditional oasis society used to deny basic human freedoms to large sections of the population (including women, slaves, serfs and sharecroppers). In such cases, instead of increased inequalities per se, it is perhaps better to speak of new inequalities based on access to external monetary resources through livelihood diversification, a process in which migration tends to play a preponderant role.

Hence, it is important to carefully consider the specific historical evolution of class or ethnic stratifications as well as the relative access of classes and ethnic groups to migration in order to assess the impact of migration and remittances upon inequalities. A recent overview of case studies on migration and inequality across Central America, Eastern Europe, West Africa and South Asia demonstrates how the mutual causality between migration and inequality varies both between and within regions, and emphasizes the need for defining which kind of migration and which kind of inequality are being analysed. To a considerable extent, "measuring" the impact of migration and remittances on inequality is an ambiguous and normative affair. For instance, conclusions on the "severity" of inequality partly depend on the weight attached to incomes of households at different points in the income distribution when calculating indices of inequality. There is also no objective, scientific yardstick with which to judge a situation in which inequality has increased, but in which the majority of migrant and non-migrant households are better off and poverty has decreased. This scenario exemplifies the ambiguities involved in attaching relative weights to distributional versus absolute income objectives.

NETWORKS OF OBLIGATION LINKING INDIVIDUALS

Massey debunks the individualist assumptions of the most influential and widely used approach in migration, the individual cost-benefit model. He reveals that the assumptions of this model, in which migration decisions are based on the calculations of a rational individual who weighs her expected gains (e.g. employment or higher salary) against possible losses (e.g. deportation), are faulty. Rather than isolated agents, people are linked to one another through social networks. These connections have a ponderous effect on migration. The two central ways they shape migration include: 1) making migration less risky for individuals by circulating information among potential migrants, and 2) feeding subsequent migration, since kinship networks allow migrants to send remittances home, making migration a viable household strategy for diversifying economic risk.

Thus, the nature of migration changes dramatically over time. The initial associated high-risk declines for individuals as more of their family and friends migrate. This is because, denser networks of migrants provide potential migrants with increasingly reliable information about the opportunities and dangers associated with the place of destination and the migration process. People in one's network also offer needed assistance, such as helping one find a job or a place to live. This facilitates the choice to migrate, making migration progressively more likely, which is what Massey refers to as "circular and cumulative causation" (Massey 1990:4). Because of this process, the profile of migrants shifts over time, from that of innovating, risk-taking youth to more typical individuals (Tacoli 1995).

Just as potential migrants expect kin or friends, who have already migrated, to assist them, so households of origin expect migrants to "help out" financially, by remitting a portion of their salary. Because of these expectations, households encourage select family members to migrate. As dense social networks reduce the risks of migration, households use migration to "diversify" economic risk. As long as the economies of places of origin and destination are weakly or inversely correlated, a viable household strategy for minimizing economic risk consists of having wage earners in both places (Stark 1991). This strategy relies on the assumption that migrants and non-migrants are *linked* through *networks of obligation* and *shared understandings* of kinship and friendship. These assumptions are not unreasonable, but shared understandings and obligation are likely to vary across members of a network. As the preceding section suggested, the cultural expectations of men's and women's behaviour in different circumstances may mean that one or the other is more or less likely to share these understandings.

Portes and Sensenbrenner suggest some theoretical concepts that might explain networks of obligation and shared understandings. Through their refinement of the terms social capital and social embeddedness, Portes and Sensenbrenner suggest four kinds of trust that may be at work to reduce transactions costs between individuals, and by implication strengthen network ties and obligations. The first two are well worn in sociology: value introjection and reciprocity transactions. The first imbues economic transactions with moral motivations resulting from socialization as the basis for trust. The second incorporates the history of past successful exchanges with the norm to reciprocate as the basis for trust.

The third and fourth types of trust are newer ideas and most interesting to the paper at hand. Bounded solidarity and the resulting trust among group members arises in particular situations where a common threat is recognized by many as a result of their shared identity, circumstance, or history. Invoking cultural symbols that reinforce this commonality serves to reinforce network ties of obligation. Finally, enforceable trust is more utilitarian and is based on the internal sanctioning capacity of the group either through ostracism or coercion. The ability of the group to enforce individual subordination to the group depends on the resources available in the community relative to resources available outside the community as well as its ability to monitor individual behaviour (through tight knit networks resulting from both physical and social proximity).

Thus far, Portes and Sensenbrenner's descriptions and concepts are used in the context of immigrant communities in places of destination as opposed to Massey's concepts, which describes the phenomena from places of origin. In both cases the concepts might be expanded to networks in both places of origin and destination. Their concepts also differ from Massey's in terms of where social change occurs. In Portes and Sensenbrenner's formulation the group, either through socialization, invocation of cultural symbols and identity, or closure and resources weighs heavily upon individual behaviour. Thus, the locus of action is found in the group, whereas in Massey's concept of circular and cumulative causation the locus of action is an interaction between the group and the individual. Combining these two concepts brings greater insight on the processes of social change both between and within places of destination and origin.

However, there is nothing in either Massey's or Portes and Sensenbrenner's ideas that would explain why men and women might behave differently. Although Portes and Sensenbrenner suggest some differentiation across class within the Cuban migrant community, there is little else to suggest within community variation. But, why would Dominican Republic men and women behave so differently? Or Thai men and women? The answers to these questions are pursued following a discussion of how networks are suggested to link time and space. This discussion is necessarily precedent because it introduces the concept of *relative deprivation*, a concept we find relevant for understanding the formation and changes in gender identity resulting from migration processes.

Networks Linking Time and Space

Work on networks and migration has further shown that individual decisions made at one point in time have profound effects upon social structures at later points in time. Moreover, they suggest that migrant networks can link economies of places of origin and destination so that they become inter-dependent. For instance, Stark et al. find that migration remittances from the United States back to Mexico have a strong impact upon inequality in the place of origin. Poorly developed migrant networks from places of origin increase income inequality in the place of origin, as few households have access to migrant income. However, this may change as migrant networks grow and more people have access to similar sources of income (Massey 1990).

In addition, labour markets in the place of origin may change with increasing migration such that the outflow of migrants raises local wages to the point that wage differentials no longer provide a motivation to move. The possibility of inequality dissipating depends on levels of inequality between places of destination and origin, and how structures of production change. For example, Massey et al. (1987) find that on average a Mexican migrant's repatriated earnings constitutes 82% of a migrant's origin household income. The wage rates differ by six times between migrants and local wage labourers.

Massey argues that earnings on this scale dwarf locally generated incomes and have profound distributional impacts on migrant communities. Some of the effects of this kind of difference result in privileging some households' access to land and resources, transforming egalitarian places into places where the social context is characterized by a few with economic and social power.

In addition, traditional relations of production also change under some contexts. In the case of Mexico, after acquiring land, some households continue to diversify risks by allocating family workers across activities, specifically sending fathers and sons to migrate, and women and children to work in agricultural production. Or, investments in agricultural technology reduce the need for agricultural wage labour and increase unemployment.

The derivative expectations about the consequences of migration assume that relative deprivation and networks of obligation link individuals and communities across time and space.

For networks of obligation, we have noted there may be significant differences between men and women (as suggested by the preceding review of the literature on gender and migration), which may differentially influence societal level outcomes. Similarly, relative deprivation operates through individual and group identity and one might expect that gender would be a significant distinction. And, therefore, the way in which people understand themselves, or construct their identity as either men or women can be expected to shape how relative deprivation operates and, in turn, social structures of production and inequality.

These ideas are incompletely developed in the migration literature and could benefit from works in the field of cultural sociology. There is a body of work in the sociology of culture that explores how people fashion identity (e.g. (Berger and Luckman 1967) and the role material things play in this that holds great promise for migration and network theories.

We will demonstrate how this work can speak directly to questions of relative deprivation and networks of obligation. We argue that different types of identity will lead to differential experiences of relative deprivation and different notions of obligation, thereby resulting in distinct patterns of migration motivation and behaviour. Although many forms of identity are relevant, we will focus on gender identity variation in patterns of migration, according to gender.

Culture, Gender, Networks and Migration

We begin with a discussion of the role of culture in a network theory of migration, theorized as a "socially embedded" and "circular and cumulatively caused" process. We consider two ways that culture enters this formulation. The first is through notions of relative deprivation and the second is through networks of obligation. Massey uses the concept of relative deprivation to designate strong desire for material goods, accompanied by a sense of entitlement, stemming from the realization that one's peers possess these goods. Relative deprivation is an explicit reference to the movement of ideas and shifting value schemes, in that it is only relevant when people's needs and desires change and can no longer be met by resources in the place of origin. Yet, Massey does not sufficiently explore the implications of this. Nor does the current formulation of network theory of migration sufficiently address the role played by networks of obligation. We discuss both and suggest that cultural meanings of gender may differentially affect the impact of relative deprivation and networks of obligation upon migration processes. We then proceed to suggest ways in which structural changes in places of origin and destination may be driven by different cultural meanings of gender, resulting in different networks and migration outcomes.

REMITTANCE EXPENDITURE, INVESTMENT AND REGIONAL DEVELOPMENT

Perhaps the most common reason for scepticism on migration and development has been the widespread belief that migrants rarely invest their money in productive enterprises, but instead spend it on consumption or non-productive investments. This belief—which also formed the cornerstone of structuralist and dependency-inspired visions that claimed that migration and remittances do not lead to, or can even undermine, development—is remarkably persistent, particularly in the policy literature. A recent report commissioned by the European Investment Bank concluded that "remittances remain primarily used for daily expenses and therefore do not have large developmental impact". Such views usually underpin ideas that governments should develop policies to "channel" remittances into productive investment.

However, the common idea that migrants do not use their money "productively" tends to have rather weak empirical foundations. Much of the research that has generated these ideas has been criticized for their serious deficiencies in methodological design. Migration impact studies also tend to neglect the fungibility of remittances with other sources of household income, which means that it is generally not possible to "earmark" migrant remittances to specific expenditures (Taylor 1999). Since the 1990s, an increasing number of studies have emerged that challenge the dim views that migrants would fritter away their remittance earnings on personal consumption (Adams 1991:719). Most studies seem to suggest that households receiving international remittances have a higher propensity to invest than non-migrant households when controlling for income and other relevant household variables. Rapoport and Docquier (2005:2) cited several studies indicating that there is considerable evidence that remittances promote access to selfemployment and increase investment in small businesses.

As with poverty and inequality, the impact of remittances on investments and economic growth in migrant-sending communities tends to change over time. In a study of the effects of temporary labour migration from five African countries to South Africa's mines on agricultural production in the countries of origin, Lucas (1987:313) concluded that migration diminishes domestic crop production in the short run, but enhances crop productivity and cattle accumulation through invested remittances and increased domestic plantation wages in the long run. A recent study of Turkish remittances shows that whereas consumption smoothing is an effective short-run motive for sending remittances, the investment motive is important in the long run. Also, Taylor (1994:100) found village economy-wide evidence that the combination of lostlabour effects and positive remittances effects may negatively affect production in migrantstaging areas initially, but eventually have a positive effect.

Activities, expenditure and investment patterns are likely to change over the course of migration and household lifecycles. Based on household data from southern Morocco, de Haas (2003) identified a sequence in which housing investments occur relatively early in the migration cycle and peak five to 14 years after initial migration, stabilizing at a high level. Most agricultural investments occurred from 15 to 24 years after migration, and investments in non-agricultural private businesses peaked from 25 to 29 years after migration.

The short-term effects of migration on livelihoods and household production in sending communities are often negative due to the immediate lost-labour effect. It is often only at a later stage—when the migrant has more or less settled at the destination, found relatively secure employment and the most basic needs of the household "back home" are fulfilled (such as food, health, clothing, primary education, basic household amenities, paying off debts and so on)— that there is more room for investments. In the meantime, households and communities have had the chance to readjust local (agricultural and non-agricultural) production systems (including labour allocation, intrahousehold task divisions) to the absence of migrants. It is only at these later stages that migrants tend to invest their money in commercial enterprises such as agriculture, large-scale housing, commerce and so on. However, the extent to which they will invest at all depends on more general investment conditions.

It is, therefore, unrealistic to expect that the full development effects of migration and remittances will materialize within the first or second decade following the onset of large-scale migration. This hypothesized relationship between the household migration stage (related to the family lifecycle) and consumption and investment patterns of households that receive remittances. To a considerable extent, this household-level dynamic model can be applied at the community or even regional levels, taking into account the fact that migration is rarely an isolated act by one individual or household, but that the migration experience tends to diffuse throughout communities once localities and regions become linked to the outside world. From this, one could hypothesize that communities and regions as a whole tend to go through different migration stages, characterized by the "innovators" stage (first pioneering migrants leave), "early adopter" stage (migration spreads throughout the community, aided by network effects) and the "late adopter" stage (migration stabilizes, and may eventually decrease) (Jones 1998b). On the basis of this model, one could further hypothesize that the full developmental effects of migration can only materialize in the second and, in particular, third stages of migration, when the majority of migrant households have been involved in migration for several decades.

The accumulated empirical evidence has refuted the hypothesis that migration automatically puts a drain on sending communities and countries and reinforces the centre-periphery gap. The counterflow of remittances and investments can partly or even more than compensate for this negative effect. However, this is not to say that the migration optimists were right. The extent to which money is remitted, and how and where remittances are spent, fundamentally depends on the migrants' social and economic position at the destination as well as on the investment conditions in the countries of origin. This explains why remittances impact so differently on different countries and communities. Whereas in some cases remittances have enabled migrants to invest in land and cattle, in other cases remittances have generally not been dedicated to agricultural improvements and instead are overwhelmingly invested in housing and land. While in some cases most remittance-driven investments have remained within the sending region (de Haas 2006), in others cases migrants prefer to invest in more distant (urban) areas outside the migrant-sending region (McCormick and Wahba 2003).

This particularly seems to be the case when sending regions lack adequate infrastructure, agricultural resources and urban centres that provide opportunities to allocate such investments. Interestingly, internal migration is associated more often with rural and agricultural stagnation or even decline than with international migration to wealthy countries, where much higher remittances enable households to substitute the lost labour and to actually invest in agricultural and other sectors.

Migrant-sending Communities

Most migration impact studies have focused only on the *direct* social and economic effects of migration, that is, the impact on migrants and their households. However, remittances may also have significant impacts on non-migrant households, and hence may reshape sending communities as a whole. Such indirect effects are usually not captured by remittance-use studies. For instance, research has tended to negatively evaluate consumptive expenses as non-developmental.

However, consumptive expenses, provided that they occur locally, can have positive impacts by providing non-migrants with labour and income. This is confirmed by empirical evidence that consumption by migrant households can lead, via multiplier effects, to higher incomes for non-migrant households. The same holds true for so-called "non-productive" investments. For example, academics and policy makers have almost universally bemoaned the high amounts of money that migrants tend to spend on housing. This is partly because such "diatribes by academics and policy makers against migrants for their profligate and unproductive ways" reflect common elitist views on the irrational spending behaviour of lower classes, which in any case have a weak or absent empirical basis.

Various empirical studies have reported that construction activities can generate considerable employment and income for non-migrants. This also applies to many other expenses such as feasts and funerals. In this way, the benefits of remittances might accrue to households other than the ones that directly receive them. These expenses increase consumption levels that may—by easing capital and risk constraints on local production—in turn facilitate local investments by migrants and nonmigrants alike. In this way, expenditure on housing and consumption may have significant multiplier effects in the wider economy.

Emigration and remittance expenditure also have the tendency to increase wages in sending regions and countries. In a Moroccan oasis, for instance, the price of agricultural labour has considerably increased, partly as a result of out-migration and increased demand for agricultural labour. While, traditionally, sharecroppers used to retain one-fifth of the yield, at the time of the study they retained on average 41 per cent of the harvest. Dependency and structuralist views have usually evaluated such wage increases as negative. However, if such wage increases occur, they reflect neoclassical predictions of factor price equalization. Although (migrant) entrepreneurs might view increasing local wage levels as negative, this is obviously to the benefit of non-migrants and immigrants living in such regions.

Narrow and Arbitrary Definitions of Investments

Besides ignoring the indirect ways in which consumptive expenses and "non-productive investments" can contribute to economic growth and employment, conventional views on migration and development also tend to rest on rather arbitrary definitions of what actually constitutes productive investments. Expenditure in areas such as education, health, food, medicines and investments in housing as well as community projects for education, health and recreational facilities (Nwajiuba 2005) can enhance people's wellbeing and ability to lead the lives they have reason to value. From a capabilities perspective on development as proposed by Sen (1999), such improvements should be considered as "developmental".

There is evidence that international remittances have a positive influence on infant health and decrease infant mortality in migrant-sending communities. Housing almost universally occupies the highest rank after consumption on the list of migrants' expenditures, and migrants have consistently been criticized for this preference. We have already seen that construction activities can have positive impacts on local and regional economies. A more fundamental argument to counter the idea that housing is "non-developmental" is that the quest to have a clean, safe and spacious house is a universal aspect of human well-being.

Criticism of migrants' "unproductive" or "irrational" expenditure behaviour also unveils an apparent inability to comprehend the difficult social, economic, legal and political conditions that often prevail in migrant-sending countries. In such insecure contexts, spending money on relatively safe assets such as houses can be a rational strategy toward securing, diversifying and improving livelihoods. In his study on the use and impact of international remittances in a rural region in Egypt, Adams made an a priori distinction between consumption, durables and investments; however, based on his fieldwork, he concluded that "on a practical level the difference between these three types of expenditures becomes blurred…from the standpoint of the individual, housing expenses should be classified as an 'investment', since new and improved housing offers possible future economic returns to the individual" (1991:705). Adams concluded that, considering the surge in land prices throughout Egypt, the high rate of inflation and the lower or even negative returns on other investments, land purchase represented a good investment from the standpoint of the individual migrant. In the same vein, Taylor (1994:101) argued that "land, housing, and other speculative investments, for which migrant families often are criticised, are a rational response to the uncertain, inflationary environments created by misguided macro-economic policies and sectoral policies that discriminate against small-scale production activities that might be within reach of migrant families".

The distinction between consumption and investments is, therefore, often blurred and the outcome of evaluations on the relative merits of such expenditure partly depends on value judgements. In fact, by suggesting that people should stay in their "mud brick houses", social scientists and policy makers risk applying different standards to others than they would to themselves. Expenditure on items such as land, housing, education, transport and jewellery can be rational, as they frequently offer better rates of return or are safer stores of value than highrisk investments in, for instance, agriculture or industry (Russell 1992). In Morocco, de Haas (2006) found that migrants consider house ownership as an important life insurance.

Community Structures and Care Arrangements

The pivotal role of migration and remittances in the social and economic reproduction of sending communities has been widely acknowledged. Only in a minority of cases has international migration provoked a proverbial rural exodus in the sense of an absolute population decline. Such processes, if they occur, instead seem to be linked to internal migration. International migration and remittances, on the contrary, enable other household and community members to continue to live in rural areas. Remittances have been ascribed an essential role in assuring the survival and reproduction of households and their maintenance in origin countries. This is why Heinemeijer et al. (1977) interpreted migration from the Moroccan countryside to Europe as a livelihood strategy of *partir pour rester* (to go away in order to stay), which corroborates the NELM and livelihood view of migration and development. This perspective not only challenges neoclassical migration theory that views migration as an income maximizing endeavour by individuals, but it also counters structuralist and dependency theories that see migration as a drain on migrant-sending communities.

While often maintaining the social and economic reproduction of communities, remittances also tend to transform social structures and care arrangements. As with the issue of migration, remittances and inequality, it is important not to automatically interpret as negative any form of change from a real or imagined stable and traditional past. On the one hand, migration can disrupt traditional care arrangements for children and the elderly; on the other hand, remittances may enable households to improve their livelihoods and to substitute family carers for paid carers. Although the social and psychological costs of separation often remain high, this gives reason to counter simplistic views on the supposedly devastating effects of migration and remittances on family life. Despite the difficulties created by the migration of household members, people tend to adapt to these new situations, which almost inevitably implies social change. For instance, King and Vullnetari (2006) contended that massive internal and international out-migration from rural Albania since 1990 has disrupted traditional social and kinship systems and has made elderly people particularly vulnerable. Although remittances cushion their social isolation, the loss of children and grandchildren through emigration has undermined elderly people's self-respect and raison d'être in Albanian family life. One of their coping mechanisms has been to follow their children abroad to care for the grandchildren, enabling both parents of the children to engage in paid work.

On the basis of his study of transnational family life in New York among Ecuadorian migrants from the Azuayo-Canari highlands, Pribilsky (2004) countered the commonly held view that male migration to the United States often leads to spousal abandonment. He found that, despite the tensions and problems faced by young couples starting to form their own autonomous transnational households, such couples often state that their relationship improved after migration. A study by Parrado (2004) of the relation between labour migration and the marriage rates of men in 43 communities in western Mexico highlighted the importance of distinguishing different scales of analysis and duration of stay when assessing the impact of migration on family life and social reproduction of families. Although at the individual level, international migration deterred marriage while migrants were abroad, after returning to their home community the remittances and savings accumulated by Mexican migrants facilitated the purchase of housing, businesses and land and as such helped them to accumulate the necessary capital to marry and start a family (Parrado 2004).

Evaluating "the" effect of migration and remittances on wider community structures and traditional institutions is an equally ambiguous and potentially value-laden affair. In Moroccan oases, for instance, migration and the concomitant partial emancipation of formerly subordinate groups of black sharecroppers has undermined the functioning of tradition village institutions that regulate the maintenance of collectively managed irrigation systems. This process contributed to the decline of these irrigation systems and diminishing water flows. On the other hand, the influx of international remittances has enabled households to pump this water through individual pumping and even to start new farms in the desert. In an indigenous Oaxacan village in Mexico, it was found that villagers regard migration as necessary, yet problematic. Although migration provides income for families, it is said to undercut traditions of community service (Mutersbaugh 2002). On the other hand, also in rural Oaxaca, it was found that some communities can use the organizational capacity of traditional governance systems to access remittances from migrants for the benefit of the community as a whole. Instead of communal labour requirements, communities can require payment from migrants and may directly solicit remittances from migrants for community projects. However, the extent to which communities can enforce these requests depends on the existing organizational strength in the community.

All in all, migration and remittances seem to be a transformative rather than a disruptive force. It is also clear that the sociocultural and economic impacts of migration and remittances are notoriously difficult to disentangle from more general processes of social change. Migration is a constituent part of a complex set of social, cultural and economic transformations that integrate emigrant communities into global social, economic and migratory systems as well as an independent factor in perpetuating and intensifying, magnifying and accelerating these processes at the local and regional levels.

Migration, Remittances and Gender

The selectivity and impacts of migration and remittances are unlikely to be gender neutral. It is often taken for granted that female migration from "patriarchal" societies forms part of household strategies such as family reunification and family formation. When women migrate alone, they are typically portrayed as passive *victims* of smugglers or traffickers, working under exploitative conditions in service sector jobs or prostitution, thereby denying them the power of agency that men are stereotypically ascribed. However, a high and increasing number of independent migrants are in fact women. Even in "patriarchal" societies, such as Mexico and Morocco, female migration is no longer exclusively a corollary to labour migration by men, if this was ever the case at all. The literature on the *impacts* of migration and remittances on sending societies also tends to ignore the gender dimension. This gender blindness has also been the major critique on the household approaches advocated by NELM, which may represent households as monolithic, internally altruistic units making unanimous decisions to the advantage of the whole group. Feminist researchers, in particular, have argued that this generalization masks intrahousehold power inequalities and rules out both individual decision making and the influence of nonhousehold members.

Gender inequality is likely to affect migration and remittance access and use as well as have a significant impact on the intrafamily allocation of social and financial remittances, making it questionable whether migration and remittances automatically enable people to challenge established gender roles. It is sometimes assumed that the migration of men encourages the emancipation of women who stay behind since in their husbands' absence, women's responsibilities, autonomy and power would increase, while remittances enable these women to assert this newly acquired independence. However, the limited empirical evidence suggests that migration and remittances do not necessarily have a structural impact on changing traditional gender roles, and may actually serve to reproduce them.

A study by Van Rooij (2000) of wives of non-migrants and migrants in Morocco challenged the hypothesis that migration contributes to changing gender roles. The lives of migrants' wives remained largely confined to housekeeping, child rearing and agricultural work. Although they tended to have more control over the use of their husbands' earnings and in child rearing, this gain in authority was mainly temporary, since migrants resume their position as patriarchs as soon as they return. Empirical research in Albania, Burkina Faso, Egypt (Taylor 1984), Turkey (Day and Içduygu 1997) and Yemen (Myntti 1984) yielded similar conclusions that migration and remittances do not lead to a permanent shift in the patriarchal family structure.

In addition, changes in gender roles are not necessarily positive. In case studies of Egyptian and Yemeni migrant-sending communities, Taylor (1984) and Myntti (1984) even suggested that the position of women might have worsened due to the growing influence of conservative interpretations of Islam that some return migrants bring back. Nyberg-Sorensen (2004:10) cited evidence from Morocco indicating that if women take over traditional "male" tasks such as harvesting as a result of migration, some of the younger men may refuse to work in what has now come to be dubbed "women's work".

Furthermore, the emotional burden of the increased responsibilities can be high. For Morocco, both Hajjarabi (1995) and Van Rooij (2000) showed that women do not necessarily appreciate the sudden increase in responsibilities and tasks, which were not theirs within the normative context of traditional society and to which they do not always aspire. As this new role is generally not assumed out of free choice, it should not be equated with emancipation in the sense of making independent and conscious choices against prevailing norms of gender roles (de Haas 2007a). However, Gammage (2004) found that, through migration and remittances, Haitian women have been able to change the political landscape of Haiti and have challenged traditional gender roles. What might play a role here is that Haiti is a predominantly matrifocal society as opposed to most European, Middle Eastern and North African societies.

Also, in the case of women who migrate, it should not be assumed that they automatically adopt the receiving country's societal norms of gender relations. A study conducted in North Carolina of four Mexican migrant-sending communities challenged the expectation that migrant women easily incorporate the behaviour patterns and cultural values of United States' society. Rather, the authors observed a process of selective assimilation in which gender relations were reconstructed within the family at the place of destination. Some elements brought from communities of origin are discarded, others are modified and others are reinforced in this process.

It is important to disentangle the effects of migration and remittances from more general processes of social and cultural change affecting migrant-sending communities. The latter are often more important, although migration may play an accelerating or reinforcing role in such processes. In particular, in the long term there may be (intergenerational) gains for women. For instance, international migration and remittances can have a distinct positive influence on the educational participation of younger women. In Albania and Morocco, it has been suggested that transformations of patriarchal power structures are more likely to be generational.

Based on their research in four Guatemalan sending communities, Taylor et al. (2006) concluded that migration and social remittances may permit a gradual erosion of traditional gender and ethnic roles, but that such changes are gradual because migrants, despite their increased earnings and awareness, run into a social structure that resists rapid change. In the Moroccan Rif, Crivello (2003) demonstrated that, by working abroad, women might enhance their roles as economic providers to the families left behind, which tends to diminish the potential stigma attached to female migration.

Both Courbage (1996) and Fargues (2006) hypothesized that—besides factors such as older age of marriage, increased female labour force participation and improved education—migration from North African to European countries has contributed to the diffusion and adoption of European marriage patterns and small family norms, and so has played an accelerating role in the demographic transition. In the case of Egyptian migration to conservative Gulf countries, the effect would be the reverse. It has also been argued that female migrants show a deeper commitment than male migrants to providing more economic support to households that are left behind.23 Blue (2004) found that females were positively associated with remittance behaviour among Cuban emigrants. However, some empirical studies have reached opposite conclusions. For instance, Semyonov and Gorodzeisky (2005) argued that Filipino men remit *more* money than female migrants do, even when controlling for income differentials between men and women.

REMITTANCES AND HUMAN CAPITAL FORMATION

Perhaps the most commonly used argument*against* migration as a potential source of development is that it deprives poor countries of their valuable human resources. Structuralist and dependency theorists have pointed to this brain drain to underpin their argument that migration undermines rather than stimulates development in origin countries, and reinforces rather than alleviates global inequalities. In recent years, this brain drain hypothesis has been increasingly questioned, allowing for a much more nuanced picture.

First, not all migrants are highly skilled. Second, the brain drain seems to be only truly massive in a minority of countries. In a quantitative assessment of the brain drain, Adams (2003) concluded that international migration does not tend to involve a very high proportion of the best educated. In two-thirds of the 33 large labour-exporting countries he surveyed, less than 10 per cent of the best-educated (that is, tertiary) population had migrated. The emigration of highly educated migrants seems to be truly massive only in a limited number of smaller countries, such as various island states in the Caribbean and the Pacific. However, even in these cases mass migration of high-skilled workers should primarily be seen as a symptom of development failure rather than the cause of this failure as such. For instance, the migration of health workers is often claimed to be extremely harmful for sending countries, and is said to have created labour shortages in the health sectors in countries such as Ghana and South Africa. However, there is limited data available to underpin such claims. On the contrary, a recent study using a new database of health worker emigration from Africa suggested that Africa's generally low health staffing levels and poor public health conditions are the result of factors entirely unrelated to international movements of highly trained health professionals. Such factors include unattractive working conditions in the public health sector and the failure to provide basic health services, which do not require highly trained personnel to deliver (Clemens 2007). This corroborates another study that concluded that migration is a symptom, not a cause, for failing health systems, and that most elite health workers would not provide basic health care to those most in need if they had stayed.

Third, labour tends to be much more productive in wealthy countries, which may, therefore, increase the capabilities of migrants and their families to improve their livelihood. Moreover, many developing countries now face mass unemployment among the highly skilled, which is often the partial result of misguided education policies, which do not reflect the true skill and knowledge needs of developing economies. In other words, there is often overinvestment in higher education and underinvestment in primary and secondary education and vocational training. This all casts some doubt on the assumption that the emigration of the highly skilled would *automatically* represent a loss. In many cases, the long-term individual and collective gains may effectively outweigh the immediate costs of migration. In fact, many governments consider skilled labourers to be an export product and thus willingly create surpluses of certain categories of the highly skilled. For instance, the Philippines educates some categories of professionals, such as nurses, for the explicit purpose of generating remittances from abroad (de Haas 2005).

Fourth, as in the case of remittance impacts, it is important to distinguish the negative shortterm effects from the often more positive, long-term effects of the emigration of the highly skilled. Depending on the social, economic and political conditions in origin countries, the departure of the highly skilled *may* have beneficial effects in the form of a counterflow of remittances, investments, trade relations, skills, knowledge, innovations, attitudes and information in the long run. Migrants have played an important role as innovating and transnationally operating entrepreneurs and investors in countries such as India, the Republic of Korea and Taiwan. It has become increasingly clear that migrants' contribution to development is not conditional upon their return, and that many migrants live transnational lives, combining activities in origin and destination countries. This corroborates evidence on the potential durability of remittances, countering pessimistic views that equate migrants' settlement and integration with an inevitable "loss" for origin countries. On the contrary, wellintegrated migrants seem to have an increased capacity to contribute to development. The extent to which they do so, however, crucially depends on general economic and political conditions in origin countries.

Finally, a "brain drain" can be accompanied by a significant "brain gain", because the prospect of moving abroad may stimulate the incentive to pursue education among stay-behinds (World Bank 2005:68). This situation might explain how a country may end up with more educated workers (a brain gain) despite the existence of a brain drain and the "educated unemployment" prevalent in a number of developing countries.

A recent study in the Philippines shows that educational expenditure in origin households increased with remittances (Yang 2004). In El Salvador, remittances tend to reduce the likelihood of children leaving school. Another survey shows that Mexican children in migrant households completed their schooling significantly more often, with the largest impact for girls in households where the mother has a low level of schooling. Based on an analysis of nationally representative household data in Guatemala, Adams (2006) found that, at the margin, households receiving internal and international remittances spend 45.2 per cent and 58.1 per cent more, respectively, on education than do households that do not receive remittances.

Analysing data from El Salvador, Edwards and Ureta (2003) found that remittances have a large, significant effect on school retention. In urban areas, the effect of remittances was at least 10 times greater than the effect of other income.

In rural areas, the effect of remittances was about 2.6 times that of other income. Two surveys conducted in Morocco equally suggest that remittances enable migrants' children, and particularly daughters, to go to school. In a case study in Nepal, Thieme and Wyss (2005) similarly concluded that international migration and remittances have a positive effect on the education of children. Besides remittance-enabled investment in physical capital, investment in human capital is likely to be important for the long-term growth prospects of developing countries. Thinking of it from a capabilities perspective on development (Sen 1999), spending on the education of children counts as a long-term productive investment and as an income assurance strategy for households and families. Such investments in their children's education are especially important for people without access to formal social security arrangements. However, whether skills and knowledge acquired through education will be deployed locally or abroad, that is, through migration, ultimately depends on the political climate, economic growth and the structure of labour markets in sending countries.

On the other hand, there is evidence that under certain circumstances migration might also create *negative* incentives for education. If the opportunity to migrate decreases the return to education, individuals may be discouraged to invest in education.

This seems specifically to be the case in migration systems predominated by low-skilled and often undocumented migration, where few if any positive externalities of education can be expected. For instance, a Mexican or a Moroccan cleaner with a university education in Spain or the United States is unlikely to earn significantly more than a colleague with only a primary education. There is indeed some evidence from Mexican household surveys indicating that international migrations have a negative effect on the level of schooling of children (McKenzie 2006).

This finding corroborates others who suggested that schooling has no effect on incentives for international migration from rural Mexico, whereas schooling has positive effects on *internal* migration incentives. In other words, the wage gain is higher for less-educated Mexicans who migrate to the United States rather than internally. Migration and remittances can thus both encourage and discourage education of non-migrants. Depending on the specific incentive structures, remittances and the opportunity to work in cities or abroad give individuals and their households the choice either to invest in or to disengage from education. Confirming this hypothesis, the empirical evidence is indeed mixed, although a majority of studies seem to support the NELM hypothesis that remittances have positive effects on school attendance and educational achievement. A point often ignored is that improved education is not only a potential result of migration and remittances, but also that the desire to obtain more education is often one of the very reasons for rural-to-urban (de Haas 1998) and international migration, and successful skilled international migrants may indeed stimulate other people to follow their path.

MIGRATION, REMITTANCES AND POLITICAL REFORM

Migration and remittances also affect social and political life in countries of origin in a broader sense. Sending countries have often had ambiguous attitudes toward emigrants. Many states have considered migration as a safety valve to reduce unemployment, poverty and political unrest and saw migration as a direct way to get rid of political dissidents.

It has, therefore, been argued that emigration could diminish pressure for domestic reforms (Kireyev 2006). On the other hand, there are strong long-term economic incentives for emigration states to strengthen ties with their absent citizens (Barry 2006).

Many sending states have become dependent on remittances to cover trade deficits and to maintain domestic stability, a situation that seems to have increased their willingness to engage with emigrant populations and increase their voice in internal political affairs. Over the past decade, many sending states have, therefore, embarked upon more inclusive diaspora engagement policies through extending special political and economic rights to emigrants and allowing dual citizenship.

Migrants often play a significant role in the societal and political debate and civil society in countries of origin. Their involvement underscores the fact that the developmental effects of migration are not limited to remittances and investments, but also include important sociopolitical dimensions. Migrants and their organizations often take an active stance in shaping their new role in the national life of their home countries. Migrants' considerable weight can eventually create a push for political and economic reforms, democratization, increasing political and bureaucratic transparency and the emancipation of minority groups in sending states.

Although migrants have recently been celebrated for their ability to stimulate social, political and economic reform in origin countries, it is important to remember that migrants, through remittances and other factors, may also contribute to sustained conflicts, for instance, by providing support for warring parties. Furthermore, migrants are often from middle-class or elite groups and, therefore, might not necessarily represent the view of the poor and the oppressed, but instead effectively sustain oppressive political systems. Again, this scenario exemplifies the difficulty of generalizing about the social, economic and cultural effects of migration and remittances. The direct effect of skilled emigration needs to be evaluated on a case-by-case basis. Furthermore, such analyses tend to be value laden. This is particularly evident when assessing migrants' political influence. Migrants encompass all possible political colours. And, clearly, there is no objective, scientific yardstick for determining which direction of political change is ultimately desirable.

Remittances and National Economic Growth

Whereas views on the impact of international remittances on social and economic development in migrant-sending societies have recently inclined toward the positive side, the impact of remittances on national economic growth and employment are rather unclear. The consequences of remittances on long-term economic development are not well understood (Kapur 2003:vii). There seems to be no conclusive evidence to sustain either neoclassical or dependency theory, because relevant studies have yielded contradictory findings. In a recent analysis of the effect of remittances on employment performance for Central and East European economies, Leon-Ledesma and Piracha (2004) found that the impact of remittances on unemployment depends on its effect on productivity growth and investment. Econometric estimation using data from 11 transition countries from 1990 to 1999 yields support for the view that remittances have a positive impact on productivity and employment both directly and indirectly through their effect on investment.

Other studies are less upbeat and mention the potentially adverse effects of remittances in that they create a strong disincentive for domestic savings and support private consumption of (imported) goods instead of financing investment, which can potentially hamper competitiveness and increase trade deficits (Kireyev 2006). Chami et al. (2005) questioned the whole assumption that remittances play the same role in economic development as foreign direct investment and other capital flows. Empirical tests of a model in which remittances were assumed not to be profit driven, but rather compensatory transfers, yielded a negative correlation between remittances and GDP growth. This finding suggests that remittances may not be a source of capital for economic development. It has also been commonly argued that large remittance inflows can contribute to currency appreciation (Dutch disease). However, there is little empirical evidence sustaining this hypothesis. A recent study claimed that Dutch disease is less likely to occur with remittances than with natural resource booms, primarily because remittances are distributed more widely and may avoid the sorts of exacerbating strains on institutional capacity that are often associated with natural resource booms.

These apparently contradictory empirical findings on the macroeconomic impact of remittances do not necessarily conflict on a theoretical level. First, as with issues of inequality and development on the community and regional levels, the positive impacts of remittances on national development are likely to materialize only in the long term (Russell 1995). Second, their impact is disparate across countries and is ultimately contingent on the social relations and economic structures in which the foreign currency becomes embedded (Eckstein 2004). Can remittances alone trigger economic growth? Probably not.

Although remittances play an increasingly vital role in securing and actually improving the livelihoods of millions of people in the developing world, it would be naive to expect that remittances alone could solve more structural development obstacles such as an unstable political environment, misguided macroeconomic policies, lack of security, bureaucracy, corruption or deficient infrastructure. Also, legal insecurity of property tends to have devastating effects on people's ability and willingness to invest.

If states fail to implement effective political and economic reform, migration and remittances are also unlikely to contribute to nation-wide sustainable development. However, if development in origin countries takes a positive turn, if countries stabilize politically and economic growth starts to take off, then migrants are likely to be among the first to join in and recognize such new opportunities, reinforcing these positive trends through investing, circulating and returning to their origin countries. This sort of investment has happened in the past few decades with several former emigration countries as diverse as the Republic of Korea, Spain and Taiwan Province of China, and might be currently happening in a country like Turkey, where many Turks living in Germany and elsewhere in Europe play a significant role as transnational entrepreneurs in Turkey's economic growth.

3

Modern Environmentalism and Social Change

MODERN ENVIRONMENTALISM

United States

The 1960s built strong cultural momentum for environmental causes, giving birth to the modern environmental movement and large questioning in sociologists interested in analysing the movement. Widespread green consciousness moved vertically within society, resulting in a series of policy changes across many states in the U.S. and Europe in the 1970s. In the United States, this period was known as the "Environmental Decade" with the creation of the United States Environmental Protection Agency and passing of the Endangered Species Act, Clean Water Act, and amendments to the Clean Air Act. Earth Day of 1970, celebrated by millions of participants, represented the modern age of environmental thought. The environmental movement continued with incidences such as Love Canal.

Historical Studies

While the current mode of thought expressed in environmental sociology was not prevalent until the 1970s, its application is now used in analysis of ancient peoples. Societies including Easter Island, the Anaszi, and the Mayans were argued to have ended abruptly, largely due to poor environmental management. This has been challenged in later work however as the exclusive cause (biologically-trained Jared Diamond's *Collapse* (2005); or more modern work on Easter Island). The collapse of the Mayans sent a historic message that even advanced cultures are vulnerable to ecological suicide—though Diamond argues now it was less of a suicide than an environmental climate change that led to a lack of an ability to adapt—and a lack of elite willingness to adapt even when faced with the signs much earlier of nearing ecological problems.

At the same time, societal successes for Diamond included New Guinea and Tikopia island whose inhabitants have lived sustainably for 46,000 years.

John Dryzek et al. argue in *Green States and Social Movements: Environmentalism in the United States, United Kingdom, Germany, and Norway* (2003) that there may be a common global green environmental social movement, though its specific outcomes are nationalist, falling into four 'ideal types' of interaction between environmental movements and state power. They use as their case studies environmental social movements and state interaction from Norway, the United Kingdom, the United States, and Germany. They analyse the past 30 years of environmentalism and the different outcomes that the green movement has taken in different state contexts and cultures.

Recently and roughly in temporal order below, much longer-term comparative historical studies of environmental degradation are found by sociologists. There are two general trends: many employ world systems theory—analysing environmental issues over long periods of time and space; and others employ comparative historical methods. Some utilize both methods simultaneously, sometimes without reference to world systems theory.

Stephen G. Bunker (d. 2005) and Paul S. Ciccantell collaborated on two books from a world systems theory view, following commodity chains through history of the modern world system, charting the changing importance of space, time, and scale of extraction and how these variables influenced the shape and location of the main nodes of the world economy over the past 500 years. Their view of the world was grounded in extraction economies and the politics of different states that seek to dominate the world's resources and each other through gaining hegemonic control of major resources or restructuring global flows in them to benefit their locations.

The three volume work of environmental world systems theory by Sing C. Chew analyzed how "Nature and Culture" interact over long periods of time, starting with *World Ecological Degradation* (2001) In later books, Chew argued that there were three "Dark Ages" in world environmental history characterized by periods of state collapse and reorientation in the world economy associated with more localist frameworks of community, economy, and identity coming to dominate the nature/culture relationships after state-facilitated environmental destruction delegitimated other forms.

Thus recreated communities were founded in these so called 'Dark Ages,' novel religions were popularized, and perhaps most importantly to him the environment had several centuries to recover from previous destruction. Chew argues that modern green politics and bioregionalism is the start of a similar movement of the present day potentially leading to wholesale system transformation. Therefore, we may be on the edge of yet another global "dark age" which is bright instead of dark on many levels since he argues for human community returning with environmental healing as empires collapse. More case oriented studies were conducted by historical environmental sociologist Mark D. Whitaker analysing China, Japan, and Europe over 2,500 years in his book *Ecological Revolution* (2009). He argued that instead of environmental movements being "New Social Movements" peculiar to current societies, environmental movements are very old—being expressed via religious movements in the past (or in the present like in ecotheology) that begin to focus on material concerns of health, local ecology, and economic protest against state policy and its extractions. He argues past or present is very similar: that we have participated with a tragic common civilizational process of environmental degradation, economic consolidation, and lack of political representation for many millennia which has predictable outcomes. He argues that a form of bioregionalism, the bioregional state, is required to deal with political corruption in present or in past societies connected to environmental degradation. Interestingly, after looking at the world history of environmental degradation from very different methods, both sociologists Sing Chew and Mark D. Whitaker came to similar conclusions and are proponents of (different forms of) bioregionalism.

SOCIETAL-ENVIRONMENTAL DIALECTIC

In 1975, the highly influential work of Allan Schnaiberg transfigured environmental sociology, proposing a societal-environmental dialectic. This conflictual concept has overwhelming political salience. First, the economic synthesis states that the desire for economic expansion will prevail over ecological concerns. Policy will decide to maximize immediate economic growth at the expense of environmental disruption. Secondly, the managed scarcity synthesis concludes that governments will attempt to control only the most dire of environmental problems to prevent health and economic disasters.

This will give the appearance that governments act more environmentally conscious than they really do. Tertiary, the ecological synthesis generates a hypothetical case where environmental degradation is so severe that political forces would respond with sustainable policies. The driving factor would be economic damage caused by environmental degradation. The economic engine would be based on renewable resources at this point. Production and consumption methods would adhere to sustainability regulations. These conflict-based syntheses have several potential outcomes. One is that the most powerful economic and political forces will preserve the status quo and bolster their dominance. Historically, this is the most common occurrence. Another potential outcome is for contending powerful parties to fall into a stalemate. Lastly, tumultuous social events may result that redistribute economic and political resources.

BENEFITS, COSTS AND THE FORCES AFFECTING PUBLIC PARTICIPATION IN EDM

Public participation in EDM is playing an increasingly important role in the protection of the environment. The forces driving the increased use of participatory practice, the benefits accruing from same, as will as the costs and potential problems are described below.

Forces Driving Stakeholder Processes

Many different forces are at work, prior to, and throughout, a public participation programme. However, the following factors have also moved the participation debate forward. People generally resist change, especially when they do not understand or agree with the goals, the methods, the sponsor or the timing of the proposed change. So, keeping the public in the dark is often a recipe for disaster. Citizens are also increasingly reluctant to defer to 'expert' government agency opinions, and are unwilling to act as sounding boards for bodies that have already made decisions, particularly when they affect their local communities. Both of these tendencies lead to a lack of public confidence and trust, unless the relevant authorities take note of them. There are growing social expectations for environmental equality resulting in part from the high media profile given to environmental issues. Findings, that minority and low income groups in the USA had been disproportionately affected by pollution and downgraded environments, resulted in the issuing of Executive Order 12898 by President Clinton.

A far-reaching programme ensued, based on meaningful involvement and fair treatment for all races, cultures and incomes in environmental decision-making. "The transmittance of 'experience', rather than knowledge, is the critical neglected dimension of decision-making, particularly as it pertains to our national decision-making"(Barkenbus, J. 1998, p.9). For example development planning in Dublin City requires largely the same expertise as rural development planning, but the experience, vision and values of the rural population may be very different to that of their city cousins. The further the EDM process is from central government, the more pertinent becomes the public participation in same, and in this context, face-to-face meetings are critical to producing real learning and trust.

Previously, with the exception of Development Plans and Waste Management Plans, public involvement in EDM in Ireland was largely restricted to the minimal fulfillment of the two "rules of national and constitutional justice, and in particular 'audi alteram partem' (hear both sides)".

In practice this meant that firstly a decision was made and this was then presented to the public for comment, a process also known as 'report and comment'. So, both sides have been heard, but one has the power, and can choose to ignore the input of the other. Changes driven by the Aarhus Declaration and Principal 10 will affect many areas of environmental regulation and planning, opening them up to far greater public participation. Alongside this is the increasing transparency of regulatory processes.

The directive on Freedom of Access to Information on the Environment (Directive 90/313/EC) SI.125 of 1998 and The Freedom of Information Act, 1997 have opened up the EDM processes to closer scrutiny by the public. By compelling the relevant authorities to release documents on request, the inner workings of government have been opened up for closer examination, and relevant information freed up to enable more effective public participation in environmental governance.

There is also a growing diffusion of information. The many portals of information available on the internet, together with the traditional media, libraries and the excellent work, in Ireland, of ENFO, all increase awareness of environmental issues.

Since the Aarhus Convention, which agreed to recognise and support the crucial role played by ENGO's in articulating opinions of an environmentally concerned public, European funding has been given to support their activities (Jeffrey, D.W. 2001). €4.62 million was distributed in Europe in 2003. In Ireland, the Department of the Environment and Local Government allocated €132,000 in 2001, and €133,000 in 2002 to build capacity in 23 ENGOs with a national remit.

This was done via a limited company known as Environmental (Ecological) Core Funding Ltd. (Morrisey, P. 2003). It was estimated in 1999 that there were some 500 International ENGOs (Environmental NGOs) world-wide that operated in three or more countries. Apart from the rapid growth of the ENGOs, there is clearly expanded interest in participation. Public unrest at the prospect of development, without formal opportunity for participation in decision-making, is increasingly responsible for expensive delays. In the UK, policing of antiroad protests has alone cost millions of pounds (Treweek, J.1999). The Shell Oil Company, in the UK, was eventually forced to adopt a major consultation programme on the fate of the Brent Spar, North Sea oil exploration rig, as a result of the international reaction to the campaign waged by Greenpeace. (Acland, A. 2002, 4-1).

Hampshire County Council, in England, with a population of some 2,000,000, had to scrap its waste management plan, following much public unrest, and start from scratch, with a well planned and successful public participation programme. A waste plan was then adopted which had broad support, and is being put into action. (Acland, A. 2002, 4-2). Many industry organizations are realizing that for their good image, public safety, and the longterm financial well-being of their members, responsible partnership with host communities is essential.

There is some evidence that corporations which build sound, responsive relationships with all their stakeholders tend to be longer lived and more successful as businesses in the long term than other corporations (Wheeler and Sillanpaa, 1997). Olson, M. and Toyne, P.(2000) also report a study which suggests a direct correlation between increased public involvement of the public in corporate affairs, and increased profits.

The Chemical Manufacturers Association in the U.S.A. (representing 90% of all chemical production) set up the Responsible Care Initiative, which sets codes of practice. There are six areas covered by these codes viz: Community Awareness and Emergency Response (CAER); The Pollution Code; The Process Safety Code; The Distribution Code; The Employee Health and Safety Code; and The Product Stewardship Code. In relation to all of these, the guiding principles exhort their members "to recognize and respond to community concerns about chemicals and our operations, and to work with others to solve problems created by past handling and disposal of hazardous substances." The adoption, by some industries, of environmental management systems, such as I.S.O. 14001, and E.M.A.S (Eco-Management and Audit Systems) shows their belief that a transparent and responsive industry is also more likely to be a viable one. E.M.A.S. requires public reporting of environmental management and auditing. Internationally, trends towards decentralization in many countries, increases in the numbers of countries with representative democratic forms of government, and conditions laid down by donor agencies on development loans, e.g. The World Bank, are some of the international forces bringing increased public involvement in EDM. Whilst it is not the intention of the author to go into detail on risk assessment and disaster management., it is worth noting that public participation should, under Council Directive 96/82/EC (Seveso ?) and the Council Decision 1999/847/EC, play an important part in both of these important areas. Wates, N. (2000) gives guidelines for organizing community risk assessment and disaster management programmes, whilst the "UK Guidelines for Risk Assessment and Management" (Defra UK. 2002) give a good introductory insight into the social aspects of risk, and in particular the factors influencing risk perceptions. These factors are listed here and are also relevant to other areas of EDM.

- o Risks which are involuntarily imposed (e.g. pollution from an incinerator) tend to be seen as less acceptable than voluntary ones (e.g. bonfires)
- o Unfamiliar risks (e.g. GMO's) tend to cause concern especially when it appears that they are poorly understood by science.

- o Activities associated with a dreaded form of death (e.g. cancer) are viewed with alarm.
- o Man-made or technological risks (e.g. nuclear power) are less acceptable than natural ones (e.g. Radon). o A risk involving a single large-scale consequence (e.g. civil aviation accident) causes more concern than risks which result in numerous small scale consequences (e.g. car accidents).
- o Alarm may be caused by risks when the consequences of exposure are delayed and cause hidden or irreversible damage (e.g. ionizing radiations).
- o Inequitable distribution of risks and benefits as a result of a particular activity is likely to make the risk less acceptable. An example here might be the remaining operative Chernobyl nuclear power stations. Employees, knowing the risks involved but needing to earn a living, would have a different view of risk to others living in the vicinity, and different again to those living 100 kms away, and relying on the electricity to heat their homes in temperatures of-30°C.
- o Activities posing a threat to certain groups such as children or future generations are generally more worrying.
- o Risks which are the subject of controversy and contradictory information generally cause concern.

Benefits of Public Participation.

The protection and enhancement of the environment is the main aim of most EDM processes, and public participation can improve the quality of both the process and the end decision. The participation process is also a learning one for all the stakeholders involved, especially if there is a free flow of information between the parties.

For the public it can often be the first experience of taking an active part in the democratic process. EDM processes benefit from the direct and immediate knowledge held by citizens and business, concerning environmental conditions in their communities and industries. Encouraging the public and other stakeholders to share their knowledge, with the regulatory authorities, fosters better-informed decisions and decreases the likelihood of environmental harm, whilst increasing project viability. Of 25 overseas projects sponsored and evaluated by the World Bank, 13 failed mainly through lack of local input. It should be realized that "wisdom is not limited to scientific specialists and government officials," (120 p.6) and that "rational analysis, carried on in ignorance of political reality, may well end up so divorced form social reality, as to be of little use to anyone."

Public participation gives broader perspectives on a particular process, and early involvement gives: added time to study issues and develop the process; enhanced credibility of the decision making process; early identification of the diverse perspectives on the issues of concern; and the generation of solution options (E.L.I. Research Report, 1997). Better-designed projects, which avoid costly delays in appraisal and implementation, can also result from early and planned consultations and public participation. For the proponent, early participation can have the added benefit of diffusing opposition to a project. If a broad based consensus is built, it can also lead to a public sense of 'ownership' (Acland, A. 2002, 4-2). The public's enthusiasm is potentially a powerful motivating force for the EDM process. Public input can also supplement scarce government monitoring, inspection, and enforcement, resources (Bisset, R. 2000).

Involvement in EDM is a learning experience giving the public insight into the governance process. If the experience is good, it powers the way for future co-operation. The converse can also be true! Experience has also shown that environmental issues are powerful catalysts of civic 9 participation and serve as a good incentive for citizens' action and responsible democracy (Technical Document 1, 1996). Executive Order 12898 introduced by President Clinton is a far-reaching programme, based on meaningful involvement and fair treatment for all races, cultures and incomes in environmental decision-making. It has done much to prevent the dumping of dirty industry on the marginalized members of the USA citizenry. The order requires state agencies, and in particular the EPA, to pro-actively seek out the disenfranchised members of communities likely to be affected by developments, or already living in depleted environments, and encourage them to become involved in the relevant EDM processes.

Costs of Public Participation

There is limited information on the relative costs of using the different methods of participation practice, although some attempt is made to quantify which describes each method. Actual costings for specific processes are given in a number of studies. Clearly deliberative processes, which are used to engage relevant stakeholders in debate, discussion and deliberation, could only be done as part of a major project. Expenses range from €20-40,000 (for a citizen jury with 16 participants for 5 days), to €200-300,000 (for 3 community advisory groups of 16 people over 6 months).

However, extensive use of participatory processes in the 'Wise Use of Flood Plains' project showed costs of about 10% of the above. Most of this funding was used to employ facilitators (Cuff, J. 2001). The costs to members of the public in time and money, as well as emotional stress in situations where access to EDM is limited, do not appear to have been estimated previously. An attempt is made to gather some facts about the first two in this study. The intensity of the stakeholder process, including commitments of time, energy and money, and the often, uncertain results, has led to a burnout phenomenon amongst many participants, and from all stakeholder groups. (Yosie, T.F. and Herbst, T.D. 1998) Excessive raised expectations about participation can lead to frustration and anger with a breakdown in trust. It is essential then to be clear with all participants as to the limits of influence of the process. Where an infrastructure project crosses planning jurisdiction boundaries or where more than one regulator is involved, the costs to the public, state and proponents are multiplied.

The increased time scale and expense involved in public participation is of particular significance in projects with a small capital funding. An international example of this would be the AIJ projects (Activities Implemented Jointly under the Climate Change Convention). These projects already require appraisal by two governments and then there is the extra of public participations costs. After this they must compete with traditional energy supply systems, where often no regulatory costs are involved.

Problems Encountered in Public Participation Practice

The main areas of difficulty affecting public participation are attitudinal, lack of capacity to deliver programmes, lack of clarity about what outcomes are possible and the lack of a legislative framework. Some aspects of these issues are addressed below. The difference between success and failure is not always clear. If the public participation process delivers a clear decision, which is then overruled by the legislature, is this a success? (E.L.I. Research Report 1997 p. 13). A good example here is the Bantry Bay Integrated Coastal Zone Management (ICZM) Project, funded for three years under the EU Life Programme. After three years of intense community activity and the drawing up and enactment of a text-book public participation plan, the Bantry Bay Coastal Zone Charter was created.

At this point, no further funding was available, and the Project was closed down. Clearly the process was a success, but the result not. There is a general lack of experience of participatory processes in Ireland, and very few stakeholders have experienced planned participation processes. There may be suspicion, cynicism, or enthusiasm, but there is unlikely to be previous training. Suspicion about participation could be from politicians, who may feel their power is being diluted, or from ENGOs that have very specific and fixed viewpoints. Cynicism could be from previous public participation processes which were poorly managed, leaving participants reluctant to try again (E.L.I. Research Report, 1997). Citizens are frustrated when they are treated as adversaries, rather than welcome participants in the EDM process........ they feel they have been invited too late in the process. Public 'hearings' often do not include 'listening'. Citizens efforts and ideas are not included in proposals and no reason given.

The resources available to proponents and government are overwhelming. Litigation and direct action at least get a reaction" (C.E.Q. 1997. p.18). Similarly, public hearings are criticised for: being held at times inconvenient for the public, establishing an atmosphere that inhibits dialogue, and conducting proceedings that intimidate the public (Lein, K.L. 2003, p.56).

The lack of a clearly defined purpose can also means that the role of the public is sometimes unclear not only to the public but to those delivering the process, with the consequence that the participation process chosen is often unsuitable for the particular EDM process. The making available of the necessary resources for a worthwhile public participation process, whether by the proponent or the regulator, by the commitment of personnel and finances, is essential. The implications for project proponents, of not having a properly planned and funded participatory EDM process, may prove much more costly, than dealing with the backlash. In many circumstances, the choice increasingly is not whether to involve the public, but how to get the best value from the chosen process.

To avoid hearing from only the activist or the powerful elite, and in order to get the widest sweep of opinion and information, authorities must reach out into the community. In this regard some activities are best avoided, for example public meetings.

In the absence of trained facilitators these can often come down to 'he who shouts loudest wins!' Lack of technical support for the public, and difficulties in getting access to information can diminish the ability of the public to play a meaningful part in EDM processes.

Public access to independent expertise in a particular technical/scientific field can prove difficult, particularly where the proponent of a project is a monopoly employer in the industry in the state. Faced with five weeks to object to a planning proposal, for example, this is a major hurdle. Added to this, it is the experience of the author that stakeholders with no technical/scientific background find it problematic to access, comprehend or evaluate data and information, especially under these short time constraints.

The feelings of powerlessness engendered by these hurdles, add to public perceptions of a lack of influence at both lower and higher levels of national and European government. "Consultations of interested parties.... can only ever supplement, and never replace, procedures and decisions of legislative bodies which possess democratic legitimacy" (COM (2002) 704. final p.4). This sense of powerlessness may be part of the reason why, even in cases where considerable energy and resources are expended, to identify individuals and groups, only a small proportion of the public ever attend participation programmes (Petts, J. and Leach, B. 2000. p.18). Public involvement may actually result in an increased level of conflict (134.p18). Becoming involved in a consultative process where the decision has already been made, or where the possible outcomes are not made clear at the outset, can lead to a great deal of frustration.

Anger may follow when the input of the public is ignored, especially following prolonged constructive engagement with an EDM process. Conflict can also occur between professionals. One source of such disagreements could evolve from the different emphases of 'scientific peer review' and 'social peer review'. The scientific peer review process is well established, and is essential to assess the technical information provided to policy makers. The parallel social peer review, designed to obtain societal acceptance and legitimacy for the decisions rendered, by contrast, does not have a set of recognised professional standards. (E.L.I. Research Report. 1997. p.14). It should also be remembered that whilst science may strive for the 'truth', the opinions of scientists are coloured by their values and beliefs. Scientists, engineers and other 'experts' should show respect in the face of 'emotional', cultural and traditional forms of wisdom. The perceptions created by a technocratic philosophy encourage NIMBY activism and further polarise communities.

The resulting deadlock frustrates the ability of planners to achieve consensus on initial issues and contributes to anti-participation attitudes. Therefore, rather than define 'NIMBY'attitudes as an irrational response to problems ordinary citizens cannot grasp, the solution is to encourage more participation not less (Lein, K.L. 2003. p.56). The misconception that the public are overly emotional, ill-informed and solely motivated by selfish interests, in their obstruction of facilities for the common good, leads to an information-based strategy. The assumption being that, 'if only the public knew the truth!' This assumes the existence of an objective truth to know (Petts, J. and Leach, B. 2000. p.9). The conflict that arises from having different bodies making decisions on different parts of the same EDM process can often confuse the public understanding and increase frustrations. For example the executive split of planning and environmental matters in some aspects of development between the Local Authority and the EPA. Public involvement in these circumstances must deal with two different agencies.

Organisations resist change, and communication blocks within organisations can prevent them from making timely responses to their publics. The established routines and organizational systems of many bodies seek to promote the 'status quo'. Organisational structures which support sustainability, and therefore public participation, are a threat to 'command and control' style management systems. Managers, who have risen to power in this style of structure, frequently resist the transition to alternative structures, which embrace public consultation (Griffiths, A. 2000). Many opportunities for public participation are laid down in the environmental legal framework. Where legislation does not specify early public involvement, then it is at the discretion of the relevant authority, and dependent on the opinion of the relevant public servant.

For example, in the development planning process, the Manager's reporting of the consultative process clearly includes the names and nature of all submissions together with his response to them, whereas in making an Air Quality Management Plan there is no legal compulsion to show how any submission might have affected the final decision.

The recent use by Cork City Council of Article 81 of The Planning and Development Act, Regulations, 2001, to enter into a public/private partnership with a company previously refused planning permission to develop the same site (TP 02/26234), leaves the public only minimal scope for comment and no route to appeal any decision made. Under section 19 of the Protection Of The Environment Act, 2003, the making, variation or replacement of a Waste Management Plan, has been made an Executive Function. This has removed the immediate political accountability of the decision-making, and so removed another route for public input.

THE HISTORY OF ENVIRONMENTAL SOCIOLOGY

Sociology has traditionally made a distinction between humans and nature. As we will see, this is precisely the problem that humans coincidentally suffer from when interacting with their surroundings. Automatically, it seems we are put at a disadvantage by forming human social structures and ignoring the larger all-embracing society of the animal and vegetal realms. If one were to think in terms of humans as an integral part of nature, and therefore inherently natural, many problems associated with the abuse of the environment should be positively affected. Classical sociology was concerned primarily with humans as a part of systems. These systems were limited primarily to the social and economic sectors of human society. The emphasis was on something akin to soul searching; looking within for solutions that are available without. As Redclift and Benton point out in Social Theory and the Environment, "The classical sociologies deriving from Weber and the German neo-Kantian tradition, and from Durkheim and French structuralism, establish (albeit by different theoretical moves) sharp nature/society dichotomies.". It seems that the traditional sociologies paid scant attention to the range that the human habitat may take, and focused more squarely on man. Let's explore the views classical sociologists held on humans and their relation to their environment.

Durkheim

Emile Durkheim was one of the founding fathers of sociology, and was the first French sociologist. To Durkheim, men were creatures whose desires were unlimited. Unlike other animals, they are not satiated when their biological needs are fulfilled. "The more one has, the more one wants, since satisfactions received only stimulate instead of filling needs." It follows from this natural insatiability of the human animal that his desires can only be held in check by external controls, that is, by societal control. Society imposes limits on human desires and constitutes "a regulative force [which] must play the same role for moral needs which the organism plays for physical needs." In well-regulated societies, social controls set limits on individual propensities so that each individual knows the eventual limit to his/her activity. Durkheim did distinguish the social realm from the psychic, biological and mineral realms, yet he saw society as a phenomenon of nature. This can be witnessed in many plant or animal settings, where associations are formed which enable the species to survive or flourish. Of the traditional approaches, Durkheim's does lend credence to the idea that environmental problems can be understood within the context of cultural production and reproduction. Durkheim's positivism and constructivism gave us the legacy of examining environmental problems as a science with observable consequences and socially constructed causes.

Positivism: This doctrine was first called positivism by the 19th-century French mathematician and philosopher Auguste Comte, but some of the positivist concepts may be traced to the British philosopher David Hume and the German philosopher Immanuel Kant. Comte was, in the main, interested in a reorganization of social life for the good of humanity through scientific knowledge, and thus *control of natural forces.*

Although Durkheim formulated an organismic theory of society where each organism must function in its own place and time in order for the whole to remain healthy, he neglected to bring the environment in which that work is being done into the picture. He did not however insist as his contemporaries did that nature was "socially produced". Durkheim introduced the notions of agency and structure to sociological theory; agency is defined as the power that humans have to operate independently of the constraining social structure. The structure itself is dependent on agency for its existence, it is comprised of such things as laws, conventions, taboos and so on. An interesting result of Durkheim's theories of agency structure is that they can be subversively used to undermine the traditional lack of attention paid to environmental problems. Agency would seemingly allow us to either neglect or care for the environment as we so choose, but the social structure could dictate certain modes of action which can be oriented towards a conservationist perspective. Further, if the environment itself were to be seen as the governing structure within which humans must operate, with the laws of nature guiding human agency, it seems against (human) nature to destroy the very structure which supports our meagre selves.

Weber

Max Weber would probably have rejected this idea of the environment as a determining structure; he was concerned primarily with humans as a system unto themselves, their being constituted the only social reality. He did not believe that sociologists (or any one else) could discover some overarching structure that was universal to humankind. Ironically, Weber devoted much of his academic life to describing the alienation of the capitalist worker, where human agency was largely overruled by the hierachical structures of instrumental rationality and beauracracy. This disenchantment stems from the separation of the workers not from their capabilities for the use of agency, but from their implicit rejection of nature in favour of capitalist business practices. The beauraucratic structure may stifle the workers, but the true distance is between the surrounding environment and their desk jobs. Some may posit that this separation of humans from their environment is a product of the technology that is being employed in these workplaces, as if technology were something alien or unnatural. We must remember however, that humans are inherently both a part of and a product of nature; how then can human constructs be unnatural? They are simply an extension of our natural ability to use tools and to communicate with one another. Weberian disenchantment is quite different, for it is the arbitrary construction of limits, punishments and rewards that make up the beauraucratic authority system. Is this really unlike the structure that we deploy against nature? Both are arbitrary, both possess too narrow a scope to assess all the complexities of a system and both impose control in a manner that tends to be destructive to the subject of the control. The worker becomes disenchanted; the environment becomes polluted.

Marx

The most "green" of the early social theories, Marxist thought usually sees any society as a system of societal relations. This allows for an understanding that social production of goods depends on relations between individuals as well as between people and nature. Marx did make a distinction between nature and society, nature was what provided the raw materials with which the labourers made their living and fed their families. Marx saw science and society in rational terms, beleiving that science was a progressive and liberating force, one that would enable humankind to gain control over nature and therefore to better control their chosen path in life. According to Marx, the appropriation of natural resources in this manner were only possible in a specific social setting.

He theorized that in the transformation of resources into goods for human consumption, humans themselves were transformed. Despite this, he thought that relations between humans and their environment was static, for they are both essentially social and common to each step of social existence. Therefore, the interactions between humans and their environment cannot provide a source of change in society; this can only occur between groups of people.

Marxist ideology relies heavily on the idea that economic development under capitalism involves the creation of value as resources are transformed into commodities. The problem is, there cannot be creation without destruction. In order to create value, we must destroy and sully valuable natural resources; not valuable as commodities, but as a life sustaining matrix upon which we all rely. The value of natural resources must always be weighed against the long term consequences of their use.

Neo-Malthusianism

Works like Hardin's the tragedy of the commons (1968) reformulated Malthusian thought about abstract population increases causing famines into a model of individual selfishness at larger scales causing degradation of common pool resources like the air, water, the oceans, or general environmental conditions. Hardin offered mass privatization or a tyrannical state to induce presumed environmental solutions. Many other sociologists shared this view of solutions well into the 1970s. There have been many critiques of this view, particularly sociologist Elinor Ostrom or economist Amartya Sen.

Even though much of mainstream journalism considers Malthusianism the only view of environmentalism, most sociologists would disagree with Malthusianism since social organizational issues of environmental degradation are more demonstrated to cause environmental problems than abstract population or selfishness per se. For examples of this critique, Ostrom in her book *Governing the Commons: The Evolution of Institutions for Collective Action* (1990) argues that instead of selfishness always causing degradation, selfishness can sometimes be the motivator of people taking care of their common property goods by changing the organizational rules of the extraction rules in their regions, in her research of durable property management systems around common pool resources that have lasted for centuries in some areas of the world.

Amartya Sen argues in his book *Poverty and Famines: An Essay on Entitlement and Deprivation* (1980) that population expansion fails to cause famines or degradation as Malthusians or Neo-Malthusians argue. Instead, in documented cases, a lack of political entitlement to resources the exist in abundance causes famines in some populations. He documents how famines can occur even in the midst of plenty or in the context of low populations. He argues that famines (and environmental degradation) would only occur in non-functioning democracies or unrepresentative states.

Eco-Marxist scholar Allan Schnaiberg (below) argues against Malthusianism with the rationale that under larger capitalist economies, human degradation moved from localized, population-based degradation to organizationally caused degradation of capitalist political economies to blame. He gives the example of the organized degradation of rainforest areas which states and capitalists push people off the land before it is degraded by organizational means. Thus, many authors are critical of Malthusianism—from sociologists (Schnaiberg), to economists (Sen), to political scientists (Ostrom)—and all focus on how a country's social organization of its extraction can degrade the environment independent of abstract population.

ENVIRONMENTALISM AS A SOCIAL MOVEMENT

The term 'social movement' designates the principal category into which social scientists have slotted the new phenomenon of environmentalism. As a prelude to examining how they have done this, it is helpful to consider briefly the relationship between objects and categories. When scientists of any variety allocate a new object to a familiar category, they do so as part of the process of investigating its place in the wider scheme of things, however that might be conceptualized.

The initial allocation is usually pro-visional; a close examination of the object may indicate that it would be better placed elsewhere. A set of broad categories thus forms an analytical framework within which the specific characteristics of objects can be examined and compared. But the categories themselves are not immutable; science leaves their boundaries open to question, and, to recall Bohannan's comment, one person's black box is another's field of investigation. It is the continuous examination of their contents that results in analytical categories being redefined. Categories and their contents are thus held perpetually (though not continually) in suspense.

This has been the pattern of social scientific studies of environmentalism as a social movement. Some analyses, probably the vast majority, have taken for granted the status of environmentalism as a social movement. They have used the category as a broad framework within which to examine the special features of environmentalism, such as its relationship with science and its global character, without questioning the boundaries of the category. Rudig et al. noted this tendency in British writing on social movements:

A notable feature of much of British writing is the frequent but perfunctory use of the term social movement without exploration of its potential connotations or efforts to set it into relevant theoretical or conceptual contexts. Typically it is undefined and is often used quite promiscuously.

This comment is presented as a criticism, and is valid as such in the context of their discussion of social movement theory. But in broader terms, every analysis needs to leave some concepts unquestioned. If everything were open to investigation, there would be no solid ground in which to anchor an interpretation, no way of tying it to a broader field of study. Thus, in two of the early empirical studies of environmentalism, Harry et al. (1969) and Devall (1970) used 'social movement' as nothing more than a convenient label. It served to locate the object of analysis within a broad typology of social phenomena, in order to relieve the reader of any concern about what kind of a thing was being discussed, and direct their attention to what most interested the analysts, in these instances, the social characteristics of conservationists.

In a similar way, McCormick referred to the phenomenon whose history he was describing as 'the global environmental movement', but paid no attention to the sense in which it might be called a movement. Numerous studies have used the label in a similar way to provide a context for analyses of environmentalism in different countries. The label signals that, in all these cases, something similar is being discussed, and that comparisons are therefore valid and possibly interesting, but suspends interest in how that broad something might itself be understood.

According to Yearley's (1994) analysis, this use of the category is more in line with the American interpretative tradition than that established in Europe. In the American tradition, 'social movement' is typically treated as an 'empirical generalization', recognized by its broad organizational features: 'more organized than protesting crowds or mobs, less formalized than political parties and more concerted than simple social trends'. European theorists have tended to identify social movements in terms of 'their perceived capacity for major social transformation', perceived, that is, by the analyst, who is drawn to search for signs of transformative capacity.

For Touraine, it is present when one class struggles against another for control of historical processes. For Melucci it is present when norms are contested and sources of power are challenged. For Eyerman and Jamison it resides in what they call 'cognitive praxis', an attempt to generate new knowledge through communicative action. A considerable amount of interpretation of observed reality is required in order to recognize any of these criteria, leaving no clear, non-arbitrary way of identifying social movements for analysis.

In addition, although it is the capacity to transform that defines a social movement, there is a tendency to regard as 'true' social movements only those which actually transform (there being no other proof of transformative capacity than actual transformation). In other words, true social movements can only be identified retrospectively, not only after a movement has been analysed, but also after its social consequences have become clear.

This effectively rules out the possibility of identifying a phenomenon as a social movement as it develops and as a framework in which to examine its special features. The European tradition, while it may have advanced our understanding of the role of social movements in a wider context, has therefore not produced the kinds of definitions which can form a useful framework for analysis. In a similar vein, Eyerman and Jamison made the observation that movements, by definition, are transitory, they live and die, and whatever innovations they introduce are either rejected or adopted by wider society. However reasonable this might appear, it could not be used as a criterion for identifying social movements empirically, unless we were to confine our studies to movements that had already died, and whose transitory nature was therefore confirmed.

Jamison et al. forged their own definition of social movements by combining transformational and organizational criteria, and in doing so claimed to bridge the divide between theorists in the European tradition, for whom social movements are sources of new collective identities, and those in the American tradition who see social movements as mechanisms for 'resource mobilization', and identify them empirically by their organizational features. However, their comparative analysis of environmentalism in Sweden, Denmark and Holland shows that their new composite definition is found wanting as an empirical tool. Environmentalism takes on different shapes in different countries, because environmentalists have to organize their activities according to the political context in which they operate.

The analysis showed that in Sweden environmentalism did not develop a distinctive oppositional character, for two main reasons. First, there are financial incentives for new organizations to formalize their structure along the lines of established political groups, with the result that 'the borders between the established and the oppositional are blurred'. Second, it is difficult for new political actors to loosen the grip on Swedish political culture, of the long-established cleavage between the socialist and bourgeois blocs. Instead, new interests tend to be incorporated into those of the existing blocs and promoted through their activities. As a result, in Sweden, 'environmentalism can hardly be called a social movement'. Thus, despite their declared intention to combine transformational and organizational criteria, the analysts fall back on the organizational when identifying social movements empirically. Although environmentalists in all three countries share the same collective identity, environmentalism in Sweden is less of a social movement because it does not possess the appropriate organizational features.

The distinction between organizational and transformational criteria is significant in relation to the perceived existence of two environmentalisms. Both the conservative and the radical forms (or indeed, in some cases, a single undifferentiated environmentalism) have been seen as displaying the organizational features of a social movement. But almost by definition, only the more radical form has the capacity to transform society, and so analysts who have understood social movements in this way have tended to restrict their use of the term to the more radical form.

Thus Cotgrove who, quoting Banks, saw social movements as self-conscious attempts 'to introduce innovations into a social system', suggested that 'something more like a coherent movement emerges' if we focus only on the groups that fundamentally challenge dominant economic values.

However, it would probably be more accurate to say that the transformative capacity of radical environmentalism has more often been seen as identifying it as a 'new' social movement. More will be said about this when discussing the relationship of environmentalism to established political allegiances.

Environmentalism as a Political Ideology

Social scientists have treated 'political ideology', like 'social movement', as a category within which to examine the distinctive features of environmentalism. Again, the term is left undefined and 'used quite promiscuously' by some analysts and subjected to quite close scrutiny by others, though this does not always yield a clear definition. Cotgrove, following Mannheim (1966), defined ideology as 'beliefs and values which are justifications for the status quo, the preservation of existing institutions and the interests which they serve'.

As such, they contrast with environmentalist perspectives which he regarded as 'utopias', visions of a better society. And yet he also referred to environmentalist ideologies, and identified the function of an ideology as 'legitimating or justifying courses of action', regardless of whether the actions concerned support or oppose the status quo.

Dobson, following Donald and Hall, also defined ideology in terms of its function: political ideologies provide 'the concepts, categories, images and ideas by means of which people make sense of their social and political world, form projects, come to a certain consciousness of their place in that world and act in it'. In this sense, ideology fulfils both cognitive and practical functions; it enables people to understand the world and their place within it, and forms a basis for action. Paehlke provided a more purely substantive definition: an ideology is 'a worldview both value laden and comprehensive', but he also saw the practical component of ideology as definitive. His aim was to develop 'a political theory with ideological potential', a potential which he identified as lying in the ability of environmentalism to present an effective challenge to the dominant political order.

From these and other studies it is possible to identify three features of environmentalism which analysts have seen as signifying its status as a political ideology: its comprehensiveness, its coherence and its practical potential. The comprehensiveness of environmentalism lies in its ability to present a vision of a complete alternative society, a 'post-industrial' and 'sustainable' society. Not surprisingly, some analysts identify this feature only in the more radical form of environmentalism.

By definition, radical environmentalism rejects a managerial and piecemeal approach to environmental change and seeks a comprehensive overhaul of society's values and institutions. Thus for Dobson, 'ecologism' is an ideology, whereas the more conservative perspective (which he calls 'environmentalism') is not.

Paehlke, however, made little of the radical/conservative distinction, and identified environmentalism in terms of a single though wide-ranging set of values. He observed that 'the opponents of environmentalism apparently saw its ideological potential before its advocates did', in that they recognized that the values espoused by environmental campaigners (respect for nature, a need to reduce waste) held far-reaching implications for social change.

The internal coherence of environmentalism has been examined at some length by Goodin (1992) who, though he did not identify environmentalism explicitly as a political ideology, analysed it in ways consistent with the concepts of ideology discussed above.

For Goodin the distinction between conservative and radical environmentalism (expressed as 'shallow' and 'deep' ecology;) is less significant than the relationship between what environmentalists value and the kinds of actions they advocate. A theory of value implies a theory of agency, in the sense that what is seen as valuable should be protected through action.

Goodin identified nature or 'naturalness' as the core environmentalist value. People value nature, he suggested, because it provides them with a context in which to set their own projects and activities and, in so doing, enables them to see some sense and pattern in their lives.

He argued that, although this theory of value has clear implications for the kinds of public policies that environmentalists might advocate, it does not necessarily hold implications for individual lifestyles. The need to see personal lives set in a larger context demands that the context itself (nature) be protected, but it also demands that personal lives be somehow distinguishable both from the larger context and from each other. It is therefore 'logically coherent', according to Goodin, for environmentalists to advocate policies which protect the natural world, while refusing to adopt a green personal lifestyle.

Goodin's analysis would seem to hold out some promise for the practical potential of environmentalism as a political ideology. Individuals are more likely to support environmentalist goals if they are not expected to give up their cherished patterns of activity. Not so Dobson's analysis which, in exploring the implications of radical ecologism, emphasizes the practical difficulties of pursuing 'Green' objectives in a society which appears receptive only to a more conservative 'green' message. He pointed out that in Britain, Green activists tend to speak with a green voice in order to make their message more palatable, with the result that the true voice of ecologism is not heard in public.

What Paehlke would call the 'ideological potential' of radical environmentalism is thus destroyed by the perceived need to compromise. In contrast, Paehlke's own analysis seems to suggest that some degree of accommodation between environmentalism and other political perspectives is necessary in order for the ideological potential of environmentalism to be fulfilled.

Paehlke saw this potential in the ability of environmentalism to present a realistic alternative to 'neoconservatism', which he saw as the dominant ideology in Anglo-American democracies during the 1980s. The ability of environmentalism to achieve this, he suggested, depends to some degree on its relationship with other established perspectives in the political spectrum.

ENVIRONMENT BECAME THE SOCIAL ENVIRONMENT

Laying the conceptual foundations for the new profession of social work, Mary Richmond (1922) acknowledged the physical environment as an important contextual consideration for practice but perceived its importance in terms of only its social aspects, asserting that the physical environment "becomes part of the social environment" to the extent that it "frequently has its social aspects". From the outset, the profession of social work was more comfortable using social science lenses to view the environment rather than perspectives from the physical or natural sciences. What happened later when the profession adopted an ecological perspective from the natural sciences? This ecological perspective was distorted to re-affirm the profession's emphasis on the social environment. Consider Gordon's (1969) work that called attention to social work's newly declared "simultaneous dual focus on organism and environment", a statement of the ecological perspective perhaps in its purest form. Gordon, however, immediately went on to declare his assumption that the organism would be "interpreted by psychological theory" while the environment could be "interpreted by sociological and economic theory". Similar to Richmond's work, here was another clear direction to understand the environment exclusively in social terms. Gordon (1981) later asserted that "the ultimate goal of social work is to bring about a balance between the realities of a person's capabilities and a person's social situation", with no mention of the physical environment at all.

Developing this ecological perspective into a functional systems approach for social work, Pincus and Minahan (1973) proposed four basic systems for practice, all of which were social (the change agent system; the client system; the target system; and the action system). From this systems perspective, "the focus of social work practice is on the interactions between people and systems in the social environment" with a goal of restoration of balance or equilibrium within immediate social systems where there had been some disruption. Considerations of the physical environment were beyond the scope of this approach. Building on these foundations, a pattern was established in the mainstream social work literature whereby the environment would be transformed into the social environment, with the physical environment disappearing altogether. No adequate rationale or explanation would be offered, and the switch was generally unnoticed or unacknowledged. Consider a few examples.

Yelaja (1985) presented the ecological metaphor as a major influence on social work with its emphasis on "the reciprocal relationships between the individual and the environment and the continuous adaptation of both person and environment to each other". Yet the very next sentence declared that "human growth and development constantly change in relation to the social environment – and the social environment changes in response to human factors". Notice the switch. Within two sentences, the "environment" became the "social environment." The physical environment had disappeared without explanation, effectively written out of the ecological equation. Miley, O'Melia, and DuBois (2004) similarly set out a promising view of transactions between people and their environments, explaining how "people affect their environments and, likewise, the social and physical environment affects people". On the very same page, however, they reaffirmed "social work's focus on social functioning" which they presented as the balance between coping efforts and the demands of the "social environment." Once again, the physical environment was dropped without explanation.

Heinonen and Spearman (2006) explained that "the primary focus of social work should not be on psychological forces, the environment, or the social structure, but on the interface or relationship between the person and the social environment". In a single sentence, the triad of person, environment, and social structure became the duality of person and social environment. While this was an interesting and relatively quick instance of the familiar switch, arguably the most efficient example comes from a generalist practice textbook by Hull, Jr. and Kirst-Ashman (2004).

Not all social work authors left the physical environment completely behind. A minority declared the physical environment to be an integral component of their worldview and foundation for practice. Sadly, many of these pronouncements were quickly undercut by less than full support for the environment in subsequent applications. Ecological language is frequently used only as window dressing for conventional approaches that subsequently ignore the physical environment in their assessment tools and practice models. Once again, selected examples illustrate the pattern. Consider that Neugeboren's (1996) book with the promising title Environmental Practice in the Human Services included only one paragraph that dealt directly with the physical environment, and this was completely focused on agency physical space (with mention made of lighting patterns, non-skid surfaces, safety features, and corridor length).

Even when the physical environment is presented conceptually as an important consideration for social work, it seldom makes the diagrammed practice model. Lehmann and Coady (2001) defined a client's environment as "any aspect of the physical, social, and cultural environment, and what is most important will vary with individuals, time, and geography". The physical environment here was an integral component of the overall environment for social work practice and a potential variable influencing human activity.

For some unexplained reason, however, the accompanying diagram of this ecological perspective labeled social and cultural contexts while completely ignoring the physical environment. Sheafor and Horejsi (2006) similarly defined the environment broadly as "one's surroundings-that multitude of physical and social structures, forces, and processes that affect humans and all other life forms" but then made a distinction between the "immediate environment" defined in terms of social systems, and the "distant environment" which included features of "clean air, drinkable water, shelter, and good soil to produce food".

For no apparent reason, nature was relegated to the distance as background. Three pages later, the illustrated model of practice featured a background labeled only as "the social environment" with no mention whatsoever of the physical environment. From central to background to obscurity in three pages!

If the physical environment is consistently dropped from the diagrammed models of practice, it comes as no surprise that the assessment tools offered in mainstream practice textbooks concentrate primarily on aspects of social functioning, social networks, and social roles. The instruments, worksheets, and interview schedules offered for conducting person-in-environment assessments generally do not include elements of the physical environment. Organizing data for an assessment using genograms and eco-maps limits the view to the social environment. There is little point declaring the natural world to be an integral part of a person's environmental context if the assessment tools used are not capable of recognizing or incorporating these aspects. Zastrow (2004) presented threats to the natural world and the associated quality of human life as falling within the scope of environmentalism but not social work. Perhaps this is the logical consequence of perceiving the environment as a social environment: social workers are concerned with the social environment while environmentalists are left to tackle issues of the natural environment. Of course, some social workers could also be environmentalists, but not necessarily. Returning to Morito's (2002) terminology, this is an example of thinking about ecology rather than thinking ecologically.

Reclaiming the Environment in Social Work

Although relatively rare, there are instances in the literature of determined attempts to place environmental issues at the core of social work theory and practice. Nearly thirty years ago, Germain (1981) raised alarm that the profession was distorting the ecological perspective by leaving the physical environment unexplored "as a static setting in which human events and processes occur almost, if not entirely, independently of the qualities of their physical setting". She argued for understanding the physical environment in terms of both the natural world and the built world, further textured by the rhythms of time and considerations of spatial location. Writing at the same time, Weick (1981) also decried social work's focus on human behaviour to the neglect of the physical environment. He proposed a dynamic matrix of internal and external environments necessary to understand and influence human behaviour.

Between 1992 and 1995, the NASW journal Social Work published four articles making a strong case for inclusion of the physical environment within the domain of social work. Describing the social work literature devoted to the physical environment as "sparse", Gutheil (1992) was concerned that this oversight could result in social workers' neglect of physical surroundings when conducting assessments. The next year, Hoff and Polack (1993) considered human/environment interaction from the other side. Rather than looking at how the environment influences human activity, they emphasized "the human threat to environmental viability" which they argued had been ignored in the social work literature.

Later that year, Berger and Kelly (1993) also called for social work's ecological model to be extended "to a full awareness of human's role in biological as well as social ecosystems". Arguing that the foundation values of the profession would also need to be expanded to support this new direction, they developed a 12-point Ecological Credo for Social Workers. Two years later,

Berger (1995) voiced the appeal once again in a provocative editorial that applied the label "Habitat Destruction Syndrome" to a global illness whereby "the human race is collectively engaged in practices that damage the environment and ensure our eventual self-destruction". The persuasive argument was that we have become desensitized to the threats to our environment and immobilized by a fear that the problem is too big for us to handle. Assuming that habitat destruction needs to be understood as the "greatest threat to our social welfare," Berger again asked why we do not "add environmental activism to social work's list of social welfare concerns".

In 1994, Hoff and McNutt published a book called The Global Environmental Crisis: Implications for Social Welfare and Social Work. Motivated by environmental threats facing humankind, the authors began with the premise that human and environmental welfare are "inextricably linked". Hoff and McNutt (1994) argued that social work and other professions will have to move beyond outdated goals of individual well-being and social welfare to adopt new models geared more towards sustainability and protection of the environment. This position received strong support in a subsequent policy statement from the National Association of Social Workers (2000):

Protecting people and the natural environment through sustainable development is arguably the fullest realization of the person-in-environment perspective. The compatibility of sustainable development and the person-in-environment perspective is a firm theoretical foundation from which to apply macrolevel social work practice to person-natural environment problems. Gamble and Weil (1997) and Gorobets (2006) sought to put this notion of sustainable development at the core of community development theory and local development practice. Similar work from Finland promoted a new "Eco-social approach" for social work.

In his book Ecology and Social Work: Toward a New Paradigm, Coates (2003) argued that the Western focus on the individual and competition has made us blind and indifferent to our connectedness with the natural world. His new paradigm calls for social work to become a major player in the transformation of society towards global consciousness and environmental well-being. Graham, Swift, and Delaney (2009) similarly placed the "environmental imperative" clearly at the top of the list of essential issues that will shape social policy into the 21st Century, observing that the profession of social work missed the boat by applying ecological theory only to issues of people and their social contexts. Centrality of the physical environment to macro level practice is given another boost in a recent textbook entitled Human Behavior and the Social Environment: Macro Level – Groups, Communities, and Organizations which includes an entire chapter devoted to "Human Behavior and the Natural Environment: The Community of the Earth". Here, in a mainstream social work textbook, are discussions of biodiversity, global warming, war, and consumerism presented as challenges to the planet and our profession.

Voices at the Margins of Social Work

While notions of stewardship, sustainability, and place may be new to the mainstream profession, they have some standing at the margins of social work. Central to rural and remote practice is an understanding of context, of locality, of place and its powerful implications for human identity, activity, and problem-solving. In rural settings, a shared history and lifestyle leads to a rural identity rooted in a sense of belonging and a profound attachment to place. How does this rural notion of "place" affect the practice of social work? Social work is not something created elsewhere and then done or imposed on rural or remote areas. It is created or made in each place (Cheers, 2004). Much of the developing literature on spirituality and social work makes reference to Canda's (1988) influential definition of spirituality as "the human quest for personal meaning and mutually fulfilling relationships among people, the non human environment, and, for some, God". Canda's original broad notion of spirituality has frequently been narrowed in the social work literature to simply an internal quality or characteristic of the individual, again without adequate explanation (Zapf, 2005). A decade after contributing the foundation definition, Canda (1998) called for social work to revisit the person-in-environment concept "in a dramatic way" because the person is "not separable" from the natural environment. Canda and Furman (1999) further challenged the profession to reconsider "what is the whole person and what is the whole environment?".

Consistent with Canda's (1988) broad definition of spirituality, deep ecology clearly rejects divisions between the human and nonhuman worlds, and suggests instead that human identity derives from an ecological consciousness. Rosenhek (2006) put it simply: "In a nutshell, the deep ecology movement reminds us that we are from the Earth, of the Earth and not separate from it". Deep ecology promotes harmony and connection among all forms of being, a mutual dependence rather than human domination of the natural world for economic gain. Diverse ecosystems have intrinsic value beyond their economic utility for extractable resources. As explained by Ungar (2002), "diversity, complexity, and symbiosis are in our own best interest". From the perspective of deep ecology, "social work practice needs to address the problems that arise from excessive and destructive human interference with nature".

In Western society, we tend to view the physical environment as separate from ourselves, as an objective thing, as a commodity to be developed or traded or wasted or exploited, as an economic unit, as property. The dominant Western worldview has been described as "hostile to nature" and antagonistic to any concept of personhood beyond individualism. In contrast, the foundation metaphor of Aboriginal traditional knowledge has been characterized in the literature as a perspective of "I am I and the Environment,". Suopajarvi (1998) explained it this way: "I'm not in the place but the place is in me", similar to Cajete's (2000) observation that "we are the universe and the universe is us". When inhabitants of a region have been there for many generations, their identity incorporates the place and their relationship to it. Through this process, Aboriginal cultural identities become tied "directly to the land and concepts of place". Graveline (1998) talked about a direct link between "geographical space and worldview". Cajete (2000) called this link "geopsyche" whereby people assume traits of a particular place they have occupied for a long time, and the place assumes human traits, in a continual process of co-creation.

From the field of international social work comes a global concept of environmental citizenship which is "motivated by principles of sustainability and sensitivity to the natural order" and serves as a link between social justice and ecology (Latta, 2007). Because protection of the environment requires collective action at the global level, the notion of global environmental citizenship pushes beyond individualism, nationalism, and the rights of one generation. The Brundtland Report (United Nations, 1987) offered a simple yet powerful definition of sustainable development as "development which meets the needs of the present without compromising the ability of future generations to meet their own needs". An International Policy Statement on Globalisation and the Environment from the International Federation of Social Workers (IFSW, 2004) calls on individual social workers and their organizations to recognize the importance of the natural and built environment to the social environment, to develop environmental responsibility and care for the environment in social work practice and management today and for future generations, to work with other professionals to increase our knowledge and with community groups to develop advocacy skills and strategies to work towards a healthier environment and to ensure that environmental issues gain increased presence in social work education.

Voices from Other Disciplines

Disciplines outside of social work offer intriguing perspectives and concepts from their experiences with interactions between people and the physical environment. From the world of art come visual expressions of encounters with physical landscapes and an historical record, preserved in visual images, of ways of thinking about the land (Evernden, 1985). The cinematic option of telling a place rather than telling a story challenges our cultural notions of place as mere scenery (Wenders, 2001). Music theorists explain the process of authoring space through narrativization, local performances, and expressions of local knowledge and rhythms. Music has also been connected with intentional movement through space through such processes as soundscapes, songlines, and musical pathways. Exploring the link between wine and place through the development of terroir wines, viticulture attempts to capture place value or somewhereness in a bottle.

Environmental psychology has been actively exploring interrelationships between environments and human behaviour, with an emphasis on multidisciplinary efforts to understand the meaning of places. The discipline of sociology has been exploring an embodied sense of place, habitus, and the implications for local life opportunities. Environmental design is involved with understanding place as a concept then applying this knowledge through active placemaking to create livable and sustainable communities. Mutual influences between people and the planet are also a focus of study in human geography incorporating discussions of belonging, identity, and place attachment (Norton, 2004). Concepts of community allegiance and rootedness have led to approaches of place-based education, actively connecting students with local environmental and social issues. A concerned focus on people and place has given rise to a new vision of education for learning to live well in place, very different from the long-standing goal of achieving context-free credentials.

Across these areas of study outside of social work, (particularly in the applied disciplines), three common themes are apparent. The first is an acceptance of place as a foundation concept that integrates human activity with the physical environment. The second is a vision of sustainability achieved through processes such as stewardship, earthkeeping, and living well in place. The third is a belief that multidisciplinary responses are needed to take on the challenges of the environmental crises we have created.

EARTH MATERIALS AND HUMAN HEALTH

Earth materials generated by both natural and anthropogenic processes have been increasingly recognized as potential sources of illness in humans. For example, inhalation exposures to asbestos, silica, and some metal-rich dusts in industrial or occupational settings have been recognized for decades as triggers for certain diseases. Health concerns also arise from exposures to other anthropogenic atmospheric particulates, such as automobile exhaust, urban air pollution, smelting and coal combustion byproducts, and debris from building demolition and incidents such as the World Trade Center collapse.

Increasingly, environmental exposures to dusts and other atmospheric particulates (such as naturally-occurring asbestos, silica, volcanic ash, volcanic gas condensates, wildfire smoke, and dusts containing pathogens) are also being recognized as potential health concerns. Soils are recognized for their potential to affect human health-as sources for dusts, sources for pathogens, and as sources for toxicity via any contained toxicants such as heavy metals or organic chemicals.

The Earth Materials and Human Health Project (EMHHP), in collaboration with medical and public health experts, is developing and applying a variety of earth science methods to help interpret the geologic links between earth materials and human health problems. The project's scientific results will provide a sound earth science basis for more informed, effective regulatory policies and remediation strategies.

The project is currently (fiscal years 2005-2009) funded primarily by the USGS Mineral Resources Program (MRP), with some additional funding from the Earth Surface Dynamics Program. The project is a follow-up of the MRP-funded Mineral Dusts and Human Health Project (MDHHP), which ran from fiscal years 2001-2004; key MDHHP activities, outcomes and publications are presented in a separate web site. This project involves extensive collaboration with other USGS personnel and projects, and also health experts in a number of Federal and state agencies. Examples of other USGS projects with which this project is collaborating include the Near-Surface Processes, Industrial Minerals, Southwest Climate Change, Transoceanic Dusts, Surveys and Analysis, Geochemical Landscapes, and Wildfire Effects projects. Health experts with whom the project is collaborating include scientists from USEPA, NIOSH, OSHA, CDC, ATSDR, Public Health Service, Colorado Department of Public Health and Environment, University of Arizona, University of Colorado, SUNY Stonybrook, and other agencies and universities.

MINERAL DUSTS

The Mineral Dusts and Human Health project (MDHHP), which ran from fiscal year 2001 through fiscal year 2004, utilized an interdisciplinary approach (involving mineralogy, economic geology, aqueous and stable isotope geochemistry, analytical chemistry, remote sensing, regional geology, and toxicology expertise) to help understand how the geologic characteristics of mineral dusts (and the source materials from which the dusts are derived) may influence their roles in human health. A key aspect of the project was its integration of earth science and health science expertise and activities.

The project's primary focus was upon asbestos and fibrous dusts related to mining, mineral processing, or mineral products, and so the project addressed environmental and human health priorities of the Mineral Resources Program outlined in USGS science planning documents. To a limited extent, the project also successfully applied the same interdisciplinary approach (in collaboration as appropriate with other USGS projects) to study potential health implications of other earth materials such as: metal-bearing mine wastes, mill tailings, and smelter emissions; dusts from dry lake beds; soils; volcanic ash; coal and coal fly ash; and dusts from building collapse. The studies identified many topics for a spectrum of earth materials where substantial further research is needed to address increasing societal concerns.

The majority of the project's funding came from the USGS Mineral Resources Program. The Mendenhall Program supported a post-doctoral toxicology position linked to the project for two years, and the Earth Surface Dynamics Program and Energy Resources program contributed support for the toxicology position.

The Mineral Dusts and Human Health project's focus was primarily on asbestos-containing dusts, although other dusts and dust sources were also investigated to a lesser extent. The project was initiated to provide impartial scientific input to help address renewed societal and regulatory concerns about potential health effects associated with exposure to asbestos. In the past, societal and regulatory concerns were focused on commercial and industrial asbestos. However, in recent years, largely as a result of significant health problems at Libby, Montana, concerns have increased substantially regarding so-called "naturally-occurring asbestos" (NOA) and other fibrous minerals that occur (a) as accessory minerals in other industrial mineral deposits (such as vermiculite deposits like those mined at Libby, and such as some talc deposits) and (b) in rock units (such as serpentinite-bearing ultramafic rocks).

The project provided insights about a number of asbestos issues that benefit a wide variety of stakeholders. The project's activities also provided information that can be used to help address some of the many unanswered questions remaining about asbestos. For example, many questions still remain about how asbestos actually causes toxicity, and whether or not fibrous but non-asbestiform varieties of the same minerals can also trigger toxicity.

Further, relatively little is known about the full range of geologic environments in which asbestos or other fibrous minerals can occur, the extent to which natural erosion or anthropogenic disturbance of these sources contributes to background levels of asbestos in the air, and the extent to which such background contributions can themselves trigger disease. Although the project's primary focus remained on asbestos and related minerals, limited studies were also carried out on other mineral particulates and/or their potential source material, including: mine wastes; mill tailings; soils affected by smelter emissions; mercury mine calcines; dry lake beds such as Owens Lake, CA; volcanic ash; various soils; coal dust and coal fly ash; and dusts generated by collapse of buildings such as the World Trade Center.

These studies demonstrated that a similar interdisciplinary approach to that developed by the project to study asbestos can provide important insights into potential health concerns tied to many other types of earth materials that may be liberated as particulates into the environment. The studies also identified many topics in this realm where substantial further research is needed to address increasing societal concerns.

The USGS Mineral Resources Program is currently (FY 2005-2009) funding a follow-up project titled "Earth Materials and Human Health" to address unresolved questions about asbestos and the potential health impacts of other earth materials such as mine wastes, soils, volcanic ash, dry lake bed dusts, coal dust and coal fly ash, and others.

MDHH Project Outcomes

Asbestos

- USGS characterization work on fibrous amphiboles and vermiculite at Libby, Montana (funded in part by the US EPA and in part by the USGS Mineral Resources Program) has provided key scientific information that is being used or will be used to help:
  a. Assess the nature and extent of amphibole contamination present at Libby, at hundreds of plants nationwide where Libby vermiculite was processed, and in approximately a million homes with vermiculite insulation from Libby.
  b. Guide remedial efforts at sites where fibrous amphiboles from Libby are present.
  c. Understand how the fibrous amphiboles at Libby and geologically similar deposit types influence toxicity

Results of the USGS activities will directly support or influence vermiculite-related cleanup activities nationwide.

- The project's geologic studies of vermiculite deposits nationwide:
  a. Indicate that not all vermiculite deposits contain fibrous amphiboles, and therefore not all types of vermiculite deposits need to be regulated as though they contain asbestos.
  b. Provide methods that are being used to help assess whether a particular vermiculite sample is from deposit types likely to contain fibrous amphiboles.
- The project's studies of the geologic occurrences of asbestiform or other potentially toxic fibrous minerals:
  a. Provide a geologic model of formation that helps explain why some types of talc deposits do not contain asbestiform amphiboles and why others do.
  b. Demonstrate that there are many possible geologic sources for asbestiform or other potentially toxic fibrous minerals nationwide. These sources, through either natural erosion or anthropogenic

disturbance, may contribute to background levels of fibrous particulates in the air, and so must be taken into account in the interpretation of epidemiological data on asbestos-related diseases, and in the development of appropriate air quality standards for asbestos.

- The project systematically compared the mineralogical, geochemical, and toxicological properties of a wide variety of asbestos-related toxicological standards. Results show that there are considerable variations in all of these properties between different standards of a given asbestos mineral. Toxicological studies do not routinely take such variations into account, which may help explain seemingly conflicting results of different studies using different standards of the same minerals.
- The project developed, tested, and demonstrated the utility of AVIRIS (Airborne Visible and Infra-Red Imaging Spectrometer) remote sensing techniques to map the occurrence of potentially asbestos-forming minerals over large areas. The technique is particularly valuable for helping evaluate areas where potentially asbestos bearing rock units may occur, but where geologic mapping is limited. This activity was carried out in collaboration with colleagues at the California Geological Survey.
- As a result of these project activities, USGS has responded to many requests for expert geologic and mineralogic information on asbestos, including:

a. A request from the American Thoracic Society to write a summary of asbestos mineralogy for its revised criteria for assessing asbestos-related disease.

b. A request to participate in the Federal Interagency Working Group on Asbestos. This Working Group is charged with evaluating current asbestos-related issues, and how these issues can be addressed by the regulatory agencies based on sound science input from science agencies such as the USGS. Regular participation by project members in this working group highlights the need for the USGS' impartial earth science input into asbestos issues.

c. Multiple inquiries by other Federal agencies, State agencies, industry, and the public for scientific information on asbestos-related issues.

d. A formal request for a project scientist to serve as an expert witness in Federal litigation related to Libby.

e. A formal request for a project scientist to serve as an expert member of a committee overseeing activities of the Congressionally mandated U.S. Navy Lung Disease Assessment Program.

PUBLIC PARTICIPATION IN ENVIRONMENTAL DECISION MAKING

The title of this study, poses several questions: What is the 'public'? What is 'participation'? What are the 'decisions' to which it refers? Starting with the last and working backwards, EDM refers to any process of decision-making where consequent significant environmental impacts are a possibility. This includes law making, planning, strategic planning, resource management planning, licensing of industry e.g. IPPC, environmental assessment (EIA), spatial planning etc. EDM can be even more complex than decision-making on other public issues.

First, environmental impacts do not respect property, jurisdiction or boundaries.

Second, EDM can involve government agencies as both manager and regulator.

Thirdly, environmental issues can provide especially heated value conflicts that require value trade offs.

The level at which the public is involved varies with the relevant legislation, and the attitude of the other stakeholders. Often it just means informing the public of a previously made decision and asking for comments, which may or may not be heeded. Sometimes it means informed consultation. Here there is exchange of information prior to the relevant authority's reasoned decision making, and all inputs are included and seen to be included.

An example of this being the River Basin Management process under Article 14 of the Water Framework Directive as described by Judith Cuff (Cuff, J. 2001). Another example would be the Bantry Bay Coastal Zone Charter. Public participation, at its apex, could also mean that the public itself, in consultation with the relevant bodies, makes the final decision itself. Examples of this can be found under the auspices of Local Agenda 21. For public participation to be effective at any level, it requires the public to be well informed and kept aware of the possibility of participation. This requires a pro-active approach from industry and the relevant public bodies.

What then is 'the public'? The public is often treated as a unitary body, whereas in reality it is a collection of numerous continually shifting interests and alliances (Ortolano), which may be in conflict with each other. The term is used as a "catch-all to describe those with an interest in a decision, other than a proponent, operator, or responsible authority". (Petts and Leach). The individuals making up a public may be involved as individuals or as members of organisations. They may become involved due to their proximity, economics, social or environmental issues, values, etc. By contrast, stakeholders, of which the public is one, are literally those with a stake in an issue and may include non-governmental organizations (NGO's), government or its agents, industry, individuals, communities etc.

Stakeholders do not always want to be involved in an EDM process, but they have the right to know if their interests are affected. They may want to become involved at a different stake of the EDM process.

ENVIRONMENTAL JUSTICE AND HUMAN RIGHTS

Another major UN initiative related to sustainable development is the Millennium Project, a massive global human rights campaign. The Millennium Summit was held in New York in 2000, following a decade of preparatory conferences and summits. Representatives from 189 countries and leading development institutions have adopted the UN Millennium Declaration. The Declaration laid out fundamental values regarded as essential to international relations in the twenty-first century: freedom, equality, solidarity, tolerance, respect for nature, and shared responsibility. It also addressed peace and disarmament; development and poverty eradication; protecting the environment; human rights; democracy and good government; protecting the vulnerable; meeting the special needs of Africa; and, strengthening the United Nations. The Millennium Development Goals (MDGs) target eight specific areas for change by 2015: 1) poverty and hunger, 2) primary education, 3) gender equality, 4) child mortality, 5) maternal health, 6) disease, 7) environmental sustainability, and 8) responsibility of developed countries toward developing countries. The MDGs were endorsed at the World Summit on Sustainable Development (Earth Summit II) in 2002.

The MDGs recognize explicitly the interdependence between growth, poverty, and sustainable development. Goal 7 directly addresses the need to ensure environmental sustainability through four specific targets: integrate the principles of sustainable development into governmental policies and programs, reduce biodiversity loss, halve the proportion of the population without access to safe drinking water and basic sanitation, and achieve a significant improvement in the lives of at least 100 million slum dwellers (The Millennium Development Goals Report, 2008). The statistics are daunting. For example, although there is not yet a global water shortage, almost half of the world's population faces a scarcity of water and water use has grown at twice the rate of the population for the past century. More than one-sixth of the world's population does not have access to safe drinking water. Although there has been a marked improvement in sanitation worldwide, in developing regions, nearly one in four people use no form of sanitation and another fifteen percent lack access to hygienic facilities. These problems are especially severe for rural dwellers, particularly in sub-Sahara Africa, but they also extend into urban slums. Slum conditions are defined as lack of improved sanitation, water facilities, durable housing, and sufficient living area. "In 2005, slightly more than one-third of the urban population in developing regions lived in slum conditions; in sub-Saharan Africa, the proportion was over sixty percent".

Several of the other MDGs are clearly linked to Goal 7. For example, people living in extreme hunger and poverty (Goal 1) depend more directly on a healthy ecosystem, have insecure rights to resources and inadequate access to information, lack participation in decision-making, and are more vulnerable to natural disasters. Universal primary education (Goal 2) is linked to sustainable development since the heavy household responsibilities of families living in poverty often prevents their children, especially girls, from attending school. In turn, school is the most critical avenue for empowering the future generation to pursue their rights as well as educating them in the principles of sustainability. Gender equality (Goal 3) addresses environmental justice since females are over-burdened with collecting water and fuel, have limited input in decision-making, and often lack access to land ownership or resources. Child mortality (Goal 4) is highest among children under the age of five due to lack of sanitary living conditions, unclean water, and indoor air pollution. Maternal health (Goal 5) is damaged due to indoor air pollution, the excessive burden of carrying water and collecting fuel, increased incidence of malaria due to deforestation and water mismanagement, and vulnerability to man-made natural disasters.

The MDGs are closely linked to the professional mission of social work, especially the call for advocacy and action toward securing universal human rights. The most recent 2009 MDG Report documented substantial progress related to the four goals of poverty reduction, universal primary education, reduced child mortality, and some aspects of environmental sustainability (e.g., ozone depletion). However, the recent global economic recession has reversed much of this progress. The report notes that environmental justice has especially lost ground. While almost every region improved the living conditions of the urban poor, progress in barely keeping pace with rapid growth of slum areas. It indicates that efforts to preserve the natural resource base are not forceful enough, especially regarding climate change, fisheries, forest, and water. The report concludes that, while we are the first generation that has the ability to eliminate poverty, apparently, we lack the resolve to do so.

There are other programs under other auspices in the UN that are related to environmental justice. The Division for the Advancement of Women held the Fourth World Conference on Women in Beijing in 1995. One of their twelve Strategic Objectives pertained to "Women and the Environment." The Platforms for Action included a detailed discussion and three action steps directed at involving women in environmental decision-making at all levels, integrating gender concerns and perspectives in policies and programs for sustainable development, and strengthening or establishing mechanisms across levels to assess the impact of development and environmental policies on women.

The World Health Organization (WHO) adopted a General Comment on the Rights to Health in 2000 which affirm health as a basic human right. This document states that this right extends not only to health care but to the determinants of health, such as clean water, adequate sanitation, safe food, housing and working conditions, and access to education and information, including sexual and reproductive health. Environmental justice is at the center of a human right to health, since medical care (treatment) has far less of an impact on population well-being than social and environmental factors.

Despite the tremendous efforts of the UN and advocacy groups from around the world, progress toward environmental justice has been slow.

Adebowale et al. (2001) argues that, despite these international efforts, environmental problems continue to worsen since implementing "soft laws" have largely failed, globalization has intensified, and resource depletion continues at an unsustainable rate.

They conclude that existing human rights approaches are inadequate (since environmental rights are not directly addressed) and argue for explicit, stronger international agreements. In the current climate of global capitalism, concern for human safety and environmental protection are consistently subjugated to economic growth and the maintenance of inefficient patterns of production and consumption. Hancock (2003) claims that this double standard accommodates the destructive forces of capitalism, which perpetuates systematic environmental degradation and human rights violations.

SOCIAL WORK AND ENVIRONMENTAL JUSTICE

The linkages between social work and human rights are explicit. Taylor (2000) argues social development is a prerequisite for social justice. Mapp (2008) notes that "a lack of social development creates situations in which violations of human rights can thrive" and specifies three main interrelated barriers to human freedom: poverty, discrimination, and lack of education. Reichert (2006) cautions that social workers often fail to see how human rights are closely linked to social work policies and practices. She identifies six primary interventions to foster basic human rights: challenging oppression, empowerment, strengths perspective, ethnic-sensitive practice, feminist practice, and cultural competence.

Social work educators have also called for the need to address environmental justice as a critical component of social and economic justice. McKinnon (2008) urges that, "social work has the opportunity to be part of the solution rather than an uninvolved bystander to the emerging environmental predicaments". While the human rights movement has a clear record of actively advocating for environmental justice, social work education (at least in the U.S.) has failed to incorporate this perspective into the curriculum. While human rights are typically discussed in terms of "spatial" relationships regarding the obligations of nations or communities to each other, the new discourse on sustainability represents a "temporal" extension to future generations (Ife, 2008).

In this global era, social work students must be assisted to engage in an informed discussion of the universal aspects of human rights and environmental justice. They must be helped to gain awareness about the pressing problems of inequality around the world (especially for children) and to identify sustainable solutions to the very real environmental crisis facing humanity today. The concept of sustainability has "long been familiar to many workers engaged in social and community development programmes". Acquiring a knowledge base that links social work practice with universal human rights, environmental justice, and sustainable development will help them to envision the world as a more just and humane place.

A paradigm shift is occurring around the world regarding sustainability and environmental justice. It has not reached a critical mass necessary for global change, since humanity has yet to respond effectively. Social work, as the helping profession that traditionally focused on linkages across systems, must actively join this movement if we are to stay relevant in the contemporary global 21st century. Our professional mission of advocating for and acting toward social and economic justice must be expanded to include environmental justice. We must overcome any remaining xenophobia and extend this commitment to the entire world, as the ecological crisis does not respect national boundaries and affluent countries have an obligation to help the disadvantaged everywhere. It is incumbent upon social work education to prepare students for this challenge, and for social work practitioners to embrace sustainability. Our very survival, and the survival of future generations, depend upon it.

THEORETICAL APPROACHES TO DISABILITY CONTENT IN SOCIAL WORK EDUCATION

Historically, disability has been explained and understood from a variety of perspectives. These views of disability span a continuum from a diagnostic-medical perspective to a complex, interactive person-in-environment perspective (Stiker, 1999). Simply put, the diagnostic-medical explanation of disability places the locus of disability internally, within an individual who has experienced illness, insult, or anomaly. This internal focus results in an interpretation of the disabled individual as defective with reference to normative physical, behavioral, psychological, cognitive, or sensory being. The interactive, person-in-environment lens, on the other hand, looks at the interaction of internal and external factors in an individual's life that creates a disabling condition. Between these two views, numerous other explanations and understandings of disability exist, including spiritual demonization or glorification of individuals with disabilities. Contemporary theorists, influenced by pluralism, a perspective which posits the phenomenon of multiple realities, view disability within the complex and diverse universe of human experience, and from this perspective understand disability as a multilevel social justice concern embedded within particular cultural, sociopolitical, economic, and relational environments. Contemporary legislation and protection prohibiting segregation and externally imposed control over the lives of people with disabilities have emerged from this perspective. But even these laws advance diverse definitions of disability. For example, Social Security defines disability as the inability to engage in remunerative employment as a result of a disabling condition, whereas the Americans with Disabilities Act (ADA) defines disability more broadly as limitation in life activities due to impairment.

The literature reveals the complexity and conceptual confusion regarding definitions and understandings of disability. However, two broad definitions of disability predominate: one locating disability as internal to individuals, and one identifying disabling factors in environments external to individuals. Therefore, we propose that social work students be introduced to these two distinct ways of conceptualizing disability.

The Diagnostic Approach to Disability

The diagnostic approach to disability is based on medical explanations of individual human conditions. In this perspective disability is defined as a long-term to permanent physical, behavioral, psychological, cognitive, or sensory impediment that renders individuals less able than those who are free of such impediments, or those with impediments from which they can recover. This perspective both essentializes disability and locates it within the individual (Shakespeare, 1996). Interventions provided by disability services are designed to be curative. That is to say, services are aimed at remediating the disability.

In large part, the diagnostic approach is based on the historic notion of illness advanced by Parsons in the early 1950s. According to Parsons (1964), illness releases the sick person from compliance with socially enforced behavioral norms. In exchange for release from behavioral obligations, the individual who is ill is expected to be compliant with, and appreciative of, medical intervention designed to cure. Not unexpectedly, the diagnostic approach to disability does not bode well for those with conditions that cannot be cured, modified, or changed by professional intervention. In this view, the individual who cannot be "fixed" remains deficient in the sense that the person appears to function in ways outside of socially acceptable norms. The diagnostic approach to understanding disability, then, classifies an individual as a deviant or as noncompliant with conventional behaviors.

The concept of rehabilitation underlying a wide variety of interventions is firmly situated within the diagnostic approach, in that most interventions are aimed at improving the function and well-being of individuals with medical diagnoses.

While fields such as occupational therapy and vocational rehabilitation are concerned with the elimination or alteration of environmental barriers that impede individual function, these fields are still based on the diagnostic approach to disability.

This orientation is apparent in these fields' concern with addressing diagnostic-functional abnormality (developmental disability, psychosis, and so forth), regardless of the locus of the interventions. An individual is referred to rehabilitation because of what is perceived to be a medical condition that limits function, and this view of disability frames the work of the rehabilitation professional, even if modification of the individual's environment is the intervention.

Within this perspective, rehabilitation practice can range from adapting an environment to fit individual limitations to Working with individuals to adapt to an environment and exhibit more normative function.

Disability as a Construct

From a constructionist approach, disability is viewed as a phenomenon constructed by factors and forces in the external environment rather than as a physical, behavioral, psychological, cognitive, or sensory inadequacy (Shakespeare & Watson, 1997).

For many people with disabilities, while physical, behavioral, psychological, cognitive, or sensory anomalies are acknowledged, they are not necessarily seen as undesirable, in need of remediation (Quinn, 1988), or even relevant to understanding the circumstance and experiences of disabled people. Central to this approach is the notion of human diversity.

A fundamental question raised by constructionist approaches to disability is why a condition such as impairment of an individual's ability to walk, which requires the use of adaptive equipment, is perceived as a disability, and a condition such as mild nearsightedness, which also requires the use of adaptive equipment, is not.

In constructionist approaches to disability, language or the terms that one calls oneself are determined by the disabled person reflecting that individual's interpretation of his or her connection to the social, political, economic, physical, cognitive, and sensory environment. Because disability is seen as a social "construction" rather than a condition which is located "with" an individual, the admonitions by professionals, and even scholarly writing venues, for those not using person-first language are not appropriate. The individual is "disabled" by a socially created set of circumstances and has the right to declare or define himself or herself as "disabled" by an environment rather than living with a disability.

Unlike the rehabilitation approach, which can also address the environment as the needed locus of change, constructionist approaches to disability attribute an individual's incapacity to function to a disabling environment in which barriers are socially erected and maintained (Hahn, 1993). Negative attitudes, limited or nonexistent physical and communication access, and the denial of rights and privileges are examples of just some of the barriers that interfere with a disabled individual's potential to actualize desired social roles such as student, partner, parent, etc..

Thus, disability is seen as inequity in how an environment responds to and interprets human diversity, rather than as a deficit to be cured, remediated, or fixed. It is not surprising that individuals with disabilities have advanced this notion of disability in direct response to models that devalue them (Oliver, 1996).

Within constructionist conceptualizations of disability, there are many different emphases, each of which has been posited as a model of disability in and of itself. For example, in the view of those who see disability as a political construction, the barrier creating the disabling condition is disempowerment caused by unequal earning opportunities for individuals with conditions that are socially constructed as disabilities.

Discrimination and exclusion from the workplace limit the disabled individual's capacity to exchange earned resources for privileges, goods, and services. For disabled people political life is an economic life wherein the discrimination, exclusion, and disenfranchisement are experienced as an increased probability of substandard wages and poverty.

According to Oliver (1996), the political understanding of disability, and we would suggest an economic understanding of disability, while not equivalent to policy, legislation, or social change, does provide direction for future political action.

Another important focus within constructionist approaches to disability is the view of disability as culture. This focus suggests that all individuals who define themselves as disabled belong to a unique group, which shares circumstances, experiences, tacit rules, language, and discourse. In this view, the notion of disability is one of group belongingness and distinction from other groups who do not share the disability identity. That is to say, anyone who identifies as disabled is disabled. Who belongs and does not belong to the culture is therefore not based on diagnosable condition, since diagnosis is irrelevant in this approach to determining who is disabled and who is not.

Those individuals who perceive themselves to be unfairly treated and perceived as undesirable by dominant social institutions are therefore members of the culture of disability in that they share disadvantage and curtailment of civil rights (Linton, 1998). Within this framework, issues involving race, class, gender, sexual orientation, and disability identification are important determinants of the shared experiences that bind people together in single, identifiable communities of concern (Charlton, 1998). Linton (1998) notes, This outrage is tied not only to the political position of disabled people, but from a materialist analysis, which identifies the "economic restrictions imposed on the individual that disable him or her".

4

Environmental Change and Refugees in Third World

An initial difficulty in dealing with 'environmental refugees', or 'environmental migrants', is that there are perhaps as many typologies as there are papers on the subject. El-Hinnawi (1985) and Jacobson (1988) started with three sub-categories of environmental refugee, namely temporary displacement due to temporary environmental stress; permanent displacement due to permanent environmental change; and temporary or permanent displacement due to progressive degradation of the resource base. In contrast, IOM/RPG (1992) drew distinctions between emergency vs. slow-onset movements, temporary, extended and permanent movements, and internal and international movements. Suhrke (1993) divided her discussion into migration stimulated by deforestation, rising sea levels, desertification and drought, land degradation, and water and air degradation, before proceeding to identify environmental pressure points at which the combination of such factors establishes a susceptibility towards environmental migration.

Trolldalen *et al.* (1992) distinguished between refugees from natural disasters; degradation of land resources; involuntary resettlement; industrial accidents; the aftermath of war; and climatic changes. More recently, the ball returned to IOM (1996), which used a six-fold division similar to that of Trolldalen *et al.*, but also drew an overall distinction between 'natural' and 'man-made' causes.

Whatever the precise definition or number of 'environmental refugees', a common feature of the literature is to talk of 'millions' of displaced people, and their dramatic impact on host regions, such that regional security is threatened. The image is one of mis-or over-use of the environment leading to progressive decline in the resource base, and possibly contributing to further dramatic (and unintended) environmental collapse. Environmentalists and conflict specialists see common cause in discussion of 'environmental refugees'; even if the linkages between environmental change, conflict and refugees remain to be proven. It is the purpose of the first part of this paper to examine the evidence for such linkages.

At first glance, the data available on environmental refugees appears quite impressive. A number of areas of the world are cited by a range of authors as being affected by environmentally-induced migration, ranging across Asia, Africa and Latin America. In *Ultimate security*, Myers (1993d, 189) starts a chapter on the potential for displacement due to sea-level rise with concern about the plight of Haitian boat people, 'abandoning their homelands in part because their country has become an environmental basket case'.

Homer-Dixon (1994, 22) draws, amongst other examples, on the evidence from South Asia, where the piecing together of demographic information and experts' estimates leads him to conclude that Bangladeshi migrants 'have expanded the population of neighbouring areas of India by 12 to 17 million' over the last forty years, whilst 'the population of the state of Assam has been boosted by at least seven million'. El-Hinnawi (1985) and Jacobson (1988) cite additional examples of environmental refugees from across the Sahel and the Horn of Africa, as well as the Soviet Union and the United States.

However, despite the breadth of examples provided in the literature, the strength of the academic case put forward is often depressingly weak. Taking first Homer-Dixon's example of migration from Bangladesh to India, caused by 'environmental scarcity', it is something of a surprise to find that, even in his own article, a number of other explanations for migration vie with that of environmental degradation. Thus migration is also associated also with rules on land inheritance, the system of water management in Bangladesh, the standard of living in India, and the encouragement of migration by some Indian politicians eager to gain new voters. At the same time, the source of Homer-Dixon's demographic information (Hazarika, 1993) casts some doubt on the statistics too-in this case, between 12 and 24 million such migrants. For example, Hazarika's estimate of migration to Assam comes not from any direct measure, but from a comparison of the 1951 and 1991 Assam census figures, adjusted for the population growth rate in 1951, which shows a notional excess population. Yet this increase could be accounted for in a number of ways, with likely candidates including: a rise in the population growth rate after 1951; undercounting in 1951 (eminently plausible in a remote region); or over-counting in 1991 (also eminently plausible given the link between population size and allocation of government resources).

Other accounts of 'environmental refugees' are little better. A search through the references cited in another recent review paper by Ramlogan (1996) reveals little concrete evidence either. Thus for migration from 'natural disasters', we are pointed again to work by Hazarika (1993), as well as to Mattson and Rapp (1991), Sanders (1990-91) and an unspecified report from the United States Embassy in Addis Ababa. Yet Mattson and Rapp are respectively a climatologist and a geomorphologist, who merely state that 'refugee migration is linked to drought and famine' rather than demonstrating the linkage; Sanders indiscriminately describes as 'environmental refugees' some 4.1 million rural-urban migrants in Northeast Brazil in the 1960s and a further 4.6 million in the 1970s, even though he admits that many areas not affected by drought also lost population as a result of poverty; whilst for Ethiopia, Ramlogan simply repeats an observation originally cited by Jacobson (1988) that one million people 'were about to move because of famine conditions'-without actually saying whether they did.

Similar difficulties emerge for the effects of 'long-term environmental degradation', where Ramlogan curiously cites the 'Black triangle' of the Czech Republic, Poland and south-east Germany as a region of out-migration due to pollution (a judgement that might be questioned by German authorities who have spent the last few decades trying to deal with in-migration!). And on the aftermath of war, Ramlogan makes the extraordinary assertion that the failure of Afghan refugees to return to their country from Pakistan is due to poor land productivity and the number of land mines-when surely the continuing conflict in their country of origin, and the largely favourable economic conditions they have experienced in exile might be considered more (or as) relevant factors.

Such problems strike to the core of the literature on environmental refugees, and nowhere more so than in the generation of statistics on its prevalence. In turn, the generation of statistics is critically dependent on the definition of 'environmental refugees', a process which might well be seen as impossible given the multiple and overlapping causes of most migration streams. In so far as distinctions between causes can be drawn, the following sections consider three different types of 'environmental migration' and the evidence that has been put forward for the existence of these phenomena. It is evidence that is far from convincing.

Desertification-induced Displacement

Out of the range of environmental migration 'types' cited above, perhaps one of the most pervasive in terms of popular recognition at least is that of the poverty-stricken (and usually African) farmer who is finally forced to leave the land because of drought, progressive impoverishment of the soil, and ultimately famine. The phrase 'desertification', conjured up in the 1970s to evoke the relentless onward march of the desert, but with its origins in colonial concern about mismanagement of the environment , evokes too the flight of humans towards less hostile lands, or more likely to 'refugee' camps. Particularly in the Sahel, but also in other 'marginal' semi-arid areas across Central America, Asia and even southern Europe, desertification-induced migration epitomises the 'threat' posed to industrialised societies by an army of the poor and starving on the move. As Jacobson (1988, 6) put it:

Desertification... has irreparably damaged millions of hectares of once productive land and made refugees out of millions of sub-Saharan African farmers. Migration is the signal that land degradation has reached its sorry end.

However, the evidence for 'desertification' causing migration in any straightforward way is somewhat limited. First, it is important to note that the concept of 'desertification' itself has come under fire in recent years, particularly as availability of satellite images of the region has improved. Thus work by Dregne and Tucker (1988) and Tucker *et al*. (1991) has shown a highly elastic response of vegetation cover to growing season rainfall, with the 'desert margin' in the Sahel fluctuating from year to year as a result.

Williams and Balling (1996, 50) question as 'equivocal' evidence that human activities have changed climatic patterns through influencing surface albedo, surface roughness, plant cover and soil moisture. Mortimore (1989) has noted that management practices that were thought to contribute to land degradation need to be placed in historical context. Overall, there is increasing talk of the 'myth' of desertification (Helldén, 1991; Thomas and Middleton 1994; Swift, 1996). If one accepts the argument that desertification itself is largely a myth, then it is not, perhaps, too great a step to suggest that desertification-induced migration is a myth too. Nonetheless, even if there is no secular trend of declining vegetation cover and land productivity in the Sahel, and vegetation recovers as rainfall increases, it is possible that stress migration might result from a temporary decline in the productivity of agricultural and grazing land during drought periods. Yet, for such migrants to be termed 'environmental refugees', it seems reasonable that environmental decline should represent the main (if not the only) reason for their flight.

In practice, such evidence is hardly forthcoming. For example, in one review of desertification-induced migration world-wide, Schwartz and Notini (1995) cite examples from Mexico, Haiti, and the Sahel, as well as the cases of north-east Brazil, and north-west India discussed above. But each case is problematic. In the case of Mexico, after a review of general environmental problems in the country, Schwartz and Notini provide only a brief discussion of an attempt to statistically correlate areas of emigration with areas of 'aridity'. They go on to admit that not all arid areas are 'degraded', that not all migration from these areas is necessarily the result of desertification. Their rather lame conclusion is that 'our discussion with experts, research, and analysis of the relevant statistics data *will likely confirm* that desertification is a factor contributing to migration from this region' (Schwartz and Notini, 1995, 82: my italics).

Elsewhere, and reliant on studies funded by the Universities Field Staff International and published by the National Heritage Institute, the evidence is little more convincing: for example, in Haiti, it is stated that deforestation and soil erosion are severe problems facing the country, but no clear link is demonstrated to migration. Indeed, for the case of emigration, it is stated that 'it is evident that most of Haiti's emigrants in recent years have been *political and* economic refugees', influenced only 'to some extent' by environmental deterioration.

In other work too, the evidence that is presented for migration as a result of drought and desertification is generally only the existence of migration from regions that are prone to such processes. A causal link to drought is seldom established, whilst in some cases, not even the existence of 'excess' migration is demonstrated. Thus Jacobson (1988) cites a number of Sahelian states in which rural-urban or north-south migration occurred during the drought period of the mid-1980s, or in which significant populations became dependent on food aid, and all of this is taken as *prime facie* evidence that these groups have been forced from desert margins because of declining rainfall.

However, within the Sahel, and indeed in other semi-arid regions, there is a tradition of migration that extends back over decades, and often centuries, and which ranges from nomadic pastoralism to long-distance trade, as well as the permanent relocation of individuals and families. In turn, these migrations, though rooted certainly in the difficult environmental conditions of the region, and the need to diversify incomeearning opportunities, are not necessarily related to a decline in those conditions. Indeed, there is now an increasing body of literature on migration, both internationally from, and locally within the Sahel region, which suggests that a simple link between poverty, environmental degradation and migration is hard to sustain.

In the Senegal River Valley, one of many source areas for migration to Côte d'Ivoire, Lericollais (1989) notes that migration has long reflected a household strategy to cope with environmental risks, which although severe, are not necessarily regarded as worsening. Studies have identified how migration plays a cultural role in the transition to manhood, as well as being economically linked to the generation of sufficient revenue to buy livestock.

Factors such as the decline of markets for traditional cash crops (which include gum arabic and cotton), the development of Senegal's groundnut basin, and subsequent mechanisation of agriculture in the delta provide additional and more recent motivations to move out of the middle and upper parts of the Senegal River Valley. Moreover, such conclusions are not limited to the western Sahel, but can be extended across the continent. As David (1995, 18) notes from an empirical study based in Senegal, Mali, Burkina Faso and Sudan:

Migration does not necessarily signify a rejection of a rural livelihood. Rather, it demonstrates that the survival strategies of rural Sahelians are not only rooted in their immediate vicinity, but are also linked into economies in other rural and urban locations. It is precisely this inter-linkage which supports rural communities and helps them to survive in such climatically unstable environments.

The picture is one of migration as an essential part of the economic and social structure of the region, rather than a response to environmental decline-a picture reinforced by numerous other studies that have confirmed the critical role of migrant remittances in household and regional economies.

The situation appears similar in other semi-arid regions of the world allegedly prone to desertification and related migration. For example, Glazovsky and Shestakov (1994) argue that currently 40 per cent of the population of the former Soviet Union are living in areas characterised by 'acute ecological situations' that are adequately described as desertification. But they also admit that migration from such areas is not new, including as 'desertification-induced migration' such movements as the migration of Mongolian tribes northwards in the second century B.C. due to drought, or the removal of population from the Khoresm oasis in the first century A.D. after the invasion of nomadic tribes which destroyed irrigation systems.

This notion of 'environmental refugees' hardly tallies with arguments about recent destruction of the ecological balance by modern society; rather, migration is again perhaps better seen as a customary coping strategy. In this sense, movement of people is a response to spatio-temporal variations in climatic and other conditions, rather than a new phenomenon resulting from a physical limit having been reached.

For the 'environmental refugees' thesis to be plausible in the Sahel and other semiarid regions, what is required is not simply evidence of migration from what have always been harsh, marginal environments; rather evidence is needed of an increase in migration at times, or in places, of more severe environmental degradation. Such a process is hinted at in discussions of 'stress migration' in the Sahel, one of five phases of response to famine identified by Cutler (1984), the others being sale of stock, wage labour, borrowing of cash or food, and the sale of valuables. Yet as Pottier (1993) observes, there are a number of analytical question marks both over developing typologies of responses to famine, and especially over assuming that these occur in a sequence, the last, and most severe of which is migration. For Pottier, migration is not an 'end result' which can be labelled simply as a 'problem', but often forms part of the solution to famine for those concerned. In each case, the dynamic causes and consequences of migration need to be investigated, not assumed. Nor are migrants from drought necessarily 'refugees' even in the broad sense of the word. Indeed, Turton and Turton reported how the Mursi of Ethiopia responded to the 1970s drought through a strategy of 'spontaneous resettlement' in which they systematically avoided distributed relief at institutional feeding points-which might 'have turned large numbers of Mursi into permanent refugees in their own country'.

Some of the evidence that does exist specifically on migration responses to environmental stress points at least in part in the opposite direction. Thus a study by Findley (1994) of emigration from the Senegal River Valley in Mali shows that during the drought of the mid-1980s, migration actually *declined* rather than increased. In turn, there was a clear reason for this, since to migrate requires an initial cash investment to pay for travel and associated expenses on arrival, and an economic downturn reduces the ability of families to make such an investment. However, there was an interesting nuance to this finding, in that whereas mainly male *migration* (defined as departure for a period of six or more months) declined, the process of *circulation* (defined as departure for less than six months, and involving many more women and children) did increase during the most severe period of the drought. In a similar vein, Davies (1996) talks of the difference between 'coping' strategies (such as temporary circulation) and 'adaptation' to drought, the latter involving more permanent and irreversible changes in livelihood, and usually an increase in poverty and vulnerability. It is less than clear that migration represents a prominent form of 'adaptation' in the Sahel.

ENVIRONMENTAL REFUGEES FROM THIRD WORLD COUNTRIES

Although environmental refugees are worldwide there are some large pockets: 4 million in the Horn of Africa, 2 million in Sahel, about 3 million in rural areas of Central China and about half a million in Mexico and Central America . The principal reason being land abuse, agriculture collapses, drought, starvation and civil war.

These places have some common characteristics. They are mostly places with high population densities, predominantly rural agriculture, poor soils; people are extremely poor and suffer from malnutrition, food and water shortage. They appear in cities, which are already overcrowded and have millions of jobless people, congested, filthy and are forced to live on bare subsistence. They are also forced from areas which are, which are targeted for rapid industrialization under national programmes. These projects are usually opposed but proceed anyway with little or no care for land destruction and/or refugees caused . In India, statistics show that about 20 million have been displaced by official projects including dams, mines, forest preserves and irrigation.

In Egypt, more than a million hectares of soil were stripped from productive farms to make bricks for the Aswan Dam. Saddam Hussain and his activities have destroyed thousands of sq. km. forcing thousands to be trapped there or fleeing to Iran. In the vast Asian Desert, the former Soviet Union's thirst for water to irrigate and expand cotton farming has intercepted the headwaters of the Aral Sea. The sea has shrunk from 60,000 sq. Km. to 50,000 sq. km. With the consequence that the salinity has raised tremendously destroying the fisheries that once have a capture capacity of 50,000 tons per annum. As a result the age-old fishermen's village have been wiped out.

During Vietnam War in 1982, according to a UN study, 15000 sq. km. of mangrove had been destroyed. Numerous bomb craters halted farming, forcing millions to become environmental refugees. In Eastern Europe, during soviet rule, more than 100 villages and Town in Northern Bohemia (now in Czech Republic) were devastated and more than two hundred thousand people suddenly become environmental refugees. .

The much talked about Narmada Project (India), which envisages the construction of 30 big, 135 medium and over 3000 minor irrigation dams is expected to displace over two lakh tribal, devastate 40,000 thousand hectares of prime teak forests and 84,000 hectares of cultivable land in the states of Gujrat and Madhya Pradesh. The Singrauli Super Thermal Project in Madhya pradesh has already submerged or cleared several hundred hectares of land displacing a large number of tribal due to bad planning.

In the case of the Tehri Dam it is expected to displace 85,600 persons by submerging the town of Tehri and 95 villages, 72 of them partially (Saad Ali, 1991). An international conference in San Francisco in 1988 termed it the "second most dangerous irrigation project in the world", apart from the fact that it is located in a seismic zone.

Environmental Refugees from Developed Countries

Fewer environmental refugees are found in industrial countries than in the Third World. Moreover unlike huge "point" sources, there are smaller, "non-point" sources. The refugees are generated mainly due to exposure to toxic chemical, air pollution, and contamination of water supply. Exposure to such contaminants can cause pathological symptoms and force victims to flee temporarily or permanently. An emerging problem is the "sick building syndrome", a complex condition where various factors like chemicals, pathogenic microbes and poor ventilation interact to make people so ill that they flee.

Apart from this, coming up of big cities in the coastlines, over earthquake zones, dense forests, mountain foothills may also contribute to refugee problem. There have been cases of refugee generation as a result of earthquake, landslides hurricane in Japan, Australia, Europe and U.S. The Hurricane Andrew, that struck the coast of Florida in 1992, created half a million environmental refugees.

ENVIRONMENTAL PROBLEMS IN FUTURE

In 1990, The Intergovernmental Panel on Climate Change (IPCC) predicted that the greatest effect of climate on population displacement would be sea-level rise, severe storms, coastline erosion, coastal hooding and agricultural disruption. The IPCC estimated that up to 360,000 km. Of coastline might be affected in future. Based on this, Myers (1992) predicted "environment refugees" in a green hose affected world to be 150 million by the year 2050. Scientists have predicted 13 million climate change environment refugees in Bangladesh, 16 million in Egypt, up to 73 million in China, 20 million in India and a million more in small countries and 50 million more for agriculturally dislocated areas by the year 2050 . While predicting the future one should not forget the "adaptation mechanism".

It is true that climate changes will have significant influence in some regions, but these changes will take place slowly giving enough time to region and communities to adapt. Although, most affected will be the poor with few options while the reach will have resources, means and government support to adapt faster in the face of environmental change. There is thus an urgent need for in-depth studies on the adaptation mechanism of different communities. How different regions cope with environmental stresses? Why resource scarcities in some regions do not cause major population immigration, etc?

What conclusion can be drawn from the above discussion?

Four general conclusions can be drawn for the above :

1. A generalized statement that environmental degradation results in population displacement overshadows a number of complexities making the prediction difficult.
2. It is very difficult to separate specific role of environmental degradation and human displacement, especially those that are "voluntary" in nature. One should remember that displacement takes place due to combination of environmental, economic, social and political stigmata. Thus segregating environmental processes from other factors is not only difficult but also distortion of reality.
3. Various literatures assure that human movement from adverse situations is a certain means of relief from environmental pressure. Although there is an old Chinese proverb which states that "of thirty ways to escape danger, running away is the best" but it is not always true and movement may not always reduce the environmental stress,

rather one type of environmental stress may be replaced by another (economic, social, political or other environmental stresses).

4. One important point, which is usually overlooked, is that whether such movements are of temporary or permanent nature.

Question thus arises whether migrants desire to return back to their homing ground, if that option is open? There are thus three important stages in the displacement process (Lonergan, 2000)

* Survival-utilizing displacement as a need for acquiring relief from environmental stresses;
* Recovery-When migrants use their movement to recover from the immediate distress and consolidate their position; and
* Improvement-a migrant may use the opportunity for improving their position and future prospects, in which case a return to their home is not likely to occur.

A statistics of all the above attitudes will decide the magnitude of the problem and severity of the environmental crises. The future National and International Policies to curb the severity of environmental refugees crises.

The four conclusions mentioned above pose difficulties in developing a scientific policy to deal with issues of environ-mental crises and population displacement. Taking into account these difficulties, two sets of recommendations can be formulated:

* Policy recommendation for assisting communities and areas under stress that may cause human migration;
* Specific policy recommendation for agencies involved in solving crisis.

Thus, despite of the complex nature of displacement, greater emphasis should be given in national developmental programmes. Major emphasis should be given or promoting sustainable development not in the field of ecology but also in nation's economic and social policies for ensuring human security. Under this broad framework micro-policies should include:

* Development of a system that will help to anticipate displacement in case of environmental crisis,
* Identification of adaptation mechanisms, and how such mechanisms can be imbibed in vulnerable communities and region.
* Development of case studies to understand how environmental degradation influences population movement and what can be done to assist those affected;
* Development of better working relationships among human rights, environment, population and NGO's related to such organizations;
* Development of politics to include refugees in the development programme to assist the affected;

* Recognition of causes environmental degradation and formation of policy framework to ensure minimum environmental impacts;

CLIMATE CHANGE AND MIGRATION

Climate change and its consequences have become a fixture for many political agenda. Controversial though discussion about climate change may be, there is international and cross-party political consensus that global warming is going to be one of the greatest political, economic and social challenges for the coming years.

In social terms in particular climate change plays an increasingly important role. The consequences of global warming already present are confronting whole societies with enormous burdens, whether this is due to increasing rainfall and floods in some areas, the scarcity of rainfall and prolonged drought periods in others, or failed harvests or a shortage of drinking water. International organisations, representatives of various governments as well as experts on climate and migration all around the world are meanwhile discussing the possible effects of climate change on global migration processes.

Climate experts assume that global warming may well lead to a global shortage or at least to a displacement of cultivable land. The reasons for this are as diverse as are the impacts of climate change; rising sea levels will lead to more frequent flooding and storms in coastal and delta regions, small island states and low-lying coastal regions could disappear completely as a result. In some regions rainfall will increase significantly, provoking periodic flooding, while in other regions precipitation will quickly decrease, rapidly promoting droughts and desertification. Soil erosion caused by sandstorms and the decline in vegetation will reduce agricultural productivity in these areas — often already low — to a minimum, potentially endangering the food supply for major regions as a whole. The creeping effects of global warming and the associated increase in extreme weather events, as well as the deterioration in living conditions, may give rise to new migration streams.

This policy brief deals with the phenomenon of *environmental migration*. It focuses entirely on the effect of climate change on global migratory movements without neglecting the environmental consequences on the regions of origin and destination. The following paragraphs will firstly contain a comparison of estimates as to how many people will be affected worldwide and an introduction of those areas where climate change is most likely to cause migration. The brief will then examine the two main controversies concerning this phenomenon: the causality relationship between environmental factors and new migratory movements as well as the legal position of the persons concerned. The conclusion emphasises the necessity of extending the protection of people affected by the phenomena of climate change at the international level, even if it cannot be assumed that there is an exclusive causal relationship between climate change and migration.

Estimates

Reliable statistical data cannot be collected as there is not an internationally recognised definition for the phenomenon of climate-induced migration. In addition, estimates are also hindered by the fact that an immediate connection between the consequences of climate change and migration cannot be clearly demonstrated. In the absence of authoritative forecasts, there is a series of estimates based on unsupported assumptions (so-called *guesstimates*). The figures vary depending on which climatic, demographic and social values the estimates are based on. Under favourable conditions, there may be only a slight increase in current migratory movements, but under unfavourable conditions even high estimates appear to be too low. In 2002 the UNHCR estimated the number of people forced into migration as a result of flooding, famine and other environmental factors at 24 million and later the number of persons displaced internally as a result of natural catastrophes alone at 25 million. The German Advisory Council on Global Change (WBGU) assumes that 10-25 % of all global migratory movements are the result of climate change and its consequences; that would be the equivalent today of an absolute number of 25-60 million migrants. *The United Nations University – Institute for Environment and Human Security*, or UNUEHS, in Bonn estimated the number of environmental migrants up to 2010 to be at least 50 million. The Intergovernmental Panel on Climate Change anticipates a total of up to 150 million migrants as a result of climate change by 2050. The United Kingdom's Stern Review bases its estimate on a review of a large number of studies and forecasts and concludes that there are likely to be 200 million environmental migrants by 2050. The figures of Oxford professor Norman Myers are also widespread; he anticipates more than 200 million environmental migrants by 2050.

Affected Areas

In addition to the estimates given above, even the size of the population in areas that will be particularly affected by climate change can provide a useful reference as to the number of people who will be facing special climatic challenges in future and who may possibly regard migration as an alternative. The United Nations standing committee responsible for determining internationally recognised terminology (*Inter-Agency Standing Committee*, IASC) has identified four important scenarios that are likely to trigger migratory movements:

It is a decisive aspect in all scenarios that climate-related migratory movements may take place both within the affected nation states and across international borders, and may be further assigned case-by-case to a continuum of voluntary migration, preventative migration and refugeeism. Such migration may also be either temporary or permanent.

Endangered states are deemed in general to be the poorly developed island states (Small Island Developing States, or SIDS), the sub-Saharan states, Asian coastal states, the Polar region, African developing states (Less Developed Countries, or LDC), the least developed countries worldwide (Least Developed Countries, or LLDC), the Near and Middle East, and Central Asia. Depending on the nature of the consequences of climate change, areas affected in line with the IASC scenarios may be divided into the following categories.

TIBETAN REFUGEES' RIGHTS AND SERVICES IN INDIA

The Chinese assault of Tibet, and the Dalai Lama's following decision to flee in 1959, resulted in the mass influx of Tibetan refugees into India that continue today. It has become clear to the Indian government, as well as to the Tibetan community in exile, that repatriation is unlikely in the near prospect. Consequently, an evaluation of India's protection of, and assistance for Tibetan refugees is necessary to ensure their treatment is in accordance with international standards. Unfortunately, such an assessment shows that there is a lack of proper protections and services; this ought to be of particular concern to the international community as India has served on the Executive Committee of the United Nations High Commissioner for Refugees (UNHCR) since 1995.

How can a country be trusted to lead an international organization dedicated to the protection of refugees when it has such unstable and inadequate refugee policies itself? Central to the assessment is India's lack of legal compulsion to provide refugee protections or services. This is largely a consequence of India's abstention from the 1951 Convention relating to the Status of Refugees and the subsequent 1967 Protocol, which, in addition to defining a refugee according to international law, outlines certain rights and services host states must afford them. With the exceptions of the customary international practice of *non-refoulement* and the obligation to provide asylum as outlined in Article 14 of the Universal Declaration of Human Rights (UDHR), India does not have international, regional, or national obligations to refugee populations on its soil (Feller 2006). Despite this, and despite the nation's refusal to accede to the 1951 Convention, India argues its current refugee policy is in accordance with international norms. However, India has no national refugee law, and no regional agreement on the matter exists.

The only mention of foreigners in Indian law are in the Registration of Foreigners Act of 1939, the Foreigners Act of 1946, and the Foreigners Order of

1948— all of which employ the term *foreigner*, broadly defined as "a being who is not a citizen of India." Among other practices, the 1946 Act and the 1948 Order allow the government to limit employment opportunities, freedom of association, and a foreigner's possessions. These pieces of legislation also restrict movement inside India and prohibit select activities, most of which are political. In fact, Tibetan refugees are only allowed in India on the condition that they abstain from political protests against China – a clear suppression of their right to political expression as afforded by the UDHR. This political suppression was particularly evident during the 1991 visit of then Chinese Prime Minister Li Peng, during which Tibetan refugee leaders were arrested and placed under police surveillance to curtail protests. A similar occurrence was witnessed during Prime Minister Wen Jiabao's 2010 visit. Human rights law grants refugees fundamental civil and political rights, yet the Indian government denies these rights to Tibetan refugees.

India's lack of legal obligation allows it to change refugee policies at will, often to reflect its current political interests. The result is a rather unstable refugee policy, exemplified in the disparity of rights and services afforded to Tibetan refugees according to their date of arrival in the country. The Indian government regarded the first wave of Tibetans arriving in 1959 with the Dalai Lama as refugees and granted them legal asylum. They were allotted land and housing – a privilege not afforded to other foreigners and one that would later be denied to newly arriving Tibetans. More importantly, these refugees were automatically given a Registration Certificate (RC). According to the Tibetan Government-in-Exile, the Central Tibetan Administration (CTA), the RC is a legal document issued by the Indian establishment that allows Tibetan refugees "the right to enjoy all the privileges enjoyed by any Indian citizen except the right to vote and work in Indian government offices" (Immigration and Refugee Board of Canada 2009).

While many question the extent of the 'privileges enjoyed' by RC-holding Tibetans, the value of the RC is not contested. The RC allows Tibetans to legally travel and work within the country, serves as an identity document, and is a pre-requisite for the Identity Certificate, which is necessary for international travel. Tibetan refugees arriving between 1959 and the 1970s also benefited from services provided by the UNHCR, which despite its tumultuous relationship with India had a temporary presence in the country. The rights and services afforded to Tibetans inward after the 1970s are scarce and indicative of a changing Indian policy—arguably in an effort to preserve Sino-Indian relations.

In 1963, the Indian government ceased to legally recognize arriving Tibetans as refugees. Consequently, those arriving after 1979 (including some arriving in the late 1960s) have had greater difficulty acquiring RCs. The newer process to acquire an RC is arduous and particularly concerning because employment, residency rights, and international travel are contingent upon this document. In addition, while the Indian government provided land to the original refugee community, newer arrivals have not been as fortunate. The denial of land by the government is troublesome considering that farming is chief to a Tibetan's income and Indian law prohibits foreigners from purchasing land. Additionally, the UNHCR closed its office in New Delhi and discontinued its aid to Tibetan refugees in 1975. As a consequence of the Indian government's lack of assistance, the CTA (with substantial assistance from NGOs) has had to shoulder the burden of providing for these refugees. Although the CTA is able to cover basic needs, they are overwhelmed and are unable to effectively address the broader social welfare of this burgeoning community (Adams 2005). Even those with the RC carry on to struggle with their refugee status.

Unable to gain Indian citizenship, they cannot vote, work for local or federal governments, carry an Indian passport, or legally purchase land. Although Tibetans possessing an RC can legally work in pre-approved segments of the economy, many employers often discriminate against them in favor of Indian nationals. This resentment originates from the belief that Tibetan refugees are adversely affecting job opportunities and that they benefit from elevated standards of services not afforded to Indian nationals. While it is believed that communal relations between the Tibetans and the Indian host community have been improving, there have been isolated reports of aggression and discrimination that have largely gone uninvestigated by local police. To further exacerbate this issue, Tibetans are not represented in the local and central legislature and thus do not have readily available avenues for redress. In 1949, when the United Nations debated legal protection versus material assistance for refugees, India argued that "the guarantee of legal rights without concomitant material assistance was a hollow concept" (Oberoi 2006, 22).

However, it has become clear that as Tibetans continue to cross the border, India has not only decreased the rights afforded to these newcomers, but too the services provided to them. Given that repatriation for this refugee community does not appear possible in the immediate future, India needs to concern itself with improving its policy toward this population— thereby affording refugees the proper protection and treatment per international standards. Signing the 1951 Convention would be the best avenue by which to accomplish this as it will lessen the burden on India by affording it assistance and services from the UNHCR and HUMAN RIGHTS & HUMAN WELFARE member states. Above all, India's lack of legal obligation should not be understood as an absence of Tibetan refugees' entitlement to proper services and protections.

TREATMENT OF THE REFUGEES

In the beginning, two large transit camps were set up in consultation with the Government of India: one at Missamari, located ten miles from Tezpur in the Indian State of Arunachal Pradesh; the other at Buxa Duar, a former British prisoner-of-war camp situated near the Bhutanese border in West Bengal. Within a few weeks after the setting up the camps, 6,000 refugees arrived at Missamari and 1,000 at Buxa Duar. As the camps could accommodate not more than 9,000 persons between themselves, simultaneous efforts were made to disperse the refugees for road building works in the cooler regions of North India to prevent fatalities due to intense heat, overcrowding, and epidemic of amoebic dysentery. The first batch of 3,394 people was sent for roadwork in Sikkim in September 1959 in several groups.

Agricultural base Settlements

The Dalai Lama's vision of exile society took root in his new headquarters, an abandoned British hill station called Dharamsala. On 29 April 1960, after a little more than a year's stay, the Dalai Lama moved to his new headquarters from Mussoorie. In Dharamsala, the Dalai Lama revitalized his small administration in exile and called a special meeting of the people's deputies and staff members on 2 September 1960 to formulate new strategy and plan. As a part of the new plan, he established a bureau (now known as Bureau of H.H. the Dalai Lama) in New Delhi to serve as the Tibetan link with the Indian Government and various international relief agencies that were coming to the refugees' aid. Similarly, the Office of Tibet in New York was also set up in 1964 to raise the issue of Tibet at the United Nations and to disseminate information on Tibetans inside and outside Tibet. Rehabilitation, however, was the instant task at hand.

Although the roadwork had provided the much-needed temporary employment for the refugees, it turned out to be not only dangerous, but also hard. The migratory and unsettled nature of the roadwork proved to be extremely hard, particularly on the children and old people. Apart from this, many road-workers suffered from tuberculosis and other communicable diseases due to lack of nutrition and sanitation, compounded by hard labour. As such, the Dalai Lama approached Prime Minister Nehru for assistance for the permanent rehabilitation of the refugees. Nehru, on his part, canvassed the State Governments for vacant countryside for the purpose. Karnataka State (in South India) immediately responded, offering initially 3,000 acres of uninhabited stretch of jungle in gently rolling hills 52 miles west of Mysore City, situated at the altitude of 2,6000 ft. above sea level. It agreed to accept initially 3,000 Tibetan refugees and provide a grant of four million Indian rupees to execute the rehabilitation project.

Soon after this, the first Tibetan agricultural resolution was set up in the middle of December 1960 at Bylakuppe, accommodating a total of 3,217 Tibetan refugees by the end of 1965. For administrative reasons, the settlement was divided into six camps, each with 500 acres. In the first few years, the settlers engaged in reclaiming land, digging wells, and constructing houses, during which they were paid daily wages and given regular rations. The settlers were divided into artificial families of five people, relatives or not, and each family was given five acres of agricultural land. They were accommodated in the three-room brick-walled, tile-roofed single story house, built on a 500-sq. ft., part of which also served as their kitchen garden. A cooperative society was set up in 1961 and later formally registered. The cooperative society procured and advanced seeds, fertilizers, and pesticides; marketed agricultural produce collectively; and provided common services such as tractors, trucks, and warehousing. Besides, the cooperative society later played crucial role in managing carpet weaving centres, flour mills, poultry farms and other ventures such as retail outlets in the settlements. In the same year, a school was opened in the settlement. When the Bylakuppee settlement was first started, a small dispensary was set up in a tent to cater to the emergency medical needs of the refugees. Later in 1964, a special complex of concrete houses was built with assistance from foreign organizations to accommodate a dispensary with inpatient facilities.

For the first five years, the settlers cultivated cotton, tobacco, rice, millet, paddy, lentils and oilseeds, all of which failed miserably. Farming in South India was so different from Tibet's unique high-altitude agronomy that many settlers became totally discouraged and helpless. However, the agony of the repeated crop-failure was solved in 1965, when a Swiss technical adviser, in consultation with the Agriculture University of Bangalore, conducted soil tests and also tested the yields of bullock-ploughed and tractor-ploughed fields. This test resulted in the cultivation of maize crop instead of cotton, tobacco, and other crops and also replacement of bullock plows by tractor plows. The new crop and methods proved so successful that, by the end of 1966, the settlement became self-supporting. Bylakuppe settlement had served as a model for planning other agriculture based settlements later. By mid-seventies, 26 agricultural-based settlements were established in India, Nepal and Bhutan, accommodating a majority of the Tibetan refugees.

Agro-Industrial Settlement

It was apparent that it was not viable to restore all the refugees in agriculture-based settlements. Not only was it hard to find relatively large tracts of land, it was also not practical to rehabilitate all the refugees in agriculture-based settlements. Many of the refugees were traditionally nomads and traders, and had no idea of farming. With this in view and also to expedite the process of rehabilitation, it was found necessary to seek other avenues of resettlement.

Thus, a plan was made to rehabilitate many of the refugees in small-scale industries. To facilitate this, the Tibetan Industrial Rehabilitation Society (TIRS) was established in October 1965, with its headquarters in New Delhi. For the next three years, the TIRS launched several small industrial projects. These included woolen mill at Bir, tea estate in Bir and Chauntra, Tibetan crafts at Bejnath, limestone quarry at Kumrao, hydrated lime plant at Sataun, fiberglass factory at Poanta Sahib, and handicraft centre in Puruwala. These projects accommodated more than 4,000 refugees. These projects were meant not only to provide adequate employment opportunities to the inmates, but also skills in different trades. In each industrial project, school and health care facilities were provided by the TIRS with funds raised from foreign agencies. Besides, the TIRS established a Himalayan Marketing Society, based in New Delhi, to market the produce of these settlements. However, many of these industrial efforts failed due to lack of technical and managerial skills. The majority of the industrial settlements gradually began to depend more on traditional carpet weaving, roadwork in summer, and woolen garment trade in Indian towns and cities in winter.

Handicraft-based Settlements

Over the centuries, Tibet had shared intimate cultural and deal relationship with its neighbouring countries. Through these interactions resulted in the development of many traditional crafts in Tibet. The traditional crafts included metal work, woodcraft, clay modelling, applique work, thangka painting, hand-made paper, leather work, woolen cloth and carpet weaving, etc. Although there were no major institutes in the traditional society to promote these trades, these arts and crafts were practiced in individual households and the products were sold out locally, or through traders to different part of Tibet. When the Tibetan refugees came into exile in early 1960s, some of the Tibetan craftsmen settled in Kalimpong, traditional Tibetan trading post in the North India, and others settled temporarily in Darjeeling and Nepal. Thus, with hope of preserving and promoting the traditional Tibetan crafts as well as to provide employment options for the refugees, the CTA, in consultation with the Government of India, set up several handicraft-based settlements as a part of rehabilitation scheme.

The first handicraft-based settlement was set up on a four-acre estate in Darjeeling in October 1959. The 13th Dalai Lama, during his exile from Tibet in 1910-11, had used the site as his temporary residence and therefore, has a special sentimental value for the Tibetans. The settlement or centre provided shelter and employment for 450 people. Education and medical needs of the inmates were also taken care of. Besides, the centre also ran old people's home and a crèche for small children.

The centre's produce, such as carpets, woolen sweaters, Tibetan women's aprons, wood carved decoration items, wooden toys, leather goods, etc. were marketed locally as well as abroad with the help of aid agencies. Encouraged by the success of the first handicraft-based settlement, other similar settlements or centres were set up in the following years. These included the handicraft centre in Dalhousie, Dharamsala, Kalimpong, Simla, Clement Town, Rajpur, and Dehradun–all in India. Similar settlements were also set up in Nepal. In these handicraft-based settlements, cooperative units were established to procure raw materials and market produce. While the cooperatives marketed the settlement's produce both in India and abroad, the settlers engaged also in individual trade of sweaters–knitted initially by themselves, but later bought from the factories in Ludhiana City in Punjab, India–to supplement their income. Each winter they set up makeshift bamboo-walled and plastic-topped stalls on the sidewalks of bazaars and marketplaces all across India. By the later half of the sixties, sweater selling became the supplementary trade of the majority of Tibetan refugees.

By 1980, only 30,000 Tibetan refugees remained on road construction work. By 1992, a total of 52, 500 people were rehabilitated in the agricultural settlements, 7,700 in Agro-Industrial settlements, and 6,400 in handicraft-based settlements, and 39,800 refugee remained outside the organized units, earning livelihood in petty private enterprises or in the Indian service industries.

New Challenges

The death of Mao Zedong in 1976 and the end of the Cultural Revolution in China and Tibet resulted in opening China to the outside world. This dramatic change also led to the opening of Tibet and the first-post 1959 contact between Beijing and Dharamsala, which took place in March 1979. Many Tibetans, both inside and outside Tibet, took the advantage of the situation to undertake the arduous cross-Himalayan journey to visit their family members and relatives. Many families met for the first time after two decades of separation. With the passage of time, a steady stream of new refugees from Tibet came to seek asylum in India and Nepal.

From 1987 to 1994, Tibet was rocked by a series of pro-independence demonstrations. The Chinese authorities reacted by escalating the machinery of repression, especially against those involved in demonstration. This made life in Tibet all the more difficult, resulting in a mammoth increase in the flow of refugees. Between 1986-1996, some 18,700 refugees arrived in India and Nepal. The situation became still worse after 1994 when the Chinese government introduced harsher policy to deal with the Tibetan nationalism in Tibet. In order to cater to the needs of these new refugees, the CTA opened a Reception Centre in Dharamsala in 1990. Later, its branches were opened in Kathmandu and Delhi. While the Kathmandu Reception Centre is supported jointly by the UNHCR and CTA, the centres in Dharamsala and Delhi are funded by the CTA with a support from the United States' Government. The rehabilitation of the children below the age of 18 and monks and nuns is comparatively easier as the children can be sent to existing boarding schools and the monks and nuns to the monasteries and nunneries in India. The rehabilitation of adult refugees is problematic. This is because most of the adult new refugees are unskilled and most of the existing settlements are overcrowded. As such, the CTA opened a special Adult Education Centre in the outskirts of Dharamsala in 1993 to provide vocational and language training to the new refugees.

CLIMATE CHANGE AND ENVIRONMENTAL REFUGEES

The origin of environmental refugees can be partially blamed on our dependence on non-reusable energy which has caused increased gas emissions into the atmosphere. These energy bi-products include carbon dioxide (CO_2), methane (CH_4), nitrous oxide (N_2O), and fluorocarbons (HCFC, HFC, PFC). These gases, grouped under the term "Greenhouse Gas Emissions", have, since the 1990's, been identified as being responsible for climate change. CO_2 is the worst greenhouse gas with a 76% distribution in earth's atmosphere; the other gases follow with CH_4 at 13%, N_2O at 6% and HCFC, HFC, PFC running at 5%.

Another reason cited in scientific literature to explain climate change is the earth's natural warming and cooling cycles. Deep-sea cores have revealed evidence that the earth warms and cools naturally on a 1,000 to 3,000 year cycle. The last cooling period may be the so-called Little Ice Age which began ca. 1100 CE. This cool period lasted for a few hundred years and then a warming trend again started; we may currently still be experiencing this trend.

The important question, however, is – whatever is causing the current climate change, be it greenhouse gas emissions and/or the earth's natural cycles — can we reverse this trend? If we could stop all greenhouse gas emissions immediately, would it change anything? How long would it take to drop CO_2 back to the level of the early industrial period when CO_2 levels sat at 290 ppm? Dr. Susan Solomon, an atmospheric scientist at NOAA's Earth System Research Laboratory and winner of the 2009 Volvo Environmental Prize, mentions in her pioneering study entitled Irreversible climate change due to carbon dioxide emissions that *"changes in surface temperature, rainfall, and sea level are largely irreversible for more than 1,000 years after carbon dioxide (CO_2) emissions are completely stopped"*. She also adds that *"increases in CO_2 that occur* *in this century "lock in" a sea level rise that would slowly follow in the next 1,000 years"*. If this is the case, humans must now be resourceful. The world's populations must decide upon a response to our changing climate.

Can we decrease the number of environmental refugees through Reforestation? The World Health Organization diagram below clearly indicates that climate change is a driving force that directly influences human populations world wide. One of the major issues identified by this chart is desertification/ land degradation. Forests are ecosystems that have sustained human life for eons. We use forests as a source of fuel for cooking and as a source for building materials. We also use forested lands as a source for many foods and medications. Wood, if managed properly, is very inexpensive, easily accessible and renewable but overuse of this natural resource has resulted in deforestation and the degradation of human environments. Reforestation is by far the most efficient way to tackle climate change and hence the most efficient way to decrease the number of environmental refugees. Prof. Norman Myers, environmentalist, authority on biodiversity and three time leading environmental prize winner, stresses in "Environmental Refugees: An Emergent Security Issue" that reforestation is the best way to embrace a sustainable development approach in countries facing difficulties in meeting human needs. Reforestation will "rehabilitate hydrological systems and watershed functions, and thus avoid floods and drying-out of river systems downstream".

Another proponent of reforestation is the 2004 Nobel Peace Prize Laureate Wangari Maathai's. She is now Deputy Minister for the Environment in Kenya. During her Nobel prize acceptance speech, she mentioned that *"A degraded environment leads to a scramble for scarce resources and may culminate in poverty and even conflict"*. She started a tree planting program in 1977 with just seven trees. This soon became the Green Belt Movement where Kenyan women are encouraged to care for seedlings obtained from native trees. These seedling are used as stock plantings for reforestation in villages. Numerous non-governmental organizations (NGOs) are now involved with reforestation in other developing countries, for example in South Korea, in China and in Turkey. The aims of reforestation projects are simple: restoration of water tables, rehabilitation of ecosystems, reduction of ambient air temperature and creation of buffer zones to decrease strong wind velocity. Reforestation with indigenous trees and shrubs also helps produce natural medicines, provide biofuel and other derived products such as honey.

One such successful reforestation program has occurred in Rio de Janeiro, Brazil. Started in 1986, it is called the "Community Reforestation Project"; the mandate of this project involved the correction of two important issues: slope stabilization and job creation. It focused on planting indigenous trees on steep hillsides inhabited by *favelas*. *Favelas* are spontaneous, unregulated settlements which consist of "*...an area, predominantly of housing, characterized by the occupation of land by low-income populations, precarious infrastructure and public services, narrow and irregular layout of access ways, irregular shaped and sized plots and unregistered constructions, breaking with legal standards*". To achieve their goals, the project concentrated on hillside improvements and on reforestation. They hired *favela* occupants to build infrastructures such as terraces, drainage canals and proper roads. These projects were specifically designed to stabilize the soil, increase water retention and reduce erosion on the steep hills. The local workers also acquired skills that were transferable to construction sites in lowland areas, providing future employment opportunities.

Instead of trying to organize massive reforestation, the project opted for planting small, scattered plots of land over a three to four year period. They also focused on the re-introduction native tree species well adapted to hilly terrain. The forest plan included planting fast growing leguminous trees mixed with native, exotic and fruit bearing trees. The project staff also began educational programs to raise the awareness of the favela populations, instructing them on how they could protect and maintain the new forested areas. Of of 54 communities who participated in this reforestation project, only two recorded tree loss. This project resulted in a decrease of urban sprawl caused by the expansion of *favelas*, the regrowth of indigenous vegetation, an increase in available food, the return of native wildlife species, the regeneration of springs, the provision of shade and the improvement of air quality.

Can we decrease the number of Environmental Refugees through Adaptation? The term 'adaptation' when used in the area of climate change is the adoption of new behaviors that will help people cope with environmental changes. There are numerous smaller examples of adaption strategies, including selecting farm animals with limited water or foliage requirements, growing short season crops or drought and pest resistant crops, and changing irrigation techniques to reduce water requirements. There are also large scale adaption methods that could help us alleviate the affects of climate change including land reclamation and climate proofing.

THE LIMITS OF GLOBAL ENVIRONMENTAL MANAGEMENT

Although steps have been taken between Rio 1992 and New York 1997 in the direction of the globalization of environmental protection, the world seems to be further away from sustainability today than it was then. With environmental globalization and the consensual concept of sustainable development, the perception of an ecological crisis, or at least of ecological limits to development, appears to have vanished: acting for environmental protection increasingly tends to be seen as a technical problem, the task of increasing efficiency and of better using resources such as science, technology, information, capital, and institutions. The cause of environmental problems is no longer perceived as linked to industrial development and ever-increasing material accumulation, but it has become the very existence of human beings. Environmental problems are understood as unavoidable, as side effects of human activities, and efforts are then directed at solving these problems.

Indeed, global environmental management and sustainable development can be seen as "problem solving" concepts, in Robert Cox's terminology, as they only represent a strategy to allow the pursuit of present lifestyles and standards.

Following Strange's call for a critical International Political Economy and the need to address the question of "who gets what, how and why," the analysis of the evolution of the system of global environmental management has revealed that it tends to strengthen the mechanisms of exclusion and inequality (Strange 1988). Global environmental management and sustainable development tend to be uneven concepts, as they do not aim at promoting the correction of global disparities. They attempt to offer a universal framework in which the global society is the unit of analysis and a large share of the blame for environmental degradation rests on the Third World. Instead of stressing affluence, over-production and over-consumption in advanced countries as the main causes of environmental degradation, it tends to suggest that problems arise from poverty. Environmental degradation is transformed from a problem of affluence into a problem of poverty. The responsibility is shifted from major polluters and industrialized countries' abuses to all inhabitants of the planet. For Chatterjee and Finger (1994), the only different element in this approach is that development is now looked at from a global perspective, making the development discourse universal.

And the New York Summit represented a step further in that direction, asserting the desirability of the globalization process and underlining its beneficial aspects. It also consolidated the role of business and industry as privileged partners of the United Nations, establishing permanent contact and consultation on environmental issues. The regulatory situation relating to TNCs and business in general has worsened greatly in the past five years. Already in 1992, the US government successfully pressured for downsizing the UN Center on Transnational Corporations (UNCTC), which had been set up to monitor the social, economic and environmental impacts of corporate investment in developing countries. Today, the UN is considering cutting a sub-group of the UN Human Rights Commission which addresses the impacts of corporations on a broad spectrum on rights issues. The main international initiatives and institution for establishing guidelines for the behavior of corporations, which could together lay down a code of obligations and rights of TNCs and states, have disappeared. In their place has come a strong and growing opposite trend to reduce and remove regulations that governments have over corporations, to grant them increased rights and powers, and to reduce the authority of states to control their behavior and operations.

The Uruguay Round for example has already granted far higher standards of intellectual property rights protection to corporations, thus facilitating further their global monopolization of technology and ability to make profit through higher prices. There are also strong pressures from Northern governments at the World Trade Organization to grant foreign companies the right of entry, establishment and national treatment in all WTO member states .

In addition, the partnership between the UN and global corporations seems to have been further strengthened in the past two years. In part due to the difficult financial and political situation in which the UN finds itself as a result of the US government's refusal to pay the US $1.6 billion it owes, the UN is now openly seeking political and economic support from corporations. At the last Davos Economic Forum in Switzerland, UN Secretary General Kofi Annan called for a human face to the global market and challenged business leaders to adhere to universal values defined by the UN and contribute to global environmental protection, indicating a broader trend of growing UN collaboration with transnational corporations.

Recently, the United Nations Development Program (UNDP) has solicited funds from global corporations with poor records on human rights, labor and the environment, such as Dow Chemical, Citibank and Rio Tinto Plc, in exchange of special UNDP sanctioned logos for use by corporate sponsors. Called the "Global Sustainable Development Facility (GSDF)," the plan calls for corporate sponsors to funnel donations to a separate entity which they will manage. In the words of the UNDP, the GSDF "brings together leading global corporations and the UNDP, to jointly define and implement a new facility to eradicate poverty, create sustainable economic growth and allow the private sector to prosper through the inclusion of two billion new people in the global market economy."

According to the internal memo, sponsors will benefit from the advice and support of UNDP through a special relationship, allowing corporations unprecedented access to UNDP's network of offices, high level governmental contacts and the knock-on effects of its reputation. The plan, revealed through a leaked internal UNDP memo, has been heavily criticized by observers and NGOs, who warn that the interests of global corporations are often at odds with the basic economic and social needs of the world's poor and the values of human rights and environmental protection the UN is meant to protect.

According to Ward Morehouse, President of the US Council on International and Public Affairs, the UN should be monitoring the human rights and environmental impacts of corporations in developing and industrialized nations, not granting special favors... Increasing collaboration will lead to a reluctance to criticize corporations which are central players in the human rights, environmental and developmental dramas unfolding every day across the globe.

To conclude, the UN and international organizations in general seem to be moving towards the adoption of a market-oriented global model of environmental governance, which sees economic globalization as a positive and integrative process. The key actors of economic globalization, transnational corporations, are taking the leading role and consolidating their influence on the system of international environmental governance. With the adoption of this project of global environmental management, one particular understanding of the world, the one promoted by business and large corporations in Western affluent societies, becomes hegemonic and appears to be universal .

Environmental concerns have been incorporated as a mere dimension of the "globalization project," understood in McMichael's definition as "an emerging vision of the world and its resources as a globally organized and managed free trade/free enterprise economy pursued by a largely unaccountable political and economic elite". This project advocates a universalized model of production, of consumption, and thus of dealing with problems of environmental protection resulting from these activities.

By assuming its universality, it tends to marginalize other knowledge and other solutions to problems of environmental protection. Interestingly enough, it was unanimously recognized that the most positive result and follow-up of UNCED was without doubt realized at the micro-level, within the Local Agenda 21 framework. In an effort to implement Agenda 21 locally, social groups have worked together with local authorities to make sustainable development a reality at the local level, often on a truly participatory basis and reflecting grassroots concern and involvement.

From a critical point of view, global management's failure, exemplified at the New York Summit, was not entirely unexpected. Indeed, the global management approach inspired by business perspectives and propagated by the international development establishment tends to strengthen the globalization process at work today, failing to counter its effects in terms of social exclusion and environmental destruction. It tends to weaken social protection and environmental protection in the name of economic efficiency (McMichael 1996).

It stands at odds with the commitment to social change and to equity that lies at the root of a critical, political economy view of global environmental politics as inserted within the dynamics of economic accumulation and social structures. The question of the ownership of natural resources, for example, is not addressed. However, environmental problems in the South are often linked to problems of resource ownership and equity. Sustainable Development as defined in Rio and reasserted in New York has been practically translated into technocratic responses to what are in reality political problems.

FUTURE OUTLOOK OF ENVIRONMENTAL REFUGEES

How many environmental refugees can we realistically anticipate in the future—or rather, how many people are likely to become vulnerable to environmental problems that could force them to migrate? Let us consider the outlook for the year 2010. The population of developing countries is projected to have grown from 1995 by well over one billion people, a 28-percent increase in just 15 years. Sub-Saharan Africa's total will have expanded by more than 250 million, a 45-percent increase, and the Indian subcontinent's by 380 million, 32 percent. The numbers of people in absolute poverty are predicted to swell from 1.3 billion to 1.6 billion. The 135 million people affected by severe desertification could well increase to 180 million. The populations of water-short countries are expected to surge from 550 million to more than one billion. If the 1990-onwards "plateauing" of crop yields continues, there will be more, and more widespread, shortfalls in food production (especially in Sub-Saharan Africa and the Indian subcontinent), while international tradable stocks will be increasingly unable to keep up with fast burgeoning demand.

The 25 million environmental refugees in 1995 had mostly become obliged to migrate since 1980, when their numbers first started to climb rapidly. In light of patterns and trends of environmental decline and associated problems such as spreading poverty and population increase, it is probable that by 2010 there will be another 25 million such refugees on top of the 25 million in 1995 if only because the impelling factors will continue to be at least as prominent for the communities concerned. (This supposes too that there will be few preventive measures of sufficient scope.) In fact, the increase could well be more than another 25 million because of increasingly degraded environments coupled with growing numbers of impoverished people. For a specific instance of the problem's scope to expand, consider the prospect for Sub-Saharan Africa until the year 2010. This is already the region with half the world's traditional refugees and at least a similar proportion of environmental refugees. Despite some advances in soil conservation , smallscale agriculture (Nigeria, Zimbabwe), reforestation (Tanzania, Malawi), anti-desertification (South Africa), and population planning (Kenya, Zimbabwe, Botswana), the outlook is unpromising. The region's population is projected to increase to 830 million people, 45 percent more than in 1995. Severe desertification may well affect more than 100 million people, half as many again as today. Ten countries are expected to be experiencing chronic water shortages or even acute water scarcity, with collective populations 5 totalling well over 400 million people. Without greatly expanded efforts to tackle the region's lack of development, per-capita GNP will probably stagnate in real terms at around $400, or little higher than in 1970.

Most important of all will be the region's incapacity to feed itself. Some 20 countries with a projected population of 440 million are expected to experience up to 25 percent shortfall in food supplies, and a further eight countries with a projected 75 million people face more severe deficits. The total of malnourished people will continue to grow, with at least 100 million destitutes obliged to live for the most part off imported food. The food deficit could well rise to as high as 30 million tonnes. Because of its exceptional poverty the region will be increasingly unable to compete in the global grain market. Food aid worldwide in 1995 was only 7.5 million tonnes, enough to make up the diets of only 10 million semi-starving people.

In addition, there will be problems of global warming. Due largely to sea-level rise and flooding of coastal-zone communities, but also to increased droughts and disruptions of rainfall regimes such as monsoonal systems, global warming could threaten large numbers of people with displacement by 2050 or earlier. Preliminary estimates indicate the total of people at risk of sea-level rise in Bangladesh could be 26 million, in Egypt 12 million, in China 73 million, in India 20 million, and elsewhere, including small island states, 31 million, making a total of 162 million. At the same time, at least 50 million people could be at severe risk through increased droughts and other climate dislocations.

Concerns for Environmental Security

All in all, the issue of environmental refugees promises to rank as one of the foremost human crises of our times. To date, however, it has been viewed as a peripheral concern, a kind of aberration from the normal order of things—even though it is an outward manifestation of profound deprivation and despair. While it derives primarily from environmental problems, it generates myriad problems of political, social and economic sorts. As such, it could readily become a cause of turmoil and confrontation, leading to conflict and violence. Yet as the problem becomes more pressing, our policy responses fall further short of measuring up to the challenge. To repeat a key point: environmental refugees have still to be officially recognized as a problem at all.

At the same time, there are limits to host countries' capacity, let alone willingness, to take in outsiders. Immigrant aliens present abundant scope for popular resentment, however unjust this reaction. In the wake of perceived threats to social cohesion and national identity, refugees can become an excuse for outbreaks of ethnic tension and civil disorder, even political upheaval. This is already the case in those developed countries where immigrant aliens increasingly prove unwelcome, as witness the experience of Haitians in the United States and North Africans in Europe. Almost one third of developed countries are taking steps to further restrict immigrant flows from developing countries. Yet measures to relieve the plight of refugees of whatever kind have drastically diminished in relation to the growing scale of the problem. Although the annual budget of the United Nations High Commissioner for Refugees was recently boosted to $1.3 billion, the agency is increasingly unable to supply food and shelter for refugees of traditional kind alone, much less to invest in rehabilitation or repatriation of these refugees. Meantime the world's refugee burden is borne primarily by the poorest sectors of the global community. In 1998 the twenty countries with the highest ratios of official (traditional) refugees had an annual per-capita income of only $750.

Policy Options

There is much scope for preventive policies, with the aim of reducing the need to migrate by ensuring an acceptable livelihood in established homelands. First of all, we need to expand our approach to refugees in general in order to include environmental refugees in particular. We cannot continue to ignore environmental refugees simply because there is no institutionalised mode of dealing with them. If official standing were to be accorded to these refugees, this might help to engender a recognised constituency for e.g. those 900 million people who endure desertification, four million of whom have become environmental refugees in the Sahel alone. While desertification entrains costs of $42 billion a year just through the loss of agricultural produce, the United Nations' Anti-Desertification Action Plan would cost no more than $22 billion a year. Yet the amount subscribed so far is less than a few billion, ostensibly on the grounds that arid-land dwellers have no constituency and hence lack political leverage.

Secondly, we need to widen and deepen our understanding of environmental refugees by establishing the root causes of the problem—not only environmental causes but associated problems such as security concerns, plus the interplay of the two sets of forces. There are many conceptual grey areas as concerns proximate and ultimate causes, the contributory roles of population pressures and poverty, the linkages to ethnic tensions and conventional conflict, and so forth. Suppose, for instance, there had been a better understanding and hence a better anticipatory response on the part of the Philippines government when the agricultural frontier closed in the country's lowlands during the late 1980s, bringing on a sudden increase in landlessness and an upsurge of migration into steep uplands in search of land. The problem could have been somewhat relieved through before-the-event measures to redistribute existing farmlands, to improve rural infrastructure, and to supply more off-farm employment, thereby reducing the need to migrate out of the lowlands.

Consider too the root causes of famine. If a famine has been human-made, it can be human-unmade, whereas natural factors can only be managed and accommodated. Just as the recurrent droughts in Sub-Saharan Africa cannot all be blamed on climate, so the recurrent famines cannot all be blamed on drought. Drought has often served to trigger famines by disrupting the social, economic and political processes that would normally ensure sufficient access or entitlement to food.

Probably most important of all is that there can be little advance except within an overall context of what has come to be known as sustainable development. This applies notably to reliable access to food, water, energy, health and other basic human needs—lack of which is behind many environmental refugees' need to migrate. In big picture terms, sustainable development represents a sound way to pre-empt the environmental refugee issue in its full scope over the long run. As a prime mode to tackle the issue, then, there would be a handsome payoff on investment to foster sustainable development in developing countries through greater policy emphasis on environmental safeguards, together with efforts to stem associated problems such as poverty, population and landlessness.

However, only select parts of sustainable development measures address the particular problem of environmental refugees. Specially pertinent, for example, would be the Anti-Desertification Action Plan as applied to the Sahel and arid sectors of the Horn of Africa, both being sources of large numbers of environmental refugees, whether present or prospective. Also warranting closely targeted responses are food-short regions within Sub-Saharan Africa and the Indian subcontinent.

Much could be achieved too through better targeting of foreign aid. The annual budget of the main source of multilateral aid, the United Nations Development Programme, is not so very much greater than that of the United Nations High Commissioner for Refugees ($1.3 billion in 1995)—meaning that the United Nations' main response in this regard tends to be rather reactive than proactive. Worse, the ten developing countries with well over two-thirds of the world's "poorest of the poor" receive only one third of foreign aid—and it is impoverished communities that serve as the source of most environmental refugees. India has 27 percent of all people in absolute poverty worldwide, yet it receives only five percent of total foreign aid. Were foreign aid to be more closely directed at impoverished people in the main countries and regions concerned, it could help to relieve the problem while it is still becoming a problem, i.e. before it becomes entrenched.

There is much too that developing countries themselves can do, and at no great cost. According to UNICEF (2000), to eliminate deaths from famine would cost little more than $0.5 billion per year; to cut malnutrition among women and children (who make up a disproportionate share of environmental refugees), less than $2 billion; and to reduce hunger among the poorest households, little over $6 billion.

All of these measures would help to reduce prime pressures generating environmental refugees. The total cost would be less than $9 billion, or $7 for each of the 1.3 billion people in absolute poverty—these being the communities that are a main source of environmental refugees. By contrast, developing countries spend an annual average of $40 per citizen on military activities. In 1999 Ethiopia assigned 13 percent of GDP to this purpose, four times the global average, even while it featured some of the largest numbers of environmental refugees in proportion to population size.

5

Rural Urban Migration Change and Sociology

Rural-urban migration has long been associated with economic development and growth in the economic literature. In particular, Todaro and Harris-Todaro-type probabilistic models that examine migration have concentrated on the expected wage disparities between rural and urban (formal) labour markets as a driving force behind migration decision. These models, which are static and partial equilibrium in nature, have virtually ignored the cost-of-living differentials across regions that arise from the presence of regional non-traded (home-) goods. Moreover, even in dynamic general equilibrium models, equations specifiying labour market clearing conditions have neglected to recognize a missing endogenous variable, the households choice of residency, and the corresponding equations necessary to cause the labour market to clear as well.

Effectively, adding these conditions to the model allows agents to move from one region to another and to bring their utility function and budget constraint with them to the new region of residency. This condition profoundly affects the spatial distribution of economic activity. Furthermore, when factor market imperfections are modelled, e.g., the segmentation in labour and capital markets across regions, these factors earn different rates of return thus greatly influencing the pattern of spatial economic development.

The main objectives of this chapter are to model the residency choice decision in the context of a dynamic general equilibrium economy, to identify the channels through which segmentation in capital markets in developing countries induces migration from rural to urban regions, and to explain how uneven economic growth may emerge as a consequence. This paper incorporates cost-of-living and income differentials across regions into the migration decision of households in a dynamic general equilibrium setting. With the use of a dynamic general equilibrium model, we can capture the migration pattern as a response to changes in cost-of-living, as well as to the evolution of real wage differentials as capital accumulates due to household savings and as the rural-urban production sectors respond to the Rybczynski-like effects of competition in factors of production. Using a model that extends the standard Ramsey-type growth model, we investigate the endogenous pattern of migration in a developing country economy in the process of economic growth and structural change. The standard Ramsey-type growth model is thus extended to include two types of households in a regional, multi-sectoral environment with capital market segmentation. In particular, to best assess the impact of capital market segmentation on the economy as a whole and on specific macroeconomic variables, a policy experiment is conducted under the cases of with and without capital market segmentation: when a policy ashock is introduced, the economy performance, as well as migration patterns are examined when there is segmentation in capital markets, and when there is a perfect capital market.

The policy experiment is conducted by lowering the labour tax rates levied on the employers in the urban formal sector. The model is calibrated to Turkish economy for the year 1997, which has a large rural population at about 42 percent of the total population as of that year. Data are compiled from Turkish National Accounts Statistics and Labour Statistics. Initial results from numerical simulations show that in a model economy with a large rural population and segmentation in its capital markets, a policy change in the economy such as reducing the labour taxes imposed in the urban formal sector induces migration from rural to urban areas, and this migration continues along the transition path to a new long run equilibrium. Large drops in output in rural areas are detected, whereas the output in the urban region grows along the transition path. However, the same economy reacts to the same policy change much differently after it undergoes an institutional reform such as the integration of its capital markets. As the economy adjusts to a new equilibrium once a policy change is introduced, relative to the case with segmented capital markets, no large changes in the macroeconomic variables occur. Especially, rural households choose to remain in the rural region.

MOVEMENT OF MIGRATION

As more and more people leave villages and farms to live in cities, urban growth results. The rapid growth of cities like Chicago in the late 19th century and Shanghai a century later can be attributed largely to people from rural communities migrating there. This kind of growth is especially commonplace in developing countries.

The rapid urbanization of the world's population over the twentieth century is described in the 2005 Revision of the UN World Urbanization Prospects report.

The global proportion of urban population rose dramatically from 13% (220 million) in 1900, to 29% (732 million) in 1950, to 49% (3.2 billion) in 2005. The same report projected that the figure is likely to rise to 60% (4.9 billion) by 2030..

However, French economist Philippe Bocquier, writing in THE FUTURIST magazine, has calculated that "the proportion of the world population living in cities and towns in the year 2030 would be roughly 50%, substantially less than the 60% forecast by the United Nations (UN), because the messiness of rapid urbanization is unsustainable. Both Bocquier and the UN see more people flocking to cities, but Bocquier sees many of them likely to leave upon discovering that there's no work for them and no place to live."

According to the UN State of the World Population 2007 report, sometime in the middle of 2007, the majority of people worldwide will be living in towns or cities, for the first time in history; this is referred to as the arrival of the "Urban Millennium". In regard to future trends, it is estimated 93% of urban growth will occur in developing nations, with 80% of urban growth occurring in Asia and Africa.

Urbanization rates vary between countries. The United States and United Kingdom have a far higher urbanization level than China, India, Swaziland or Niger, but a far slower annual urbanization rate, since much less of the population is living in a rural area.

- Urbanization in the United States never reached the Rocky Mountains in locations such as Jackson Hole, Wyoming; Telluride, Colorado; Taos, New Mexico; Douglas County, Colorado and Aspen, Colorado. The state of Vermont has also been affected, as has the coast of Florida, the Birmingham-Jefferson County, AL area, the Pacific Northwest and the barrier islands of North Carolina.
- In the United Kingdom, two major examples of new urbanization can be seen in Swindon, Wiltshire and Milton Keynes, Buckinghamshire. These two towns show some of the quickest growth rates in Europe.

Cause

Urbanization occurs naturally from individual and corporate efforts to reduce time and expense in commuting and transportation while improving opportunities for jobs, education, housing, and transportation. Living in cities permits individuals and families to take advantage of the opportunities of proximity, diversity, and marketplace competition.

People move into cities to seek economic opportunities. In rural areas, often on small family farms, it is difficult to improve one's standard of living beyond basic sustenance. Farm living is dependent on unpredictable environmental conditions, and in times of drought, flood or pestilence, survival becomes extremely problematic. Cities, in contrast, are known to be places where money, services and wealth are centralised. Cities are where fortunes are made and where social mobility is possible.

Businesses, which generate jobs and capital, are usually located in urban areas. Whether the source is trade or tourism, it is also through the cities that foreign money flows into a country. It is easy to see why someone living on a farm might wish to take their chance moving to the city and trying to make enough money to send back home to their struggling family.

There are better basic services as well as other specialist services that aren't found in rural areas. There are more job opportunities and a greater variety of jobs.

Health is another major factor. People, especially the elderly are often forced to move to cities where there are doctors and hospitals that can cater for their health needs. Other factors include a greater variety of entertainment (restaurants, movie theatres, theme parks, etc) and a better quality of education, namely universities. Due to their high populations, urban areas can also have much more diverse social communities allowing others to find people like them when they might not be able to in rural areas.

These conditions are heightened during times of change from a pre-industrial society to an industrial one. It is at this time that many new commercial enterprises are made possible, thus creating new jobs in cities. It is also a result of industrialisation that farms become more mechanised, putting many labourers out of work. This is currently occurring fastest in India.

One of the last houses of the old Russian village of Lukeryino, most of which has been demolished over the last 30 years to make way for 9-story apartment buildings in the growing city of Kstovo, such as the one in the background

In recent years, urbanization of rural areas has increased. As agriculture, more traditional local services, and small-scale industry give way to modern industry the urban and related commerce with the city drawing on the resources of an ever-widening area for its own sustenance and goods to be traded or processed into manufactures.

Research in urban ecology finds that larger cities provide more specialized goods and services to the local market and surrounding areas, function as a transportation and wholesale hub for smaller places, and accumulate more capital, financial service provision, and an educated labour force, as well as often concentrating administrative functions for the area in which they lie. This relation among places of different sizes is called the urban hierarchy.

As cities develop, effects can include a dramatic increase in costs, often pricing the local working class out of the market, including such functionaries as employees of the local municipalities. For example, Eric Hobsbawm's book

The age of the revolution: 1789–1848 (published 1962 and 2005), stated "Urban development in our period [1789–1848] was a gigantic process of class segregation, which pushed the new labouring poor into great morasses of misery outside the centres of government and business and the newly specialised residential areas of the bourgeoisie. The almost universal European division into a 'good' west end and a 'poor' east end of large cities developed in this period." This is likely due the prevailing south-west wind which carries coal smoke and other airborne pollutants downwind, making the western edges of towns preferable to the eastern ones.

Urbanization is often viewed as a negative trend, but in fact, it occurs naturally from individual and corporate efforts to reduce expense in commuting and transportation while improving opportunities for jobs, education, housing, and transportation. Living in cities permits individuals and families to take advantage of the opportunities of proximity, diversity, and marketplace competition.

Environmental Effects

The urban heat island has become a growing concern. Urban sprawl creates a number of negative environmental and public health outcomes. For more than 100 years, it has been known that two adjacent cities are generally warmer than the surrounding areas. This region of city warmth, known as an urban heat island, can influence the concentration of air pollution. The urban heat island is formed when industrial and urban areas are developed and heat becomes more abundant. In rural areas, a large part of the incoming solar energy is used to evaporate water from vegetation and soil. In cities, where less vegetation and exposed soil exists, the majority of the sun's energy is absorbed by urban structures and asphalt. Hence, during warm daylight hours, less evaporative cooling in cities allows surface temperatures to rise higher than in rural areas. Additional city heat is given off by vehicles and factories, as well as by industrial and domestic heating and cooling units. This effect causes the city to become 2 to 10° F (1 to 6° C) warmer than surrounding landscapes. Impacts also include reducing soil moisture and intensification of carbon dioxide emissions.

Changing form of Urbanization

Massive urbanization in Delhi, India resulted in tremendous strain on the city's infrastructure. The planned Dwarka Sub City can be seen in foreground while the unplanned and congested residential areas of West Delhi are visible in the background.

Different forms of urbanization can be classified depending on the style of architecture and planning methods as well as historic growth of areas.

In cities of the developed world urbanization traditionally exhibited a concentration of human activities and settlements around the downtown area, the so-called *in-migration*. In-migration refers to migration from former colonies and similar places. The fact that many immigrants settle in impoverished city centres led to the notion of the "peripheralization of the core", which simply describes that people who used to be at the periphery of the former empires now live right in the centre.

Recent developments, such as inner-city redevelopment schemes, mean that new arrivals in cities no longer necessarily settle in the centre. In some developed regions, the reverse effect, originally called counter urbanisation has occurred, with cities losing population to rural areas, and is particularly common for richer families. This has been possible because of improved communications, and has been caused by factors such as the fear of crime and poor urban environments. Later termed *"white flight"*, the effect is not restricted to cities with a high ethnic minority population.

When the residential area shifts outward, this is called suburbanization. A number of researchers and writers suggest that suburbanization has gone so far to form new points of concentration outside the downtown. This networked, poly-centric form of concentration is considered by some an emerging pattern of urbanization. It is called variously exurbia, edge city (Garreau, 1991), network city (Batten, 1995), or postmodern city (Dear, 2000). Los Angeles is the best-known example of this type of urbanization.

Rural migrants are attracted by the possibilities that cities can offer, but often settle in shanty towns and experience extreme poverty. In the 1980s, this was attempted to be tackled with the urban bias theory which was promoted by Michael Lipton who wrote: "...the most important class conflict in the poor countries of the world today is not between labour and capital. Nor is it between foreign and national interests. It is between rural classes and urban classes.

The rural sector contains most of the poverty and most of the low-cost sources of potential advance; but the urban sector contains most of the articulateness, organization and power. So the urban classes have been able to win most of the rounds of the struggle with the countryside...". Most of the urban poor in developing countries able to find work can spend their lives in insecure, poorly paid jobs. According to research by the Overseas Development Institute pro-poor urbanisation will require labour intensive growth, supported by labour protection, flexible land use regulation and investments in basic services.'

Planning for Urbanization

Urbanization can be planned urbanization or organic. Planned urbanization, ie: new town or the garden city movement, is based on an advance plan, which can be prepared for military, aesthetic, economic or urban design reasons. Examples can be seen in many ancient cities; although with exploration came the collision of nations, which meant that many invaded cities took on the desired planned characteristics of their occupiers. Many ancient organic cities experienced redevelopment for military and economic purposes, new roads carved through the cities, and new parcels of land were cordoned off serving various planned purposes giving cities distinctive geometric designs. UN agencies prefer to see urban infrastructure installed before urbanization occurs. landscape planners are responsible for landscape infrastructure (public parks, sustainable urban drainage systems, greenways etc) which can be planned before urbanization takes place, or afterward to revitalized an area and create greater livability within a region. Concepts of control of the urban expansion are considered in the American Institute of Planners.

New Urbanism

New Urbanism was a movement which started in the 1990s. New Urbanism believes in shifting design focus from the car-centric development of suburbia and the business park, to concentrated pedestrian and transit-centric, walk able, mixed-use communities. New Urbanism is an amalgamation of old-world design patterns, merged with present day demands. It is a backlash to the age of suburban sprawl, which splintered communities, and isolated people from each other, as well as had severe environmental impacts. Concepts for New Urbanism include people and destinations into dense, vibrant communities, and decreasing dependency on vehicular transportation as the primary mode.

MIGRATION AND GENDER LITERATURE

The paucity of research on gender and migration until the 1990s has recently been redressed by critical reviews of migration models and a new surge in research. Most of the current discourse is descriptive. It asks questions like: How are male migrants different than female migrants? How is their decision-making process distinct? How do their reasons for migrating vary? How similar are their remittance behaviours? Are the consequences of migration different for men and women?

A few studies have shown that it is not only gender but position within the household that seems to matter: such as daughter, wife, mother, or head of household. Other studies examine intra-household resource allocation, inter-personal negotiations within the household, and changing gender roles. For example studies of rural households in the Philippines find that poorer households are more likely to send young women family members to the city as seasonal migrants. The sex-segregated, urban labour force structure insures steady short-term income for women in jobs with little opportunity for upward mobility. This socio-economic structure enables households to maintain control over young, female migrants, whose tenuous labour market situation makes them likely to continue to rely on the option of returning home.

In Thailand, Curran (1995 and 1996) finds that although both sons and daughters are equally likely to migrate, daughters are more likely to remit wages. Expectations about migration and remittances follow a similar pattern. In addition, sibling order position is an important determinant of remittance behaviour. Middle daughters are the most likely to remit wages and middle sons the least likely. This difference is explained through qualitative evidence that middle daughters work hard to insure a place in the family as they face a tenuous urban labour market, in the hopes of garnering parental resources through inheritance in the matrilineal and matrilocal society. Middle daughters occupy a more tenuous position than oldest or youngest daughters relative to parental resources. Oldest daughters, given the earlier timing of their marriage, are assured of some resources from parents and youngest daughters carry the burden and opportunity of being expected to care for their elderly parents and inherit the family house and a majority of rice fields. Among sons, middle sons have little to gain in investments from their parental households and therefore return little of their migrant earnings. They rarely receive opportunities for secondary education from their parents for two reasons: oldest sons receive it for Buddhist merit accruing to parents and youngest sons because family resources (through the pooling behaviour of daughters) are likely to have accumulated to afford educating younger siblings (Curran 1996).

The particular insight from the studies on gender, households and migration (in Latin America and Southeast Asia) is not unified family strategies influencing individual behaviour. Instead the insight is that there are complex negotiations (either implicit or explicit) between family members where the outcomes are dependent upon both cultural expectations of each gender as well as the relative resources (power) available to each family member. The preceding studies show how cultural expectations and economic opportunity associated with gender shape migration and its impact upon society. Studies of Latin America offer some examples in which migration processes can actually challenge gender roles. We review results from three Latin American studies and provide additional evidence from our own research in Thailand.

In the case of Peru, Deere (1978) shows how land reform in the 1950s has a differential effect upon peasant households. Richer households are able to finance the purchase of hacienda parcels (available when haciendas were broken up as a result of land reform), whereas poorer peasant households are forced to become wage labourers. Migration becomes common among a significant proportion of the poorer households, in response to limited jobs at home. Usually, the male head of household seeks work abroad, leaving behind an extended family of married women, their children, and their parents. In this new family structure, Deere finds that women and children gain increased decision-making power and responsibility within the household. The high rate of divorce or separation upon migrant husbands' return, suggests that women refuse to compromise their newly acquired egalitarian gender expectations when the "man of the house" reclaims his authority. However, the move to equality is only partial. For, although women gain greater power within the household and acquire more egalitarian perceptions of themselves, their husbands' migration makes them financially poorer, due to the loss of their incomes and limited labour market opportunities for women (Deere 1978).

Similarly, Guendelman and Perez-Itriago (1987) find that among seasonal Mexican migrants, gender roles are realigned in the process of migration. For seasonal migrants where the women also work, marital relations improve in the place of destination, in that there is more sharing of decision-making and cooperation. Non-working wives of seasonal migrants suffer because, separated from their kin, they become more dependent upon husbands in the place of destination. However, upon their return to the place of origin, workingwomen are forced to realign their gender roles, and the non-working women actually perceive more freedom, as they rediscover kinship support networks.

Further, Hondagneu-Sotelo (1994) finds that gender roles also shift depending on the pattern of migration and length of stay in the place of destination, whether men migrate individually and bring wives or girlfriends later or whether migration occurs as a family. In the case of the former, gender roles are more likely to be differently constructed in the place of destination than in the place of origin (Hondagneu-Sotelo 1994) Grasmuck and Pessar (1991) examine family migration from the Dominican Republic to the U.S. and find that the process has profoundly different implications for the men and women within the household. Men view migration as temporary and are eager to return home, thereby regaining traditional gender privileges. In contrast, women often hope to postpone or avoid return because they realize it entails retirement from work and the loss of newfound freedoms. As a result of these different outlooks, a struggle develops over finances. Men save to facilitate return migration, while women spend large amounts of money on expensive, durable goods, such as a home and home furnishings, so as to root the family securely in the United States and to deplete the funds necessary to relocate.

In the Thai example, although Curran (1995, 1996) finds substantial rural cultural expectations that daughters remit to their natal household, more recent studies suggest a weakening of this effect. Increasingly this expectation is coming into conflict with opportunities and cultural models offered women in the urban fast lane and a lack of opportunities for men who have little education. In fact, there is some evidence that parents' expectations of sharing inheritance and care giving is shifting away from daughters to the child (or grandchild) who shows the most interest in the farm and household. This may create a space for a redefinition of gender roles, where sons take on more care-giving roles (given their limited urban labour market opportunities) and thus expect to inherit parental resources. In sum, the gender and migration literature reveals how women and men's migration experiences differ. It also demonstrates how the household mediates between macro-economic structure and individuals. Finally, it shows how cultural expectations associated with gender are both reproduced and transformed within the household. However, its extremely micro perspective means that it does not tackle large societal patterns of migration. Better at this is Portes and colleagues and Massey (1990). Massey uses a sophisticated theory of networks and the concept of "relative deprivation" to link individual experiences with societal structures. Portes' and Sensenbrenner's work posits that macro cultural and economic influences work through networks to affect individual behaviour. It is to this that we now turn.

Migration and Networks

Concurrent with, but largely isolated from the gender and migration research are theories of migration, development, and networks, advanced most convincingly by Portes (1997), Portes and Sensenbrenner (1993), Massey (1990, 1987), and Stark (1991). These compelling theories have broad implications for social and cultural change. They point to mechanisms inherent in migration that create momentum and lead to the augmentation of migration over time. They also show how patterns of migration and networks transform internal economies, for instance, when remittances result in greater inequality in the community of origin (Massey et al. 1987). Finally and most importantly, they show how social structures and individual positions within structures (social capital and embeddedness), such as migrant enclaves, can influence individual identity and behaviour (for better or worse) (Portes and Sensenbrenner 1993).

Building on Portes and Sensenbrenner's work we will argue that networks are not only powerful conduits for instrumental information (Massey 1987, 1990), but that they also transmit values and cultural perceptions. Drawing on Berger (1967), we will demonstrate how beliefs become and remain meaningful if and only if one is integrated into networks of individuals who share those beliefs. If one fails to participate in such networks, which Berger calls plausibility structures, then one's beliefs are not confirmed or reinforced by others, making them susceptible to erosion. On the other hand, exposure to new networks with different beliefs will serve to challenge one's established world-view and offer alternative value systems. We will demonstrate how migration and migrant networks facilitate this process, leading to cultural transformation, in particular, in male-female relations. Many of our examples will draw upon research about rural-urban migration in Thailand. But the hypotheses put forth are expected to be just as applicable to other types of migration or movement across social and physical space. We begin with a review of the work by Massey because his concept of cumulative causation provides the background and tools for understanding Portes and Sensenbrenner's ideas about embeddedness and social capital as they relate to migration. A review of the migration literature by Massey (1990) is useful for understanding how patterns of migration and networks can catalyse large, national and international patterns of social change. Below, we summarize the theory and its insights for migration and social change in some detail. Its key insight is that networks serve to link individual and household decisions to larger social structures and have a cumulative effect over space and time. We focus upon how *networks of obligation* link individuals (both migrating and non-migrating), *relative deprivation* motivates migration, and *trust* structures the content and formation of migrant network ties. Each of these concepts is inherently cultural in their construct and our discussion highlights how this is so.

STATUS OF THE RURAL ENVIRONMENT

The ecosystem within which all rural activities are conducted encompasses the air we breathe, the waterbodies surrounding us, and the land we walk on. Unfettered human activity can compromise the ability of the environment to support our kind, a condition usually referred to as environmental degradation and detrimental to our future. India supports approximately 16 per cent of the world population and 20 per cent of its livestock on 2.5 per cent of its geographical area, making its environment a highly stressed and vulnerable system. The pressure on land has led to soil erosion, waterlogging, salinity, nutrient depletion, lowering of the groundwater table, and soil pollution-largely a consequence of thoughtless human intervention.

The extent of land degradation, the loss in capacity of our major water reservoirs and the decline in water level in wells in the past few years is alarming. Soil erosion from overgrazing, and intensive cultivation and soil degradation from excessive use of agricultural chemicals, have wide-ranging implications. Agricultural activities that cause land degradation include shifting cultivation without adequate fallow periods, absence of soil conservation measures, cultivation of fragile lands, unbalanced fertilizer use, faulty planning or management of irrigation. Improper agricultural practices are usually observed under constraints of saturation of good lands and population pressure leading to cultivation of'too shallow' or'too steep' soils and ploughing of fallow land before it has recovered its fertility. Overgrazing and over-extraction of green fodder lead to forest degradation through decreased vegetative regeneration, compaction of soil, and reduced infiltration and vulnerability to erosion. Annual environmental costs for India in 1995 were estimated at US$ 9.7 billion, of which surface water pollution, land degradation and deforestation contributed 84 per cent. Deforestation with shifting agriculture, over-exploitation for fuel wood and timber collection, and mining activities are also causes of serious concern. Deforestation causes degradation when the land is steeply sloping, or has shallow or easily erode-able soils, and when clearance is not followed by good management.

Over-cutting of vegetation to obtain timber, fuel wood and other products is frequent in semi-arid environments, where fuel wood shortages are severe. Overgrazing causes a decrease in vegetation cover which is a primary cause of erosion. The data provided by the National Remote Sensing Agency and Forest Survey of India based on satellite imagery, 80 Mha of 142 Mha of land under cultivation is substantially degraded and about 40 Mha of 75 Mha of land under the forest department has a canopy density cover less than 40 per cent. Perhaps the most widely recognized environmental problem is the pollution of water resources by industrial discharge, household waste, sewage, and agricultural chemicals. Water scarcity induced by mounting population density and growing economic activity in the face of fixed resources, depleting water tables, and silting of reservoirs has led to rapid decline in the quality of life in rural India.

Existing irrigated areas are displaying serious water-stressed situations, as both reservoirs and groundwater sources continue to get depleted. Consequently, the agricultural output from irrigated areas also seems to be more vulnerable to weather shocks than earlier. The problem is compounded by the fact that provision of cheap power encourages farmers to use excessive water. While this problem is widely acknowledged, a holistic policy framework to address the problem effectively is missing. India's biodiversity is gradually narrowing. Maintaining viable populations of species-whether plant or animal-is crucial in biodiversity conservation requiring the protection of important ecosystems, habitats, and the ecological processes of which they are a part. The loss of biodiversity in shrinking forests as well as in threatened marine and wetland ecosystems has strong adverse impacts in store.

Ecological Footprint

Ecological footprint analysis is an accounting tool that estimates the resource consumption and waste assimilation requirement of a defined human population or economy, in terms of a corresponding land area. Such an analysis encompasses many human needs and aggregates them into a single figure, expressed in global hectares per capita per year, which can be used to shape environmental policies. Because of the complexities involved in determining an eco-footprint, very little analysis has been undertaken at the rural scale globally, although country eco-footprints are estimated and published annually by the World Wildlife Fund.

The global ecofootprint, based on 2001 data was 13.5 billion global hectares, which exceeds the global bio-capacity by 21 per cent, or 0.4 global hectares per person. Although India's eco-footprint over the last forty years is almost constant at around 1 global hectare per person available bio-capacity per person has fallen as its population has almost doubled. The consumption patterns of the large middle class, residing mainly in urban areas will shape its eco-footprint in the years to come and it is here that the rural areas have a role to play in holding the footprint down to reasonable levels by engaging in sustainable farming practices. It must also be noted that the footprint is a very human-centric concept, talking about hectares of land to be set aside for humans without any consideration for other species.

Impact on Human Health

Globally, among the biggest dangers from farming is the continuous exposure to and the unsafe use of chemicals necessary for agriculture. In India, however, the danger to human health from such environment and pollution related causes are not given their due importance as accidents from farm machinery, with a fatality rate of 22 per 100,000 farmers. Fatality apart, chronic exposure to air and waterborne chemicals can have adverse health effects, which sometimes, can be difficult to measure because of problems in isolating individual chemical effects. While certain cause and effect relationships are not easy to identify, cumulative effects are likely to be most critical. Cancer risk could be high from nitrate, metals, as well as pesticides; other problems like adverse hormonal functions, liver damage could also take place. Moreover, toxic chemicals and pesticides in air, water, and earth enter body tissues and breast milk, through which they are passed on to infants.

For example, the impact of spraying endrin and endosulfan on cashew plantations in the 1970s to combat pests in the Kasargod district of Kerala has been so persistent that in one village alone, 156 cases of health disorders were recorded from 123 households between 1990 and 2001. These included 49 cancer cases and 23 mental retardation cases among several others. Moreover, endosulfan residues, several times the minimum permissible limit, were found in water, milk, vegetable, and fish, putting the village communities at risk even three decades after spraying of the pesticides.

THE GREEN REVOLUTION AND LAND TENURE

One of the objectives of those concerned with agrarian reforms was to increase production. In the countries where food shortages are chronic-India and Pakistan-as well, agrarian reforms have been justified by the necessity to increase the production of basic foodstuffs. Since the measures were mostly restricted to a redistribution of control over land but brought about little change in the traditional cultivation, little production increases ensued from the reforms. The lack of measures to change cultivation caused the two countries to depend largely on cereal imports with the ensuing economic and political consequences. In the second half of the sixties, technological changes took place in agriculture which exercised a strong influence on the production level. The yield increases resulting from the Green Revolution were so obvious that, within just a few years, the new technology had taken over in all of the regions where it was possible to apply it. It was remarkable that these large yield increases bad been achieved without institutional changes in the agrarian sector. This soon led to the assumption that it was possible to develop agriculture without institutional reforms and that one could do without complicated agrarian reforms. However, this soon proved to be an erroneous conclusion. A more comprehensive analysis of the process shows that numerous bottlenecks arose due to the prevailing agrarian structure and that the implications of the Green Revolution actually made a change in the agrarian structure even more necessary.

The Process of the Green Revolution

The increased production in agriculture as a result of the utilisation of new varieties with a high yield potential in conjunction with more water, fertilizers, and pesticides is called the Green Revolution. The new varieties are not of themselves high yielding, but rather, genetically, they are a yield potential which can only develop if sufficient water and plant nutrients are available. If these are lacking, the yields are sometimes lower than those of local varieties. As is often the case as far as high bred varieties are concerned, they are susceptible to diseases and require careful plant protection measures, Besides, on account of their low resistance and rapid degeneration, the varieties must be replaced by newly bred varieties after only a few years.

When the new seeds are grown with sufficient water, fertilizers, and pesticides, the increases in the yields are astonishingly high. Many a farmer has, from one year to the next, harvested three times as large a wheat yield from the same area using the new seeds. This obvious increase in the yield caused the new varieties to be rapidly adopted. During the first years, the shortage of seed, and not a lack of readiness to utilize it, constituted a bottleneck when the new varieties were introduced. All the same, one should be conscious of the narrow limits of this technological change that is misleadingly called a "revolution." It is not a general breakthrough in agricultural production. The changes apply primarily to the cultivation of wheat and rice, whereas the other cereals are hardly affected. Thus, cereals from the arid regions as well as cotton, pulses, and oil plants are more or less excluded.

As far as rice is concerned, the problems are far more difficult. The new rice varieties require not only that irrigation be available, but also make great demands on the quality of irrigation. The varieties suffer damage from too much as well as too little water. Thus, while controlled irrigation is necessary, frequently an irrigation system is used that consists of rain water overflooding the upper terraces and flowing down to the lower terraces so that the amount of water cannot be controlled. In such cases, it is a definite necessity to improve the irrigation systems before the new varieties can be successfully cultivated.

Since irrigation is an indispensable factor for this new technology, regions which depend on rainfall are implicitly excluded from partaking in these changes. But in India and in Pakistan, only about one third of the arable land is irrigated. This results in tremendous regional differences. The Green Revolution is restricted to irrigated regions and, therefore, to regions which have always produced better yields and thus belonged to the wealthier states. The regional differences became, therefore, even more pronounced.

Similar differences in participation are found according to farm size. Better information, a greater capacity to take risks, and readiness to adopt innovations explain why the large farms adopted the innovation at an early stage, In addition, they had the advantage of obtaining high subsidies during the first years and better prices for seed production. Small farms followed later with some hesitance. In some cases, tenants were forbidden to use the new seed. The more delayed adoption by the small farms can also be explained partly by the initially poor baking quality when the technology which existed in the villages was used and by its poorer taste. Even after the initial phase, the large farms were more advantaged than the small ones. There is no doubt that the new technology can be split up. Seed, fertilizers, water and pesticides can be used on small as well as on large areas. They are therefore neutral as far as farm size is concerned. However, this is no longer true in the case of tractors and pumps. In trying to improve the new opportunities by utilising machines, the large farms had, therefore, advantages. However, the different farm inputs are still more important. In this aspect, the large farms have decisive advantages. They are better informed, have better transport facilities, and more credit, and, when capital goods are scarce, they are frequently more likely to be supplied on a preferential basis. The new technology utilises to a greater extent purchased inputs, i.e., that are not produced on the farm. Thus, the interdependence with the market, capital expenditure, and thus risk are increased, especially for inexperienced farmers. Formerly, crop failures could be overcome by tightening ones belt', but this no longer helps if one has considerable debts to be paid to the farm input suppliers.

But precisely the risk ensuing from climatic fluctuations cannot be eliminated. Soon, there were crop failures because the farmers had not learned how to react promptly to infestation with disease. For those who were in a better economic position, the integration in the market economy and simultaneous implementation of the technological innovation meant new possibilities of action. For the economically weak, the path leading to market integration often led to new dependences.

Likewise, under the aspect of the overall economy, the Green Revolution has not brought advantages alone. It is true that the yield increases in the two countries improved the supply of foodstuffs for a few years. This was more lasting in India because the necessary research stations were built to produce the constantly required new varieties. Today, Pakistan is still or again dependent on cereal imports.

Moreover, the intensified utilisation of purchased inputs has not made production less expensive and has led to considerable price increases. The utilisation of inputs previously unknown to the farmers can easily damage the environment. Quite often, pesticides and herbicides are applied in a wrong concentration. But increased irrigation also has consequences. The ground water level is raised and the risk of salinisation is increased. Many regions have irrigation but insufficient drainage. In some regions, the water reserves also decrease. The overwhelming production increases also distracted from several alternatives. In countries where 20-30% of the harvest is lost, it would surely be less expensive to reduce the losses than to increase production at high costs, especially when increasing oil prices bring about a considerable rise in the cost of inputs.

It must also be mentioned that the Green Revolution meant increased production at drastically rising social costs. The society subsidises seeds, finances research stations, invests in fertilizer factories and irrigation systems, builds roads, and organises farm systems. Since part of the higher yields can be attributed to these expenses incurred by the society, and not to the efforts of the individual farmers, some of the profits should be skimmed off and go to the government for further economic development. But this is not taking place due to the prevailing power structure.

The Green Revolution is therefore a mixed blessing. It brought about decisive advances in agricultural production, but also serious economic and social problems. It is important to realize that these problems are not actually the consequences of the new technologies per se. They are the result of the prevailing economic and social conditions which only become more evident. Therefore, it cannot be a matter of putting a stop to new technology but, at the most, to keep it within bounds. It is important to take measures to solve the prevailing problems, especially the deficiencies in the agrarian structure so that new technologies no longer lead to negative consequences. The problem of the man-land relations following the Green Revolution becomes even more crucial. As will be shown in the following, the prospects in that respect have sooner diminished. This becomes especially evident if the implications of the agrarian changes for various strata of the rural population are more thoroughly examined.

Improving Land Access for India's Rural Poor

India contains the largest numbers of both rural poor and landless households on the planet. And, the two are related. Landlessness is the best indicator of rural poverty in India, better than either caste or illiteracy. Indian leaders have been well aware of the connection and the country has taken substantial policy and legislative steps to address the problem since independence. Perhaps no country has matched the volume of land reform legislation produced by India since its independence in 1947. India's experience is yet another reminder, however, that adopting well-intended laws, by itself, does not guarantee good results. From the perspective of most rural poor, India's land reform laws have not had the desired effect; and some legislative provisions have resulted in perverse and unintended consequences. Today, India's poorest households still struggle for access to rural land and land tenure security.

The story of land reform in India need not end here, however. With relatively modest revisions, some of India's existing policies and laws can further their original intent of increasing the poor's access to rural land and providing for secure land tenure. Other areas require more drastic measures. Old land reform approaches, such as blind adherence to land ceiling legislation and tenancy reform, need reconsideration. Narrowly conceived and ineffective programmes that ignore local realities must be terminated.

The time has arrived for policymakers to take inventory of its land reform experience, distill lessons learned, and more innovatively use land laws, policies, and programmes to broaden land access and strengthen land rights for the poorest and least empowered of India's poor. The "land route" is not the only route out of poverty, but in a country where landlessness is the best predictor of poverty, it is a route that cannot be ignored.

Land reform in India over the past 50 years was founded on legislatively driven efforts to provide the rural poor with access to agricultural land. Since Independence, most of the legislative energy to increase land access was funneled into three areas: the abolition of intermediaries, tenancy reform, and enactment of ceilings on land holdings.

This chapter is a summary review of those efforts and it attempts to distill some broad lessons that might inform possible policy paths ahead. The perspective is that of an outsider-a non-Indian land lawyer with comparative experience on land policy and law reform in many other countries who has also spent considerable time conducting field research on the topic in India. The paper reviews India's efforts to provide the poor with access to rural land through the enactment of laws and policies to extinguish intermediary interests (section II), regulate tenancy relationships (section III), set ceilings on land holdings (section IV), allocate government wasteland (section V), and allocate house sites to the poor (section VI). For each, the paper examines the extent to which those laws have been successful in increasing land access, and makes an initial effort to distill lessons learned for moving ahead.

Abolition of Intermediaries

The first wave of land reform legislation after India's independence concentrated on the abolition of intermediary land right holders between the tillers and the government. While these efforts are largely of historical significance, a summary review is warranted because the efforts provided a foundation for subsequent land reform initiatives and because they provide some broad lessons still applicable today.

At the time of Independence in 1947, Indian agricultural land was administered under three broad types of land tenure systems: the zamindari system, ryotwari system, and mahalwari system. The zamindari system was the most widespread, covering 57 percent of cultivated land in British India. Under this system, the British regime had declared feudal lords (zamindars, jagirdars, talukdars, etc.) and other persons previously designated as land tax collectors to be proprietors of the land. Although such persons (all of whom became generally referred to as zamindars) had not previously owned much or any of the land given to them, the British administrators dubbed them owners with permanent rights and contracted with them for the payment of land revenue (tax). The empowerment of zamindars transformed the tillers of the land into tenants whose fortunes were dependent upon the wishes and whims of the zamindars.

The zamindar's estates ranged in size from a few acres to tens of thousands of acres. Over time, the larger zamindars freed themselves from the burden of managing their estates and collecting rents from cultivators by leasing out the rent-collecting rights. In some areas, several layers-in some areas as many as 50—of intermediary rights separated the zamindar from the actual cultivator, with the zamindars seated at the top level, at the feet of the state. At all levels, intermediaries gleaned their principal income from the monetary difference between the amount of rent they collected from the layer below and the rent they were obligated to provide to the layer above. The zamindari system of receiving rent through levels of legally recognised tenure holders was generally more developed in northern India than in south or central India. This system prevailed in Bengal, Uttar Pradesh, Bihar, Rajasthan, Bengal, and Orissa, and parts of Assam, Andhra Pradesh, and Madhya Pradesh.

The second broad type of land tenure system was the ryotwari system, which covered about 38 percent of cultivated land in British India. The ryotwari system prevailed in much of southern India including present-day Maharashtra, Karnataka, Tamil Nadu, as well as most of Andhra Pradesh and Madhya Pradesh and parts of Assam, Bihar, and Rajasthan. The ryotwari system recognised individual cultivators (ryots or raiyats) as proprietors of their land with generally recognised rights to sell, lease, mortgage, and otherwise transfer their land. The system did not legally recognize any kind of intermediary interest between the cultivator and the state; the proprietors paid land revenue directly to the colonial administration. Nonetheless, informal intermediaries of the zamindari type emerged even in areas where the ryotwari (and mahalwari) systems had strongholds. While some raiyats were owner-cultivators, many rented out part or all of their land to tenants, mostly sharecroppers.

Only approximately five percent of British India's cultivated land was administered under the third type of land tenure scheme, the mahalwari system. Under this system, land revenue was assigned to and paid by entire village units (mahals). Peasant farmers contributed shares of the total amount of land revenue owned by the village in proportion to their holdings. The mahalwari system existed in most of present-day Punjab and Haryana, as well as parts of Madhya Pradesh, Orissa, and Uttar Pradesh.

The existence of intermediary interests, particularly within the zamindari system, led to highly inefficient and inequitable results. British authorities had assumed that by giving the zamindars and other tax-collecting authorities proprietary rights and fixed tax amounts, efficient collaboration between landlords and tenants would surely follow. The authorities assumed that the zamindars would provide managerial expertise, technical knowledge, and capital, and the tenants would supply their labour—a complementary relationship that would increase agricultural production and productivity. Such symmetry of contribution was never achieved on a large scale. Instead, "the sole concern of the parasitic groups of intermediaries was to extort the largest possible share of the produce of the land without making any contribution whatsoever to agricultural production."

Initially, the colonial administration gave the zamindars free rein to manage their tenants as they pleased. As the British authorities began to recognize that many zamindars were mistreating tenants through practices such as rack-renting and summary evictions, they introduced various limited pieces of legislation, starting with the Bengal Tenancy Act of 1885, that gave some protection to certain categories of tenants. These efforts were inadequate to curtail the abuses. In particular, the laws offered little or no protection to tenants under zamindar's self-managed or home farms and those under the ryotwari system.

The abuses of the zamindari system attracted attention during the struggle for independence, and in the period immediately following Independence, as the country's new leaders turned their attention toward land reform, they gave particular attention to the abolition of intermediary interests in land. The effectiveness of their efforts reflected the extent of discontent with the intermediary system. The injustices practised by zamindars, coupled with their support of the British colonial administration, fuelled the political will to undermine or eliminate intermediary rights to land.

The Indian Constitution, which grants states exclusive authority to enact land tenure legislation, provided a starting point. Soon after assuming power, several state governments initiated action to extinguish intermediary interests. By the end of the 1950s, almost all states had enacted legislation aimed at abolishing intermediary interests upon the payment of compensation. Results were mixed. On one hand, the legislation transformed some 20 to 25 million "superior" tenants into landowners or "government tenants" holding land directly under the government, placed large areas of privately owned forests and wasteland under state ownership, and altered the rural power structures. On the other hand, the laws to abolish intermediary interests fell well short of their potential because of the protracted nature of the legislative process, the shortcomings in the legislative content, the complex and time consuming procedures for implementation, and the role of the judiciary in frustrating the intent and implementation of the laws. The positive results and the shortcomings of the laws as a whole are discussed below.

Positive Results

The laws to abolish intermediary interests brought an estimated 20 to 25 million erstwhile tenants into a direct relationship with the State, with many if not most of the beneficiaries in Uttar Pradesh and West Bengal. The economic benefits realised by beneficiaries were somewhat limited for at least three reasons. First, many of the tenants who were brought into direct relationship with the state had already received some tenure security and rent regulation from tenancy laws enacted prior to independence. Second, most of the state laws required the former tenants to make payments to the government for acquiring ownership rights (to offset the compensation paid by the government to the intermediaries). Third, most of the state laws obliged the beneficiaries to pay annual land revenue (tax) at an amount equal to what they had been paying the intermediary. The legislation significantly reduced forced labour, agrestic serfdom, and other forms of oppression prevalent in many parts of the country, and forced the zamindars to share power with the beneficiaries, their erstwhile "superior" tenants, most of whom belonged to the upper and middle castes. These beneficiaries gained increased social status and, more gradually, increased political power.

In addition to the social and political gains of beneficiaries, the abolition of intermediaries brought large areas of cultivable wasteland, forests, and abadi land (house plots and other land in villages) under state ownership. States subsequently distributed a considerable amount of this land to poor beneficiaries. The legislation to abolish intermediaries also reduced the multiplicity of legal land tenures that previously existed and thus simplified and clarified land tenure law in most Indian states. Uttar Pradesh, for example, had some 40 types of legally recognised tenure types before the adoption of legislation to abolish intermediaries reduced the number of tenure types to three. Especially in a country with substantial illiteracy in rural areas, complexity of land tenure law tends to disfavour the poor; the more educated and well-off are more capable of understanding, using, and taking advantage of the law-to the disadvantage of those less capable, usually the poorest.

Shortcomings

The legislative shortcomings resulted in harmful consequences and missed opportunities. Most significantly, the laws created the impetus for zamindars to evict substantial numbers of tenants forcibly. Employing legal and illegal methods, the zamindars were particularly successful at evicting "non-superior" tenants (including tenants-at-will, under-tenants, and sharecroppers), many of whom had farmed the land from which they were evicted for generations.

Substantial loopholes and flaws in the law allowed zamindars to accomplish much of these evictions through largely legal means. In every state, legislation permitted ex-intermediaries to retain their home-farms or "personally cultivated" land; only a handful of states placed a limit on the size of such home-farm land retained. The legislation loosely defined "personal cultivation" to include cultivation through sharecroppers, servants, and wage labourers. Most state laws even allowed the intermediary to evict tenants from land he had not been "personally cultivating" but now wished to "personally cultivate," and the legislation allowed the ex-intermediaries to select the land they wanted to retain. Only West Bengal and Jammu & Kashmir simultaneously adopted land ceiling limits to restrict the total amount of land ex-intermediaries could own. The lengthy processes of adopting and implementing the laws, coupled with administrative indifference and judicial delays, frequently allowed zamindars to use other illegal and extra-legal methods to evade the law including: (1) fictitious partition of properties; (2) influence of the village officials for manipulative changes in land records; and (3) registration of tenants as farm servants or wage labourers. The states generally compensated the ex-intermediaries more than adequately for the rights they did lose, at a substantial burden to the state exchequer. According to the National Planning Commission Report, the compensation paid to the lowest slab of ex-intermediaries reached as high as 15 to 30 times of their annual net income. Frustratingly, most did not repay the favour: the ex-intermediaries were generally disinclined to invest their compensation in industry or other worthwhile economic activities.

Finally, while state laws often granted tenants the right to purchase lands from willing landlords at set rates, these provisions had serious shortcomings that precluded any significant change in landownership patterns. Prices fixed for land were high, particularly given the limited nature of the landlord's rights, and instalment payments spaced within too limited a period of time. The end result: an opportunity for tenants to become owners slipped by. In sum, the legislation abolishing intermediary rights gets mixed reviews. Most informed observers praise the beneficial impacts; the legislation reduced (and in cases entirely extinguished) the feudal nature of agrarian relationships in many parts of India. Observers also note that despite the deficiencies of the legislation, the states implemented this phase of India's land reforms more successfully than the land ceiling and tenancy reforms that were to follow. However, flawed legal provisions and less-than-effective Gunnar Myrdal's assessment, in contrast, emphasises the end of the reign of powerful intermediaries as semi-feudal chiefs, while acknowledging that inferior tenants drew essentially no benefits from the reform. Finally, Wolf Ladejinsky observes:

> *Despite opposition and administrative and technical problems, the zamindari tenures were virtually abolished. Not all have been benefited equally and not all 20 million cultivators affected have received permanent, heritable, and transferable rights. Nevertheless the effort was a great step forward for reconstruction of Indian agriculture.*

ORIGIN AND DEVELOPMENT OF RURAL SOCIOLOGY

Rural sociology is a new branch of sociology with studies being carried out from 19th century. The prominent scholars engaged in rural sociology during this period were-Sir Henry Maine, Etton, Stemann, Baden Powell, Slater and Pallock etc. The period of 1890-1920 in America saw the rural societies facing many socio-economic problems which attracted the attention of the intelligentsia thus establishing study of rural society as an academic discipline. The appointment of Country life Commission by Theodore Roosevelt was an important landmark in the history of rural sociology. In 1916 the first text book on sociology was published by J.N Gillettee.

It was first originated in the United States of America. It has taken more than half a century to become established as a distinct academic field or professional study. The main contributors to the development of rural sociology are-Charles Sanderson, Burtherfield, Ernast Burnholme, John Morris Gillin, Franklin H. Giddings and Thomas Nixon Carver. It was President Roosevelt who, through the appointment of 'Country Life Commission' gave a good encouragement to the development to the rural sociology in 1908. The report of this Commission encouraged the studies of rural society.

In 1917 the Department of Rural Sociology was set up by the American Sociological Society. In 1919, a 'Rural Sociology Department' was established under the chairmanship of Dr. C. J. Galpin. The Great Depression of 1930 provided another stimulus to the growth of rural sociology.

In 1937, 'Rural Sociological Society' was formed. It started publishing a professional journal 'Rural Sociology' containing results of rural sociological research. C. J. Galpin of University of Wisconsin developed techniques for defining and delimiting the rural community. His approach is still popular today.

The Great Second World War gave yet another fillip to the growth of rural sociology. The destruction caused by the war demanded reconstruction. The reconstruction work brought further encouragement to the science. By 1958 there were about 1000 professional rural sociologists in America. Rural sociology crossed the boundaries of America and became popular in Europe. A European Society for Rural Sociology was formed in 1957, and a similar organisation was started in Japan also. In developing countries, the role of the rural sociologists is primarily in the applied field of more effective planning and operation of rural community development programmes.

The Second World War caused heavy destruction and damage to human society which needed reconstruction. As a result rural sociology got an impetus in USA. The main concern of rural sociology came to be the understanding and diagnosing of the social and economic problems of farmers. More emphasis was placed on issues such as the internal structures of community life and the changing composition of rural populations than on their relationships with land or the social aspects of agricultural production. Theoretically rural sociology remained caught up in bipolar notions of social change whereas rural often got defined as the opposite of urban.

Rurality was conceptualized as an autonomous sociological reality. The identification of rural sociology with rural society has also raised questions about its relevance in the western context where no rural areas were left anymore and almost the entire population had become urbanized.

In response to these critiques of rural sociology a new sub-discipline of sociology emerged that operated largely within the functionalist paradigm and was preoccupied with the study of the community life of rural people. This sub-discipline known as sociology of agriculture focused its attention on understanding and analysing the social framework of agricultural production and the structures of relations centered on land. It raised questions about how and on what terms the agrarian sector was being integrated into the system of commodity production and about the unequal distribution of agricultural incomes and food among the different social categories of people. The sociology of agriculture also distinguished itself from peasant studies on the grounds that its focus was on capitalist farming where the production was primarily for the market, not on peasants producing for their own consumption by using family labour. Thus it claimed more kinship with the tradition of the political economy of agriculture or agrarian studies. At the methodological level, historical inquiries became as relevant as ethnographic/empirical studies. This conceptual shift during the early 1970s also helped in bringing sociologists working on agrarian issues in the western countries closer to those concerned with agrarian transformations in the third world.

SCOPE OF RURAL SOCIOLOGY

The scope or subject-matter of rural sociology is basically the study of rural society with all its complexities. According to Lawry and Nelson, 'The subject-matter of rural sociology is the description and analysis of the progress of various groups as they exist in the rural environment.' The main tasks of rural sociology can be mentioned here. They are as follows,

1. Rural Community and Rural Problems.
   This includes the characteristics and nature of rural community and its problems.
2. Rural Social Life.
   This includes various aspects of the rural people.
3. Rural Social Organization.
   This includes the study of various rural social organizations and institutions including family and marriage.
4. Rural Social Institutions and Structure.
   This includes the study of dogmas, customs, traditions, morals, conventions, practices and various political, economic, religious and cultural institutions
5. Rural Planning and Reconstruction.
   Rural sociology has great practical applications. Hence rural planning and reconstruction are also the main tasks of rural sociology to be dealt with.
6. Social Change and Social Control in Rural Social Setup: It is here we

study the impact of city on rural life. The mechanisms of social control of the rural society are also examined here.

7. Religion and Culture in Rural Society.
   Religion plays an important role in the rural set up. Culture of rural society exhibits striking peculiarities. These come within the domain of rural sociology.
8. Rural Social Processes.
   Different social processes such as cooperation, competition, integration, differentiation, isolation etc., that take place in rural society are also studied in rural sociology.
9. Differences between Urban and Rural Society.
   The study of rural society includes the differences between urban and rural society also.

IMPORTANCE OF RURAL SOCIOLOGY

The practical value of the study of rural sociology is widely recognised today. As long as the villages and the rural society assume importance, the rural sociology shall continue to acquire importance. The value of rural sociology can be understood by the following points:

1. Rural Population is in Majority: The world's is more rural than urban. More than two-third of people of the world live in villages. It is the village that forms the basis of society. Rural sociology is inevitable for the study of the majority of the population.
2. Intimate Relationship between the Land and Man: Man is born out of land and his entire culture depends on it. Land has been the part of and parcel of human life. Progress starts from the village. The type of land partially conditions the type of society and the opportunities for human development. This close relationship between man and land has also been recognised by economists and political scientists.
3. Villages and Rural Life from the Source of Population: Cities normally grow out of towns and villages. No city can come into existence all of a sudden without having a rural background. A village, when improved and thickly populated, becomes a town or city. Thus it is the village population that forms the source of urban life.
4. Psychological Approach to the Rural Life: Rural progress, rural reconstruction or improvement of rural societies is possible only when the people have correct idea about the rural way of life and problems. Rural sociology touches upon the rural psychology and provides a good understanding of the rural people and their society.

"All of us know," for example, that people prefer to live in cities because there are more opportunities, services, and great personal fulfillment. "Everyone knows" that successful business and economic development must stay focused on metropolitan locations to maximize transportation and labor costs. "Everyone knows" that many of our small towns and villages are in distress and that even though the *unsettling* of the countryside may be a national tragedy, it amounts to no more than a natural process that will continue to occur over the next century.

Defining Rural

There are many ways to define areas that are "rural." Although the general idea of specifically conceptualizing "rural" areas came into use in the 1920s with its basis in sociology, many, if not most, of the current explanatory frameworks evolved to provide guidance for the distribution of government monies or to perform a census of places and people. As a corollary to these classification systems, there persists the traditional assumptions that tend to go along with the word "rural," assumptions that are often ungrounded and at best belie the diversity inherent in areas typically grouped together as "rural" or "nonmetropolitan." For instance, it is a commonly held belief that farming is a mainstay of most rural economies. In fact, fewer than one-fifth of rural counties in North America now have a significant economic dependence on farming, and the 20% of nonmetro counties that have farming as their principal economic base contain less than 10% of the nonmetro population (Deavers, 1992). Moreover, the geopolitical boundaries that usually serve as the basis for these classifications often are not optimal.

The Urban-Rural Imbalance

Since 1950 it should be clear that metropolitan settlement structure leading to urban conglomerations is the dominant growth form of the world. Metropolitan areas will account for 70 percent of the net growth in world population during the 1990s-an additional 67 million people every year. Other than natural increase, the prime engine of metropolitan growth is rural-to-urban migration. It is, however, important to note that rural-to-metropolitan trends have changed directions several times in the latter part of the 20 Century. It would appear that change, rather than stability, is the typical demographic and economic situation for most of the world's rural and nonmetropolitan areas at the end of the 20th Century. The United Nations reports that 43 percent of the world's population lived in urban areas in 1990; a 34 percent increase since 1960. In the next several years (2005), the world will pass a historic milestone: more than half of its population — or more than three billion people — will live in cities. At the turn of the century, only 14 percent of the Earth's population called cities home — and just 11 centres on the planet had more than one million inhabitants.

Now there are 400 cities with populations of at least one million, and 20 megacities with populations exceeding 10 million, with a half dozen of them approaching or exceeding the 20 million level. While the developing world still flocks to core cities, much of Europe, North America, the Russian Federation, and Australia are reversing the process: emptiness at the center and growth on the edges-or the new "Edge City" metropolitan areas.

At the halfway mark of the 21st Century, more than 70 percent of the world's population will live within the metropolitan framework (an area now loosely defined up to 40-100 kilometres from the older urban cores). In most more developed nations, especially in North America and Europe, the urban-rural distribution now stands at 75-80 percent metropolitan to 20-25 percent rural.

The most common factor contributing to rural-to-urban migration is rural unemployment resulting in part from rural areas having higher fertility levels than urban areas, according to Lori S. Ashford, a senior policy analyst with the Population Reference Bureau (PRB). A shortage of basic technology in rural areas also promotes out-migration and environmental degradation; it has led to a serious shortage of arable land in many communities throughout the developing world. While the growth of cities can contribute to economic progress, the study notes that problems arise when urbanization "occurs so rapidly that it strains the ability of urban governments to provide housing, sanitation, public safety, and other necessary services— and when there are not enough jobs."

The New Paradigm

The relationship between government and economic development began to change marked during the late 1970's and early 1980's. The beginning of the 1980's saw many less developed countries heavily borrowed and unable to service their debt. The physical plant and infrastructure fashioned in the 1950s and 1960s-often of exceptionally poor quality-created high levels of service costs that even the most developed nations could not bear. Hardest hit were the rural economies and regional settlement patterns resulting in a virtually unabated flow of resources to the metropolitan areas. The final result was the beginning of the demise of the centrally-planned economy and the ushering of the "Age of Austerity." The concept of integrated population and development planning had to be adjusted in light of the changes brought about by this austerity.

Many planners and development analysts regarded the goals of development under austerity as self-evident and non-problematic, seeing the only problems as concerning how to attain them. The new paradigm recognized that both the environment and human settlement where *open* systems and regulated by things happening beyond local and national boundaries-*the Global Economy*-and greatly affected by natural and human imbalances.

In short, the *urbancentric* view of the world was called into question, especially the prevalent notion that the purpose of rural areas was to provide food, fuel, and cheap workers. The new paradigm not only recognizes the connectivity of the urban-rural spheres, but also addresses the issue of rural vitality. For, unless rural areas are revitalized, the metropolitan centres must ultimately provide the rescue funds and resources to support the countryside.

The solution is what we typically call *economic development*. In principle, the new paradigm called for self-sustaining economic growth and social policy designed to provide the requisites of existence and citizenship. While the former can help provide the fuel for the latter, we must be under no illusion that growth itself will fulfil basic needs.

The New Century Approach to Rural Planning

The most important question to be asked is "are rural areas and country towns sustainable as working and living communities?" Many rural areas have proven to be *persistent*-they have sustained while both inner city and suburban area have declined in the face of metropolitan spread. The only reasonable conclusion that can be reached concerning this persistence is their *diversity*. Less than a century ago the rural economy depended almost entirely on resource extraction, agriculture (and support service to agriculture), and fishing.

Economic Diversity

The rural areas that show the most favorable growth and economic strength have their economies based on recreation and tourism. Throughout most of North and South America, Western Europe, Australia, and New Zealand the lure of the natural environment and tourism (place and historicity) are significant parts of their economies. Firms and industries built around the exploitation of amenities show exceptionally strong growth and are a world leader in providing new jobs.

Are rural economies built around tourism and amenities sustainable? Thought on this question is decidedly mixed and generally negative. Tourism, in one form or another is the world's second largest industry. As a whole, this activity *mines* and *extracts* wealth in the form of money and exports the final resources to metropolitan areas where the corporations and trusts reside. Tourism is dependent on wealth and increasing affluence-it is not an activity within reach of the world's poor. Thus, there is a closed cycle of events whereby tourism and amenity based economies demand ever increasing affluence and affluence itself is associated with migration to metropolitan areas. Tourism and amenity jobs are among the lowest paying service industries in the world- or what is termed minimum or subsistence wage in most countries. The firms that service the local industries are labor intensive and built around employment in food service, lodging and accommodation, information assistance, maintenance, and service sales to the travelling public. Since most tourism is seasonal, the industry depends on high migration rates based on *boom and bust* seasons that in turn demand the cheapest labor available. Factors such as poor seasonal weather, higher transportation costs due to both profit taking and increasing costs for fuels can send a local economy into shambles within a short period of time-causing some of the highest unemployment rates in any industry. Finally, there is the long term (and often conflicting) goal of greater economic sustainability in local areas based on tourism and amenities. The goal is to extend visiting seasons by creating greater opportunity to capture market share of tourism monies. Since 1980 the most popular methods in the western world are gaming or gambling, conventions/meetings, and multiple use recreation (golfing, theme parks, and similar facilities). The controversy over gaming/gambling as a supplement to economic diversity continues in a worldwide debate. Regardless, it has achieved phenomenal rates of return and now appears to be reaching saturation as larger scale enterprises are developed. Wage and salary incomes paid to industry employees are among the highest in rural areas.

Remoteness

Remoteness is the one characteristic that all true rural areas share in common. It is viewed as both an asset and a major liability. Many development specialists and rural sociologists take the stance that remoteness and isolation is an asset. They argue that small structure, vertical leadership, and cooperation are important strengths that contribute to ethic and social identity. Although they acknowledge that interlocal cooperation with regional towns is important, they also counter that individual community ties are the most important process in local development. They imply that to dismiss the importance of local pride, concern, and problem solving capabilities would ignore much of the community's true resource base. On the other hand, current economic development practice now strongly encouraged in rural areas promotes inter-community cooperation, assimilation with other communities, and common work towards development. This is based on the theory that small size and remoteness is *the* major inhibitor of development efforts. Thus, the other side of the problem is how to overcome distance factors in rural areas. In general, remoteness factors are related to four major policy choices in central planning: transportation, critical service deliver, communications, and jobs skills/training. Communications, more specifically telecommunications amounting to both advanced systems of current technologies, and emerging forms of real time delivery, are predicted by many to be the total planning solution for rural areas. Unlike transportation outcomes, which must overcome*place to place* remoteness, telecommunications offers the hope of *in-place* service and need delivery. It is attractive, if for no other reason, because it offers quick and incremental *upgrade paths*-often at a decreasing marginal costs-rather than enormous sunk costs experienced in transportation and regional development.

The final factor to be discussed, because it serves to impact the cost of remoteness, is job skills/training. No society or societal sector in the global world can afford to concentrate its educational and development resources solely in metropolitan areas.

Yet, decentralization of educational resources and development ranks exceptionally high on the list of major expenditures of any nation aspiring to greater sustainability and vitality. Both public and private systems have responded throughout this century to deliver education, jobs skills, and general training to remote areas-both in-place and through regional centres coordinating with outlying communities. But, it would appear that, even with local self-help and capacity building programs, the delivery of these vital services is reaching maximum effort under present funding and technology.

Lack of Resources

A lack of basic resources to meet rural residences' needs is repeatedly shown as a major factor in a community's inability to sustain and maintain community identity and commitment. Resources are understood to mean both fiscal (material) and human and therefore most planning solutions employ a two-pronged set of policies designed to increase resource capacity. Efforts to redirect material resources to rural areas have been ongoing throughout the 20th Century and far out number programs targeted towards urban areas. Worldwide, major efforts include wide-ranging programs such as education (extension), farm and price supports, direct grants-in-aid, revenue sharing, new towns, and health care-to mentioned but a few.

No comprehensive assessment of the effectiveness of these programs exists, but few will venture to say that trillions of dollars poured into rural development has not made a difference in the shape of the nonmetropolitan sectors of our countries. Many rural sociologists argue that it is the scarceness of resources, the need for austerity, and the concomitant appreciation for the assets that do exist that creates the unique blend of community and sustainability thought to be prevalent in the world's nonmetropolitan areas. On the other hand, it is also widely argued that it is the dependence of small communities on others for aid that creates a limited perspective or community vision and a clearly articulated path into the future. Whatever blend of perspective, it is abundantly clear that the request for resources is an all-consuming factor in the life of small communities.

Work Diversity and New Rural Industries

Much of the local economic development (L.E.D.) literature promotes the development of new rural industries (RIs) as one path to a sustainable countryside. There is little argument that one of the keys to attaining a vital, living countryside is increased job opportunity and quality employment. Although RIs lag behind new service enterprises as the fastest growing component of the rural economy, nevertheless, they play a critically important role in rural economic diversification. However, a minority of rural researchers point to the rise of RIs, specifically in developing regions, as a sign of distress rather than positive rural development. Tambunan [1995] and others argue that there are two quite different conditions under which rural labor might shift from traditional agriculture, fishing, forestry and extractive pursuits: (a) when labor is pulled or "attracted" out of agriculture into better non-agricultural opportunities; or, (2) when labor is "pushed" or forced out of agriculture by declining employment opportunities into relatively worse RIs (marginal occupations) whose capacity to absorb large quantities is achieved at the cost of extremely low, and possibly declining incomes.

The first type of RIs (attracted) are typically run on a more or less stable basis with a business goal of surplus generation and growth using hired labor and a certain degree of technical sophistication. This is in contrast to the second type of RIs which are often seasonal, run with the help of unpaid family labor, using rather primitive technology catering mainly to local markets. The argument against sustainability and a total planning solution is that a heavy presence of the second type of RIs denotes increasing poverty in the region. Some researchers note, therefore, that the presence of the second type of RIs can only be justified on the basis of their labor intensity and not productivity or income gains.

Building Local Capacity as a Route to Sustainability

Throughout North America, much of Western Europe, Australia, and New Zealand, community generated rural revitalization (generally termed Local Economic Development-or LED) is currently a matter of considerable profile. A prominent feature of this activity is what is termed the *process related dimensions* of rural LED-meaning that the capacity of individual communities to bring about a better future for themselves depends in no small measure on how well they are equipped in terms of leadership and team related skills. The root challenge of all rural communities must be the shaping of new strategies responsive to the enduring realities of rural economies and cultural life-high unemployment; persistent poverty; deteriorated social well-being; lower earnings; and diminished health care-as well as changing national and global circumstances. Revitalizing "rural" must include the participation of small communities in search of positive change, whereby local people are encouraged to think more about their futures and to put into practice their ideas for securing those futures. Capacity building, therefore, deals mostly with the ability of local people to solve problems. These *process dimension programs* seek to bring about change by forging new skills within rural communities related to leadership, mediation and conflict resolution, group processes, understanding the business of government, and the articulation of a shared vision. In the simplest terms, capacity building can be defined as increasing the ability of people and institutions to do what is required of them [Newlands, 1981].

Counterurbanizing the Countryside-Evidence of Change?

Throughout this century migration flows worldwide follow a recognizable pattern: from rural to urban, from mountains to plains, from undeveloped countries to developed countries. These population flows are marked by diversity, complexity, and change leaving many of the small, remote rural areas in a final stage of disintegration. Thus, population reversal (*counterurbanization*) has become one of the hallmarks of a sustainable, living rural countryside.

On a worldwide scale, recent literature assesses counterurbanism as occurring throughout much of the world-albeit at very diverse rates. In truth, the evidence for urban population dispersal is strong while the proof for rural rejuvenation is weak. As noted, the reasons for this phenomena are diverse and complex, and should not be confused with temporary labor migration, but from an overall standpoint there are three controlling factors.

First, it is important to understand that the predominant growth form in the world today-metropolitanism-is undergoing considerable change. Traditional rural communities lying within 65 to 120 kilometres of the metropolitan fringe show a strong propensity to expand in population size and economic diversity. This large sphere of distance influencing surrounding fringe areas, sometimes called *penturbia* or the *component economic area,* is quite possible the final wave of spatial development of large urban centres before urban agglomeration occurs. Forces associated with this change are many, but predictable. In the U.S., it is often associated with the quest for more affordable housing, less computing to work, educational opportunities for children, lifestyle and amenities. Since most-if not nearly all-of the communities within the 65-120 k growth ring are classified as rural or small town (ranging from 15,000 to 5,000 and under), it is not surprising that demographers report new rural growth and counterurbanism. Second, not all of the more remote rural areas have experienced depopulation. Fully 25-30 percent of communities in the more developed countries report that small towns have gained in population during the past 30 years. Again, the factors associated with this growth are complex, but can be said to center around several major causes. The presence of tertiary (university) education systems is important, as is the location near major transportation links. The main factor, however, at least in North America and Western Europe, are amenity rich areas attracting lifestyles, tourism, recreation, elderly retirement, and land investment opportunities. Third, although the most remote rural communities show considerable aggregate population loss, some (but not many) seem to have beat the odds and sustained or even exhibit growth while their neighboring communities have perished. The evidence for this counterurbanism is sketchy at best and relies mainly on individual case studies rather than aggregate data, and for every success story there appears to be dozens of declining towns.

THE VILLAGE ENVIRONMENT

Population densities are high in Bihar, and these villages are no exception – according to the census data for 2001, 695 persons per sq km in Pokharia and 1,379 in Dubaili Biswaspur (compared with 881 for Bihar as a whole and 312 for India). Moreover, population growth is rapid. Between 1981 and 2001 the population of Pokharia almost doubled and that of Dubaili Biswaspur increased by over 75%. Literacy rates have been rising but at a very slow pace. According to the 2001 Census, even after excluding the 0-6 age group (illiterate by definition), over 50% of men and over 80% of women were illiterate in both villages. The last decade has, however, seen a revolution in school enrolment. New schools have opened and school attendance, especially of girls, has risen rapidly.

Within the villages, occupation remains dominated by agriculture, and the proportion of agricultural labourers has been rising – from 31% of all (main) workers in 1981 to 60% in 2001 in Pokharia, and from 50% in 1981 to 72% in 2001 in Dubaili Biswaspur according to the census. In 2001, 28% of workers were classified as cultivators in Pokharia and 22% in Dubaili Biswaspur. In Pokharia holdings are small – no household had more than five acres in 2009. In Dubaili Biswaspur some larger holdings were reported, but only six to eight households out of the 215 in Mazgama West tola were reported as having more than eight acres. Apart from traditional occupations such as basket-making, fishing and other caste occupations, there was little non-agricultural employment in these villages.

There are few *pucca* houses, and most houses are made of traditional materials, mud and thatch (though, often now, with a corrugated iron roof), while many of the poorer households still live in simple constructions of bamboo and thatch. Access to drinking water has improved since 1999 with an increase in the number of handpumps, though some problems of water quality subsist, especially in Pokharia, where one-third of households do not have their own supply, and in the SC locality of Mazgama. Village roads and paths and drainage show little sign of improvement, and sanitation facilities are still virtually non-existent.

The most striking and visible change concerns communications. Hard to reach in the 1980s, today the villages are only 6 km, along a good pucca road, from a four-lane dual carriageway.

This means that they are within easy reach of the local block headquarters throughout the year, and also only 40 minutes by autorickshaw from the main district market which is in turn only a few kilometres from the district headquarters.

There were many more electricity connections in 2009 than in 1999, both legal and illegal, although electricity is available only four to five hours per day and is not used for agriculture because of its unreliability. A few solar street lights have been installed, mainly outside the houses of influential villagers. There is a mobile phone in the majority of households, even among the poorest groups. There has been some growth in the number of shops, with seven in Pokharia and three in Mazgama and several more on the road nearby, in addition to a weekly market.

CHANGES IN AGRARIAN RELATIONS

The key change observed in 1999 was the shift towards market relationships, especially in the labour market. Since earlier research had connected agricultural backwardness with semi-feudal social and economic relationships, there was reason to expect that market forces, combined with improved communications, would unleash the unfulfilled agricultural possibilities of a region with abundant groundwater and reasonable soils, and a considerable potential for triple cropping.

Agricultural Production

Between 1981 and 1999, agricultural production rose substantially as a result of both increased yields and increased cropping intensity. This rise has continued over the last decade. Estimating trends in agricultural output is perilous, because of variation between cultivators and seasons, but the levels of "normal year" agricultural output in these villages, in volume terms, seemed to have increased by at least 20% in the decade. Normal wheat yields were generally reported at about 2,400 kg/ha in 2008-09, compared with an average around 2,000 kg in 1999. Aghani paddy yields were more variable, but mostly over 3,000 kg/ha compared with 2,000 to 3,000 kg in 1999.

The main source of this increase seems to lie in a continued spread of tube well irrigation, combined with the almost universal use of high-yielding varieties and fertiliser. Some farmers also use pesticides, and a few new composting methods. The spread of improved techniques may have been encouraged by migration. Migrants returning from Punjab are aware of the more advanced agricultural methods used there, and this may facilitate adoption locally.

By 2009, there were sufficient numbers of borings and pumpsets for virtually all the cropped area to be irrigated. Over-all cropping intensity has increased as a consequence, but the cropping pattern has not changed much, with the exception of a decline in jute, to some extent, replaced by maize, and some increase in the *garma* (summer) crop (maize and paddy), connected with the spread of irrigation. The growth in output has no doubt come more from higher yield than from increase in the area sown. Pulses continued their long-term decline, and there were small areas of vegetables and fruit. It is noteworthy that there was little development of new, higher value commercial crops. Paddy, wheat and maize still accounted for 88% of the entire cropped area in Dubaili Biswaspur and 68% in Pokharia according to official data; and these figures are probably under-estimates, since local respondents reported even higher proportions of sown areas under cereals. Increased yields need to be set against higher input costs (high-yielding seeds, irrigation, fertiliser, pesticides and labour), which can be substantial. Labour costs in particular have increased, while the price of foodgrains declined relative to the price of all goods up to the beginning of 2008, compared with 1999 (although it recovered in 2009). Nevertheless, detailed estimates of production costs still suggest that cereal production can be highly profitable.

There have been some changes in livestock, notably a precipitous decline in the number of bullocks, because of their replacement by tractors, but on the other hand, some growth in the number of milch animals, notably among smaller cultivators and agricultural labourers. However, these are mostly local rather than cross-bred varieties and milk production is exclusively for local and domestic consumption. There also seems to have been some increase in the numbers of goats and poultry.

There is evidence here of the spread of improved techniques and growth in agricultural output. But despite improved communications, increased yields have not led to much increase in the marketing of agricultural products. This is a sign that increased output has, to a large extent, been absorbed by a growing population. Only 10% of the most important crop, Aghani paddy, is marketed in Pokharia, and 20% in Mazgama (but higher proportions, 40 to 50% of the garma crop). About half of wheat produced is commercialised; jute and maize are essentially commercial crops, but they are grown on a much smaller area than paddy and wheat. Overall, it appears that growth is not based on structural change in the production system, but rather on the intensification of an existing model. Elsewhere in Bihar, investment in the production of vegetables, fruit, flowers and medicinal plants has contributed to growing incomes, but there is no sign of such developments in these villages. And some basic disadvantages, notably vulnerability to drought and flood, have not been resolved. Improved irrigation has made agriculture more resistant to drought, but some crops, and in general, the Aghani season, re-main mainly rainfed. Flood is even more problematic. While these villages were not affected by the devastating 2008 Kosi floods, in another year it can easily be their turn; a river passes through Dubaili Biswaspur which has frequently flooded in the past. Low lying areas often remain waterlogged. These risks still discourage high levels of investment in agriculture, and call for improved infrastructure.

Labour Relations and Wages

The market for labour has continued to tighten in these villages, and wages have risen sharply. In 1999, local wages were found to have doubled, in real terms, since 1981. Between 1999 and 2009, they rose by another 50%. In 1999, casual wages (full time, male) were mainly in the Rs 25 to Rs 35 per day range. In 2009, the main range for agricultural work was Rs 67 to Rs 95.11 The Bihar consumer price index for agricultural/rural labourers rose by

76.4% from April 1999 to November 2009, the relevant dates for our investigation, so in 1999 prices the wages observed in 2009 were in the range of Rs 38 to Rs 54, i e, a 50% real increase at both bottom and top of the range. Almost half of this rise came in the last one year between the two visits in December 2008 and November 2009. Women's wages had risen more than men's. Typically Rs 20 per day in 1999, normal wages were reported as Rs 57 to Rs 74 in 2009, a rise in real terms of 58% to 105%. There was still a wage differential between men and women, but it was of the order of 15% to 30%, rather than the 20% to 50% observed in 1999. However, there seemed to be more variability in women's wages, with the lowest slack season wage reported as only Rs 37.12

These rises in wages were accompanied by increased variability in the labour market. There was much greater diversity than in 1999 in wage rates between villages and crop operations. For instance, jute harvesting and retting was paid more because it was hard work, and there was some growth in contract work, weeding a specified area for instance, where the remuneration was negotiable depending on the area and the abundance of weeds. There was also a substantial seasonal variation. The most likely cause of these increases in wages is the withdrawal of labour from the local labour market through large-scale temporary migration to other parts of India. Increased output could, in principle, be a factor, but agricultural growth has only been of the same order as population growth, and non-agricultural output, other than construction, remains small.

The immediate consequence of the tightening labour market has been to raise the cost of cultivation, and to increase competition for labour among cultivators. It should also have increased the incentives for mechanisation. But apart from tube wells, only two types of mechanisation are widespread: tractors for ploughing and threshers. Transplanting, weeding and harvesting re-main labour-intensive, and labour use for weeding and harvesting rises with yield. It is, therefore not surprising that cultivators complain of labour shortage, notably during the monsoon months of *Asarh*, *Sawan* and *Bhado*. The labour-intensity of jute cultivation is said to be one reason for its decline; harvesting and retting of jute coincide with the paddy harvest in Punjab and Haryana, so there is a direct competition between local and distant employers.

There have been differential effects across different sizes of landholding. For many small cultivators, opportunities for migration are more attractive than own cultivation. Some rent out their land, while they migrate for work, while in others women and children replace migrant male labour. Middle peasants, who were previously hiring in labour, are squeezed by the tight labour market, and may see a fall in net income. Larger cultivators, on the other hand, may have enough market power to assure a supply of casual labour at peak times, and are so better placed to take full advantage of the potential of improved seeds and cultivation practices.

Interestingly, some of the mechanisms of the semi-feudal system are still present in this new economic environment, but they function in a different way. The main exception is attached labour, which has disappeared – the labour market functions essentially on a casual, daily basis. Tenancy, on the other hand, is if anything more widespread than before, especially in Mazgama. It remains dominated by sharecropping where both inputs (fertiliser and irrigation) and outputs are shared 50:50 between landowner and tenant. Some new practices have also developed, such as fixed payment in kind for the whole year, or a smaller share for the landowner (noted in particular for the garma season). But tenancy, which is renewed annually, no longer plays a central role in economic control. Indeed, in a reversal of previous practices, it now seems that larger landowners rent in land from small landowners.

Indebtedness too appears to be as widespread as ever, much of it to traditional moneylenders at high interest rates. But the inflow of money from migration means that debts can be repaid, and indebtedness seems to be much less important as a mechanism of social control. In addition, access to institutional loans may have improved. One small cultivator-cum-agricultural labourer was able to borrow Rs 50,000 (used for his daughter's marriage) from a bank because he owned some land.

The practice of remunerating harvest labour with a share of the crop has survived the strengthening of market forces, but like daily wages, the shares have become more variable, depending on the yield and the quality of the grain – with a larger share being paid to labour where the crop is poor. The range was between one-eighth and one-twelfth for paddy and wheat, although oneeighth was the most common for paddy, as against one-ninth in 1999, suggesting some increase in the equivalent daily wage.

However, given the rise in the casual daily wage for other operations, harvest shares no longer supply a bonus as they did in the past; it is likely that real wages are not very different from those in other agricultural operations.

All in all, the picture is one of increasingly atomised and diversified labour relations. There is effectively no organisation of labour within the villages, except the organisation of groups of migrants, and wage relationships appear to be individualised and short-term. The disappearance or redefinition of the old "semi-feudal" mechanisms has not necessarily changed the economic and social hierarchy. In some of the old "semi-feudal" families, it seems that a new generation of cultivators has adapted to the market, and their market power may permit them to invest in a more productive agriculture.

MIGRATION AND THE LABOUR MARKET

Migration has become a way of life in these two villages, as it has in many parts of Bihar. In 1999, there were already migrants to northwestern India from the majority of households, especially poorer households. Migration was almost exclusively male, short-term and seasonal, mostly between one and six months at a time. Since then migration has if anything increased further (respondents uniformly reported this), with a greater diversity of migration destinations and durations, and some move towards longer-term migration, especially to urban areas. But there is still very little permanent migration, in the sense of definitive departure of households from the village. The original reason for the growth of migration was lack of employment in the village. This reason continues to be cited by respondents, but nowadays cultivators in the village complain of labour shortage, so lack of local employment may no longer be the main factor.

The increases in local wages seen above have narrowed the gap with other parts of India. In 1999, wages for casual daily labour in northwestern India, both urban and rural, were reported as Rs 60 to Rs 65 per day, about double the wages in these Bihar villages. In 2009, migrants were reported to be getting Rs 100-Rs 150 per day in agriculture in Punjab and Haryana; compared with the wages observed in the villages of Rs 67-Rs 95 per day, the gap is down to about 50% on average. In urban areas migrants were said to be able to earn Rs

4,000-Rs 6,000 per month in a variety of casual jobs, though observations in Delhi suggest that these numbers are on the high side. All of these figures are for adult males. Very few women migrate for economic reasons. Agricultural work (transplanting of paddy, harvesting of paddy, wheat or sugarcane) in Punjab, Haryana and nearby still seems to account for at least half of all migration. One important change has been the elimination of the middle man. Since virtually all migrants have or have access to mobile phones, it has become common for farmers in Punjab to call villagers in Bihar directly when they need labour for harvesting – this contact, of course, being carried over from year to year. Groups of villagers then migrate together, and at the place of destination they live and work together. This migration is typically for two to four months at a time, depending on the availability of seasonal work. In addition, there has been a considerable increase in migration to Delhi and other urban locations, where employment includes construction, commerce and factory work. Durations are longer; a common pattern is for the migrant to stay away for four to six months, return for a month or two, and then leave again. Married migrants leave their wives and children in the village. Only one case was recorded in Pokharia of a woman migrant, engaged in domestic service in Delhi, and none in Mazgama.

Migration, as noted above, is surely the primary reason for the rise in local wages. It is often argued that the National Rural Employment Guarantee Scheme (NREGS) has a similar impact, because it both creates demand for labour and (in principle at least) pays legal daily minimum wages (Rs 89 in 2008, Rs 97 in 2009), which are higher than prevailing agricultural wages. However, in these villages there are few NREGS projects, and the volume of employment created is at least an order of magnitude less than that obtained through migration. At most, NREGS is a supplementary factor. A similar comment can be made about the recent growth in public sector construction, notably of roads, which is also sometimes identified as a source of increased labour demand, but which is again only a secondary factor in these villages. Migration, therefore, continues to be the primary driving force for rising incomes among the poor. As noted in 1999, taking into account both the additional employment of migrants and the higher wages in the village labour market, migration probably raises the incomes of labour households by a factor of two to three. Among the better-off households, there are frequent reports of children (mainly sons) getting secondary or vocational education outside the village. At this level, family and community networks are important. The Muslim community of Mazgama has connections with a business network both in local towns and spread across India, extending to west Asia, which provides opportunities for the second generation members of well-off families.

A form of migration that has developed recently concerns young boys aged 10 to 14, migrating to Moradabad, Delhi or Ferozabad to work in factories making bangles, toys, carpets or steel pots and dishes. This concerned some 25 to 50 households in Mazgama (out of 250). In Pokharia south tola, about 15 boys were migrating for work. The phenomenon had grown in the last two or three years. In Mazgama it was reported that children migrate in small groups. A contractor from outside the village advances their travel expenses and gets back a percentage of the children's wages (10% was mentioned). The boys concerned basically lived at the worksite, where they were given food, clothing and lodging, and a wage of Rs 600 to Rs 1,000 per month for the first year, and Rs 1,000 to Rs 2,000 thereafter. They would come back to the village from time to time (especially for major festivals), but would be spending 8 to 10 months in the year away. One respondent had a 12-year old son who was doing this in a bangle factory near Delhi, and who was also studying – there are perhaps some elements of apprenticeship in this process. The son called home regularly – the mobile phone again! – and was reported to be "happy". The overall impact of migration on the local labour market is considerable. First, there is the impact on women's work and responsibilities, which we consider below. Second, cultivators widely complain of both labour shortages and of the high cost of labour. Migrant workers do, however, tend to return for the local paddy and wheat harvests, and to a lesser extent at other peak times. Third, migration also generates new skills, and there was at least one example of a person working as a tailor in Jaipur who did tailoring work in the village during spells between migrations. Skills developed in construction, in carpentry and certain other occupations may also have an outlet in the village.

The decline in wage differentials between Purnia and northwest India is striking. It suggests that migration is contributing to wage equalisation across India, and so bringing incomes in Bihar up towards the Indian mean. In fact, these labour markets are now interconnected. Unskilled wages are rising less fast than other incomes in Delhi and surrounding areas, and the inflow of migrants is surely part of the reason. The long-term dynamics of the process are unclear, but the male labour reserve in these two Bihar villages seems to be close to exhausted. That might explain the shift towards child labour. There is, of course, a female labour reserve that has hardly been tapped.

Migration generates a considerable volume of resources, both in the form of remittances and savings. Bihar has become one of the main destinations for remittances within India. If what is observed in these villages is repeated across rural Bihar, the order of magnitude of the resource flow into the State could amount to 4%-7% of net state domestic product. From the point of view of the dynamics of development, these resources could be an important new source of investment. On the whole, however, this is not the case. Most respondents indicated that the primary use of remittances was for food, clothing, health and house repairs – i e, meeting basic needs – and education. However, in some cultivating households savings of migrants were used for current agricultural inputs – seeds, fertilisers – and one respondent had purchased a cow while others had purchased calves. Some had improved their houses, bought consumer durables (TV, radio, mobile phone) or repaid loans. Increase in dowry was also mentioned (although this may be a transfer between households rather than final consumption).

There were some isolated reports of land purchase or purchase of agricultural equipment. However, it was clear that relatively little of the resources generated by migration was going into production; perhaps this is not surprising, given that migrants came mainly from lower income groups.

IMPACT OF MALE MIGRATION ON GENDER RELATIONS

The migration of men has had some impact on the workload of women, on their responsibilities within the household and on their mobility. In 1981, women were seldom going outside the village, except to visit relatives or for severe health problems. Men went to the market and made all the household purchases. In 2009, women had more frequent contacts with the outside world. They went to the market (as a small group of women or with a male relative but also alone if need be), and in Pokharia some women mentioned going to the temple, to fairs and to bathe in the Ganga. However, mobility restrictions still affected young married women who had not borne children. De facto head of household when men migrate, women have more responsibilities regarding the children's schooling, taking family members to the doctor and house repair. They are also more involved in the management of money. When in need they borrow from relatives or the local moneylender. However, they keep regular contact with their husband thanks to the spread of mobile phones.

While women have always played a role in agricultural production, their importance has been growing. The increase in cropping intensity, higher yields and the absence of men has increased the demand for female and child labour. In 1999, they were mainly involved in harvesting; in 2009, more women reported also doing transplanting and weeding, while women from landowning families would oversee cultivation. There has been a substantial increase in milch animals in particular among smaller cultivators and agricultural labourers. Women assume multiple roles ranging from animal care, grazing, fodder collection and cleaning of animal sheds to processing of milk and livestock products. This increased involvement of women in agriculture includes both work on own farm and wage labour. While above a certain level in the social hierarchy women still do not work for wages, it appears that the threshold has been rising, so that, for instance, women in small peasant households who previously would not undertake wage work are increasingly reporting that they do some agricultural labour outside their own farms. The reduction in the wage differential against women also increases the incentive for women to enter the labour market.

THE ROLE OF THE STATE AND THE INSTITUTIONS OF GOVERNANCE

Since 1999, there have been important changes in the political environment of the state. The Janata Dal (United)-Bharatiya Janata Party (JDU-BJP) government led by Nitish Kumar, which came to power in 2005, was widely seen as more effective than its predecessors. In the block office in Kasba, the block development officer reeled off an impressive list of programmes which were in operation.

This was not just on paper; activities and impacts of many of these programmes could be observed in the villages. This is in sharp contrast to the situation in 1999, when state presence was weak. It may be too simplistic to attribute this only to a change of political regime, for other factors such as improved communications and awareness levels presumably also played a role. But the political change was certainly an important factor. While we did not attempt a systematic survey of government programmes at the village level, we asked questions about awareness, impact and functioning of a variety of programmes to respondents from different social groups.

First, as noted above, there have been marked improvements in communications as a result of public investment in roads, noted by many respondents as a major dimension of progress.

There has also been a substantial increase in school enrolment and attendance. This is the result of policies on both supplyand demand-sides – on the supply-side through the three new schools that have opened in and around these villages and the hiring of additional teachers; on the demand-side, through scholarships for girls and a midday meal programme, which had started shortly before our visit, although it was far from running smoothly in Pokharia.

The improvements in public health are more modest. There are anganwadi centres for child development in both villages, but they do not serve all segments of the community.

The continued demand for medical treatment from local quacks is also indirect evidence that the public health system is not meeting local needs, and it was reported that visits by block level medical staff were infrequent. However, vaccination campaigns seem to have been effective and the Janani Suraksha Yojana (JSY) promoting institutional child delivery has scored some successes. There are many beneficiaries of programmes for income transfers of various sorts. The housing scheme for backward classes and SCs (Indira Awas Yojana, IAY) reported an increasing number of beneficiaries.

In Mazgama 20 out of 30 households in the harijan tola had received some benefits from the programme. In Pokharia the impact was quite visible since the IAY programme is essentially the only source of *pucca* (brick) houses, of which several had been built or were under construction. The scheme has been in operation for many years, so the cumulative number of beneficiaries is a significant fraction of the village population – said to be 29 households (out of 163) over 10 years.

The public food distribution system is more problematic. In 2009 villagers below the poverty line were entitled to 15 kg of rice, 10 kg of wheat and three litres of oil per month at subsidised prices. The identification of households below the poverty line raises many problems which we will not go into here. But in these villages, a voucher system was in operation which made it easy to verify the distribution. This showed that in the SC tola of Mazgama, oil was regularly available but grains were distributed only about one month in two in the five months preceding our visit. According to the manager of the shop, in the other months, there was no delivery. When grain was available, however, the full quota was distributed.

Employment under the NREGS was, as noted above, of secondary importance because of migration. While there were several projects under NREGS elsewhere in the panchayats within which Pokharia and Mazgama fell, there was little activity within these two locations – there had been only two projects in the previous two years, of which one was reported as generating 30 to 45 days of work for 25 men and 15 women. But no women from these two villages reported work under NREGS. Some 70 to 80 households had job cards in Mazgama, but in the absence of local projects they did not seem to be used.

A number of other income transfer programmes report fairly large numbers of beneficiaries, the largest being the (national) oldage pension scheme, reaching, according to official data, individuals in about 15% of households below the poverty line in the panchayats concerned – and new applications which had recently been submitted would, it was stated by panchayat officials, double that number. According to official records there was also a substantial number of recipients of widow's pensions, and small numbers receiving other benefits. Respondents made little reference to receipt of income from such programmes, but their impact can only be verified at the household level.

Disappointing Development Programmes

In contrast to these "social" programmes involving cash transfers and employment creation, state policies concerned with promoting economic development seemed to be much weaker. In principle, a variety of agricultural extension programmes exist involving loans and subsidies for investment, provision of inputs and training. But there was little impact of these programmes. A small number of loans for investment in irrigation was reported in Mazgama.

Larger farmers were aware of the programmes for the distribution of new seeds and fertilisers, but complained that distribution was less than promised or of poor quality. There were demands for state borings to reduce the cost of irrigation. Many government programmes operate only on a pilot basis in a small number of blocks or panchayats, and there seem to be large opportunities which are not being exploited, e g, to support the development of milk production, or fruit and vegetables. There was little or no government support for the development of nonagricultural activities.

There was a general assumption, among village respondents, that a substantial proportion of government funds in most of these programmes was diverted into private pockets. One local official said that in the IAY housing programme, the beneficiary receives Rs 24,000 out of the Rs 35,000 allocated, with the difference taken by a middle man and public officials. Government schemes such as NREGS were diverted towards the interests of more influential sections of the village. Problems with the midday meal programme were reportedly, partly, because a local official was demanding a percentage. What was striking was less the examples of corruption which were cited than the lack of concern among respondents, who appeared to accept this as normal practice.

In order to ensure that these various programmes reach their intended beneficiaries, there are issues of governance at all levels – state, district, block and panchayat. Both of the villages studied are part of much larger panchayats, and respondents tended to portray their villages as relatively disadvantaged within that framework. This is perhaps not surprising in Pokharia, with a backward caste majority and no influential leaders or large landowners. There was little participation in the meetings of the gram sabha, the assembly of the panchayat, and little reference to its deliberations. Mazgama, on the other hand, is a significant tola of a larger village, and the location of a substantial mosque and market. Nevertheless, respondents in Mazgama believed that activities under government programmes such as NREGS were biased towards the village where the mukhya of the panchayat lived. However, there was much more participation in the gram sabha than in Pokharia (it was reported that there were 200 participants in the last meeting, although this refers to the panchayat as a whole (eight villages) and not only to Mazgama).

Conversations about the functioning of the panchayat revealed a distinct conservative bias, for instance, with respect to the effective participation of women, which did not seem to be particularly welcome. The 50% reservation of seats for women in panchayati raj institutions has led to the election as mukhya of a woman from a better-off household in Dubaili Biswaspur in 2005. But her role is only nominal and her husband assumes her responsibilities; it was said that real power lay with the panchayat secretary.

She had not attended any meeting prior to her election and since then she attends with her husband. Her lack of experience is obviously a drawback. A learning process is therefore necessary but will it lead to more effective empowerment? Beyond the political institutions, there was little effective organisation within the village. A cooperative existed on paper, but was not functioning in reality. There were no self-help groups despite the existence of a long-standing government programme to promote them. Of course, religious organisations were present and active.

6

Migration and Socio-Cultural Change

Recent research on migration, gender and remittances show distinct and disparate behaviours and practices that raise a number of questions and suggest the need for a more complete theory of migration that incorporates notions of cultural dynamics as they relate to behaviour and societal outcomes. For example, migrants to the U.S. from the Dominican Republic show distinct savings and remittance behaviours. Men save to take money home and women do not, instead investing in their new local environs and purchasing durable items. Rural-urban migrants in Thailand also show distinct remittance behaviour. Although men and women are equally likely to migrate, women remit wages and gifts to their parents' home at a significantly higher rate, and are expected to do so.

However, more recently there is some evidence that gendered remittance patterns are changing, where men are possibly remitting almost as much as women. 2 In some studies of Mexican-U.S. migrants-men predominate in the migrant streams and remit their wages. And, in a final, illustrative example, Indonesia women migrants come and go from their parent's households, borrowing money, sometimes returning with money, but rarely is there an expectation to do so. Is there an explanation for these disparate and very different stories of migration, gender, and remittances? And, what are the societal effects in places of destination and origin of such different behaviours? There are clearly elements of varying gender identity, household relations, and the role of networks in each of these very different contexts. In order to understand how these elements might be related and used to understand migration processes, as well as provide insights on how gender inequality is exacerbated or redressed through migration, we examine recent developments in the migration literature and view them through the lens of cultural sociology.

During the last twenty years there have been three important developments in the field of migration. The first development has been the recognition that there are significant differences between men and women in terms of motivations, risks, and norms governing and promoting their movement and assimilation, as well as differential consequences. The second development has been the incorporation of social network concepts to model a more dynamic migration process. And, the third development has been the recognition that migration decisions are not made by atomistic individuals but conditioned by membership within households and communities. However, with the exception of a few qualitative studies these three developments have occurred independently of each other and remain relatively distinct.

To incorporate the insights from the literature on gender and migration, we focus upon three key concepts that have emerged regarding the role of social networks, households, and communities for affecting migration processes. The three key concepts we interrogate are: "social embeddedness", "circular and cumulative causation" (Massey 1990), and "relative deprivation" (Stark 1991). We propose considering these three concepts through the lens of a third area of research, the sociology of culture, and we draw upon ideas about identity formation, trust, and normative expectations. Our empirical examples come primarily from Thailand where we draw upon both secondary and primary data but also from secondary data from Latin America and the Caribbean migrant experiences. In our effort to demonstrate that social networks and gender are essential elements for understanding migration and cultural change, our discussion refers to international, internal, permanent, and temporary migration. We begin our analysis through a brief review of the three developments in the migration field.

We then conceptualize how these three literatures might be usefully synthesized with each other and relevant work in the sociology of culture. In our view, culture is an essential component for understanding the meaning given to individuals (gender), their actions (migration), and their relationships (network ties). This in turn influences the way inequality is produced or redressed. In the conclusion, we discuss how measurement of networks might be improved by these insights and synthesis. We also suggest that by synthesizing these literatures we can refine theories of social change and the structuring of inequality in relation to migration processes. Our contention that a more complete theory of migration and cultural change could be built by considering the combined and mutually reinforcing implications of the three developments in migration and the sociology of culture parallels work by demographers studying fertility, who have recently returned to theorizing about the role of ideas working through networks to influence behavioral change.

This treatment of culture as dynamic contrasts with earlier work by demographers whose structural-functionalist perspective regarded culture as a stable, coherent, and externally imposed force that served social "functions" within communities (e.g. dissipating conflict or anxiety) (Hammel 1990). This newer literature's use of networks is mostly confined to the transmission of instrumental information, although in some cases, the transmission of ideas like the value of children, smaller family size, economic aspiration, or mobility is also discussed. The work of Watkins and colleagues suggests that societal norms, values, beliefs, and practices are reproduced and transformed within interpersonal interactions. This theoretical field of inquiry has encouraged links between the fields of Demography and Anthropology. The availability of complex, multilevel, longitudinal data, more rigorous methodologies, and field experiences that yield stories about conversations and social interactions are expected to allow demographers to better predict fertility and contraceptive behaviour. In this paper we build on this tradition, widening the scope of interest to migration and cultural change.

POPULATION, MIGRATION AND DEVELOPMENT

The relationship between MDGs and population trends and structures has started to be considered, but there is still need to improve our knowledge of how demographic mechanisms, including migration, influence progress towards MDGs attainment. This book will mostly consider the situation in Pacific island countries and major migration countries in South, East and South-East Asia, including China and India. While the relationship between population, migration and MDGs is difficult to assess in large and interdependent Asian countries, linkages appear more clearly in small Pacific countries where the impact of migration is much more important. Although lessons learnt form the Pacific may not be replicable in larger economies, it contributes to improving our knowledge of the effects of migration on population and MDGs.

MIGRATION TYPES

Migration types are not neutral on its impact on population and development. In Asia, due to lack of political agreement on long-term and permanent migration schemes, such as green cards, migration consists mostly of 'guest workers' on short-term contracts that can be extended (Asis 2005, Abella 2005). Singapore has developed medium and long-term contracts for highly qualified migrants. Chain migration patterns have developed with unskilled construction workers migrating from Myanmar to Thailand; semi-skilled Thai workers migrating to Taiwan, Singapore, while Malaysians migrate to Singapore, Korea and Japan.

Family reunification exists mostly for high qualified migrants. However, schooling of migrants' children has been addressed by several host countries including Singapore, Japan and Korea. Student and work contract migrations have consequences on age and sex of migrants. Students are youth; males migrate more often for industry jobs and women for services jobs. Age plays different roles according to types of migration as rim countries migration schemes grant points according to age. Despite forecasts of increasing shortages on labour markets in host countries (Mason), migration policies are still mostly oriented toward a restrictive selection process and temporary migration. This certainly reduces the level of legal flows and result in higher undocumented migration the characteristics of which are less precisely known.

In the Pacific, some Polynesian countries, except Tonga, are former New Zealand colonies and benefit from special access to New Zealand: Cook Islanders, Niueans, Tokelauans are all New Zealand citizens, and Samoans benefit from a special quota. Tuvaluans and Tongans (in Polynesia) and Kiribati (in Micronesia) also have some access to New Zealand under the Pacific Access Category (PAC), as does Vanuatu (in Melanesia)i. Former US affiliated islands: FSM (Federated States of Micronesia) and RMI (Republic of the Marshall Islands) have special access to the US and to US territories (Guam and American Samoa). The special schemes have resulted in large scale migration, with free movements to New Zealand for selected groups of Polynesians, extended to Australia for New Zealand residents in the frame of the Trans-Tasman Travel Agreement, and resulting in the development of transnational communities with frequent circulation, as well as overstaying, between islands and New Zealand, further including Australia and the USii. Large scale circulation also applies to Micronesian migration towards the US. These two networks are typical of Pacific migration. Such schemes are made possible by the small size of island states and have resulted in mass migration from some island countries. But, although free movement would enable return migration and circulation, this has little developed beyond visits for Christmas and family events, and it has not resulted in much brain circulation that would enable more rapid economic development.

Labour migration has a long history in parts of the Pacific, initially for work on plantations, later for work in phosphate mines, and more recently through recruitments of seamen from Tuvalu, Kiribati and to a lesser extent, Fiji. There is also migration from Fiji to UK to work in military and to the Middle East to work as security personnel. Fiji is also largely affected by brain drain, with nurses migrating to rim countries and secondarily to Middle East. Shortages in nurses in Fiji have resulted in migration of Pilipino nurses. While Cook Islanders migrate to New Zealand, shortages in the tourism industry are filled by Fijians on short-term contracts. These are Pacific cases of chain migration.

DEMOGRAPHIC IMPACT OF MIGRATION

The impact of migration on population trends and structure is well known but flows have drawn most of the attention and, actually, a precise measure of flows is needed to assess the demographic impact of migration. Beyond uncertainties on the size of flows, data on stocks are also unavailable, with Singapore and Malaysia, among others, not publishing data on nonresident population. Would such data be available, comprehensive estimate of the impact of migration in a long-term perspective - answering questions like: what would be the population of the Philippines or the Cook Islands if there had been no migration since 1960 or 1970 - would be purely theoretical because fertility would certainly have been different on the long-term had migration not taken place. More simply, we shall try to consider the current impact of migration on population trends and structure from the latest censuses in Asia and the Pacific, with more attention to a few countries. Consequences of migration on population growth are well known. They include, as regards purely demographic impacts:

- Reduced population growth for emigration countries and higher growth for immigration countries - the former is usually considered favorable to developing countries;
- Changes in sex ratios according to gender differentials in migration patterns, with various directions being possible in both emigration and immigration countries - imbalances are usually considered unfavorable;
- Changes in age structures: increased dependency in emigration countries and reduced dependency in immigration countries – the former is considered unfavorable in the frame of the demographic window theory (Mason 2006, Mason 2001, Bloom, Canning 2001). Social and economic impacts are many, but the most commonly stated relate to:
- The labour force: depleted working ages and brain-drain from emigration countries and increased labour force and brain-gain in immigration countries, the former are considered unfavorable - however, migration releases tensions on the labour market;
- Family breakdowns reflected by increased headship rates for females in emigration countries and more frequent lone persons and 'not related' or 'other relatives' members of households in host countries – the direction of related effect is not well established

The impact of migration at regional level is more rarely mentioned but it deserves to be considered, mostly as it involves populations of very different size, like in the case of China and India on one side and South and South-East Asia on the other. Economies have become interdependent in the frame of a well established system of regional migration. In emigration countries with labour surplus, migration is a safety valve that reduces unemployment and underemployment, while in immigration countries with labour shortages, migration supports economic growth – however labour surpluses and shortages need to be considered at sectoral level. The beneficial effect of emigration as a safety valve is limited in larger countries like China and India that can 'export' only a minor part of their unemployment and under-employment because receiving countries have not the capacity to absorb it and need to protect their labour market through migration and work policies (Rallu, 2001). For instance, in China, rural underemployment was estimated to be well above 100 millions people and the region, not even the world economies cannot integrate such numbers of unqualified migrants. Nevertheless, the migration pressure of China in the region remains a concern for smaller South-East Asian countries, with Chinese setting up retail businesses and taking a large share of small trade. While there is a regional circulation of labour force at various levels of qualification and sectors of the labour market, there is also an extra-regional migration to Middle East or to developed countries of the Pacific rim and the West. Thailand, Myanmar, Malaysia, Indonesia, Bangladesh, Pakistan and Sri-Lanka are largely involved in intra-regional migration (as well as extra regional migration to the Middle-East). But China, India, the Philippines and Viet-Nam have a large part of their migration directed towards rim countries and to the West.

At intra-Pacific level, migration of Pacific islanders is quite limited with only Fiji, Cook Islands and Palau attracting immigrants: mostly through regional organizations and the University of the South Pacific for Fiji and in tourism industry and construction in the Cook Islands (mostly Fijians) and Palau (mostly Micronesians). Fiji and Palau also have Asian migrants, mostly Filipinos, on work contracts in health and tourism. However, Cook Is and Fiji are mostly emigration countries. Palau experienced increasing emigration of its youth and Asian net migration declined in 2000-2005. Most of Pacific islanders' migration is directed towards rim countries: Australia, New- Zealand and the USAiii as well as to US and French territories but the latter rather consists in more or less closed US and French regional networks, that however include Asian migration, mostly for US territories. The mass migration from the Pacific, in the frame of preferential access to rim countries, results in important reduction of population growth in island countries.

MIGRATION, DISTRESS AND CULTURAL IDENTITY

Migration is a process of social change where an individual, alone or accompanied by others, because of one or more reasons of economic betterment, political upheaval, education or other purposes, leaves one geographical area for prolonged stay or permanent settlement in another geographical area. It must be emphasized that migration is not only a trans-national process but can also be rural–urban. Any such process involves not only leaving social networks behind (which may or may not be well established) but also includes experiencing at first a sense of loss, dislocation, alienation and isolation, which will lead to processes of acculturation. A series of factors in the environment combined with levels of stress, the ability to deal with stress, and the ability to root oneself according to one's personality traits, will produce either a sense of settling down or a sense of feeling isolated and alienated.

Rural–urban migration is more likely to be for economic or educational reasons, whereas migration across nations may be for social, educational, economic or political reasons. Thus reasons for migration, prior preparation to the act of migration and social support will all enhance an individual's coping mechanisms. In addition, acceptance and welcome by the new nation will also be significant in the genesis of stress and how the individual deals with such stress. In this paper, the focus is on migrants and not refugees and asylum seekers who have a different set of problems.

MIGRATION AND MENTAL DISORDER

In a classic study, Ödegaard reported that the rates of schizophrenia among Norwegians who had migrated to the USA were higher when compared with Norwegians who had stayed back in Norway. This study set the standard for further studies comparing rates of schizophrenia and other psychiatric illnesses as well as for comparing those who had migrated and those who had been left behind or who had not chosen to migrate. Although Sashidharan has argued that the same principles of migration and its impact on whites cannot be considered exactly similar to the stress and impact on African–Caribbeans, it can be argued that the process of migration, sense of dislocation and alienation must contribute to the stress on the individuals and their families even though their experiences of alienation and dislocation will be different both at individual and group levels.

Several studies in the UK have demonstrated high rates of schizophrenia among the migrant groups especially African–Caribbeans in the UK. These studies have shown consistently high rates of schizophrenia. Cochrane and Bal postulated four hypotheses, in order to explain the increased rates of schizophrenia among migrants.

Hypothesis One

The first hypothesis for the high rates of schizophrenia among migrants states that the countries from which migrants originate themselves have high rates of schizophrenia. This hypothesis, although superficially attractive, has no evidence in reality. The World Heath Organization has enabled good quality multi-centre data collection on this topic and from this, Jablensky *et al* reported that rates of narrow definition (core) schizophrenia were not dissimilar across different cultural settings.

The study included three centres in developing countries, and these showed no difference in incidence rates of core schizophrenia, although there were wide variations in rates of broad schizophrenia. The rates from India are not dissimilar compared with Western rates.

Recent studies from Jamaica, Trinidad and Barbados have all demonstrated lower rates of schizophrenia when compared with rates among African–Caribbeans in the UK. Had the rates in the sending countries been genuinely higher, it would have been possible to explain some of the variation on the basis of genetic vulnerability, pregnancy and birth complications or neurological factors. However, no such increase has been demonstrated.

Hypothesis Two

The second hypothesis of self-selection suggests that those who are predisposed to mental illness (especially schizophrenia) are more likely to migrate. Such mobility can be attributed to inherent restlessness as a prodrome of the illness or a feeling of wanting to get away from a community that may be stigmatizing the mentally ill individual. The migration of patients with schizophrenia into urban areas confirms the drift hypothesis, and yet the fact that the urban environment may well contribute some yet unknown vulnerability has not been totally disproved. Although the hypothesis that psychologically vulnerable people tend to migrate is superficially attractive, it fails to provide a full explanation. If this were indeed the case, then the rates would be much higher in the first generation of migrants and then gradually drop in subsequent generations, which is not the case. Also the rates are not elevated in all migrant communities—only in some.

It can be argued that the individual has to be particularly healthy in order to jump all the hoops of immigration that are put in their way. The first phase of migration (lasting the first few years) appears to show relatively few health problems owing to the younger age structure of the migrant. In the next phase lasting from 5 to 10 years, when the individual has settled, the problems of acculturation and alienation may contribute to development of stress, which may produce psychological symptoms. In the following phase after 10 years or so in the new setting, the migrant may feel worse especially if they have not been successful in meeting their aspirations and are impeded by social constructs such as racism, and social structures such as unemployment, poor housing and the like.

Hypothesis Three

This hypothesis states that migration in itself produces stress, which, in vulnerable individuals, leads to psychological morbidity. Theoretically this should lead to a proportionate increase in common mental disorders as well. However, available data do not support this. Also, as the rates of schizophrenia appear to be higher 10–12 years after migration has occurred, it would appear that there may be other intermediary factors that contribute to stress and elevated rates. It is conceivable that it is not the stress of migration but the stress of living in an alien culture that may be more relevant. Furthermore, factors such as cultural identity, self-esteem, patterns of attachment and prolonged periods of separation from one or both parents may play some role in the genesis of mental disorders.

Hypothesis Four

It has been argued cogently and repeatedly that elevated rates of schizophrenia among migrant groups are the result of misdiagnosis because clinicians fail to understand the cultural background of their patient and do not take into account cultural explanations of the groups they are either treating or diagnosing. However, this remains a spurious argument. Most of the research studies that have recruited patients from various migrant groups have done so on the basis of symptoms rather than research diagnosis. The emphasis on symptoms and not diagnosis may enable the clinician to overcome some of the problems experienced.

Hypothesis Five

An additional possible explanation that was not discussed by Cochrane and Bal but that is very probable is the ethnic density effect. It is likely that where migrants live together, especially with others from the same community around them, this may work as a protective factor for some psychiatric illnesses. Although shown in one study only, the comparable equal rates of schizophrenia among Asians and whites may be explained by the fact that there were large numbers of Asians living in the particular geographical areas—the population reaching 50% in some parts. However, high population density may well lead to other psychiatric conditions such as common mental disorders or increased rates of deliberate self-harm, through the mediation of an underlying culture conflict. When political and economic upheavals and natural crises lead to mass migration, this may produce a sense of hopelessness and helplessness in the individual leading to a depressive effect. Social assimilation may be affected and may not occur for a number of reasons.

Therefore a sense of deculturation or alienation emerges that further adds to the sense of failure, loss and poor self-esteem. In these conditions it is likely that the migrants and their dependants develop depressive symptoms. If there are additional factors such as discrepancy between achievement and expectation, it is likely to contribute to a sense of dejection, leaving the migrant psychologically vulnerable. Why this vulnerability leads to psychosis in general and schizophrenia in particular is difficult to explain and deserves to be studied in its own right in relation to social networks and support systems.

When individuals migrate from one nation state or culture to another, be it for temporary or permanent residence or for economic, political or educational purposes, there is every likelihood that aspects of that individual's cultural and ethnic identity will change. The degree of alteration will be determined by a number of factors—individual, kinship and societal. The changes may be transient, semi-permanent or permanent; some individuals may not undergo any changes in identity at all.

7

Social Development and Change of Society

The Jajmani system is a basic feature of traditional village socio-economic organisation in India. It is a clear example of the organic division of labour in the Durkhemian sense. Beginning with the famous study of Wiser in 1936, many sociologists and anthropologists have focussed attention on the nature and dimensions of the Jajmani system and the rules governing the relationships between the Jajmans (service receivers) and the Kamins (service givers) in different parts of the country. While Wiser (1936) stressed the reciprocity of the relationships and the nature of cooperation between different castes despite the traditional hierarchy that separates them, Beidelman (1959) looked at these relationships and services as essentially based on the principle of superordination and subordination and the consequential process, of exploitation of the subordinate Kamin (service) castes by the superior Jajman (landlord) castes.

Other studies, by and large, follow either of these approaches. Gould (1958), Pocock (1962) and others, however, emphasised the ritual aspect of the relationship from the viewpoint of the Hindu notion of purity-pollution as the basis for the Jajmani relationships, relegating the economic aspect to a secondary position. The fact, however, is that the Jajmani system functions in the village as a socio-economic and religious system born out of the traditional organisation of inter-caste relationships. As M.S.A. Rao puts it:

It is, therefore, imperative to restrict the Jajmani system to the economic and ritual service relationships. Other relationships such as caste, kinship, patron-client, tenurial do over lap. But all these should not be subsumed under the Jajmani system. To do this is unreal and highly misleading. Jajmani system is not by itself the whole of the feudalistic system... but is only a part of feudal and semi-feudal system.

Depending upon the practices and overall functioning of the village system, the relationships between Jajmans and Kamins could be either cooperative or exploitative in nature. In feudal regions, such as the former Hyderabad state, the Jajmani relationships received official recognition in such a way that each Kamin caste was expected to render services to visiting officials in lieu of a gift of land received from the government or the feudal lord, the gift being enjoyed hereditarily. The studies of Orenstein (1965), Ranga Rao (1980) and Raju (1979) also explain this.

Like any other traditional organisation the Jajmani organisation has also been subject to change. In this connection some authors have tried to indicate the nature and types of changes that have been taking place in the spheres of socio-economic and ritual activities of the village organisation. Notwithstanding the variations in the nature of changes in different villages the important viewpoint that emerges in all these studies is that the nature of Jajmani relationships and the mode of payments are undergoing a change under the impact of modernisation and economic development. However, this point requires a much more systematic, analysis.

Objectives and Method of Analysis

This paper tries, from a comparative perspective, to analyse the process of change in the nature of Jajmani relations and the pattern of occupational mobility among the Kamins in three villages at different levels of development. The three villages chosen belong to the same socio-cultural region but differ in the general level of development. In order to decide the level of development, some indicators were chosen and accordingly a set of three villages was selected from the coastal Krishna district of Andhra Pradesh. The criteria for classification were the differences in the facilities available in the three villages. These three villages were thus designated as developed, semi-developed and less-developed.

A total of ten sets of facilities were chosen and scores were shotted, to each facility. The score strength of a major item was divided among certain specified sub-facilities and the villages were classified on the basis of the total score Strength of each.

The socio-cultural and ecological backgrounds of the three selected villages are much the same. But, as is evident from the total score strength, the infrastructural facilities available in the first village (developed) are more as compared to those of the other two villages, with the second village (semi-developed) being better than the third (less-developed). However, the literacy levels in the three villages are not in that order. This difference may largely be due to the fact that in the semi-developed village not only the upper castes (Brahmins, Kammas and Bhatrajulu or Kshatriyas) but also a majority of the 138 Madiga (exuntouchable) families who have turned Christians are educated unlike theHindu Madigas in the other two villages. In the less-developed village, the majority of the population consists of the upper castes and this explains its number two position in education. In the developed village, out of 485 as many as 200 from the lower castes are uneducated, which explains the lowest literacy rate in it. The Kamins who largely belong to the lower castes are much less educated than the Jajmans.

The occupational structure of the villages shows that agriculture and related occupations constitute the primary source of income, for the villagers. The number of.people practising modern occupations is relatively high in the developed village, followed by the semi-developed and less developed villages. Data show that more people practise caste occupations in the less-developed village than in the other two villages. Agriculture in the less developed village is not as mechanised as in the developed and semi-developed villages.

SOCIAL DEVELOPMENT AND PROGRAMME OF ACTION

The Copenhagen Declaration on Social Development recognizes the urgent need to.address profound social problems, especially poverty, unemployment and social exclusion that affect every country and sets as the task of the governments to address both their underlying and structural causes and their distressing consequences in order to reduce uncertainty and insecurity in the life of people.

It adopts a broad view of social development, as meeting the.material and spiritual needs of individuals, their families and the communities in which they live. This can only be achieved through social and people centered sustainable development. As an aspect of sustainable development, there is a commitment to the protection of the environment. Social development is inextricably connected with economic development, for some of its primary goals the eradication of poverty, unemployment and social exclusion depend on it.

The Declaration identifies a number of factors that have prevented the goals of social development from being achieved: chronic hunger, malnutrition, illicit drug trade, organized crime, corruption, foreign occupation, armed conflicts, illicit arms trafficking, terrorism, intolerance, xenophobia and incitement to racial, ethnic, religious and other hatreds. Many of these factors are connected with the violation of human rights. It is therefore not surprising that the Declaration places considerable emphasis on human rights and democracy in order to achieve these goals.

Indeed more than any other international declaration, with the exception of the Declaration on the Right to Development the Declaration places human rights at the centre of development. It states, for example, that.democracy and transparent and accountable governance and administration in all sectors of society are indispensable foundations for the realization of social and people centered sustainable development.

At another point it refers to the acknowledgement that social and economic development cannot be secured in a sustainable way without the full participation of women and that equality and equity between women and men is a priority for the international community and as such must be at the centre of economic and social development. The Declaration places particular emphasis on the eradication of poverty, and this is perhaps its closest connection with human rights.

Poverty is the greatest cause of the denial of human rights. It is obvious that poor people enjoy a disproportionately small measure of economic rights such as education, health and shelter. However, they are equally unable to exercise civil and political rights, which would require not only an understanding of the dynamics of society and access to public institutions, but also confidence in them.

They are for the most part unable to use the legal process to vindicate their human and legal rights. Nothing destroys confidence so much as poverty. Poverty also compels people into the violation of the rights of others, particularly of their own children and women. Child labour is essential to the survival of millions of families throughout the Third World and, increasingly, so is prostitution.

Bonded labour is a direct result of poverty, and its exploitation by the well off. Poverty produces massive inequalities, and the subordination of some groups to others in circumstances that deny them their basic dignity. The first of the principles and goals enunciated in the Declaration, and a central theme of the Programme of Action, is a commitment to.a political, economic, ethical and spiritual vision for social development that is based on human dignity, human rights, equality, respect, peace, democracy, mutual responsibility and cooperation, and full respect for the various religious and cultural backgrounds of people. More specifically, governments have agreed to.promote democracy, human dignity, social justice and solidarity at the national, regional and international levels; ensure tolerance, nonviolence, pluralism and nondiscrimination, with full respect for diversity within and among nations.

They have undertaken to promote universal respect for, and observance and protection of, all human rights and fundamental freedoms for all, including the right to development, and to ensure that disadvantaged and vulnerable persons and groups are included in social development. Particular mention is made of the right of self-determination of all peoples, in particular of peoples under colonial or other forms of alien domination or foreign occupation and support for indigenous people in their pursuit of economic and social development, with full respect for their identity, traditions, forms of social organization and cultural values. Without trying to exhaust the references to human rights in the Declaration, the last paragraph of the first Commitment is worth quoting: As suggested, reaffirm and promote all human rights, which are universal, indivisible, interdependent and interrelated, including the right to development as a universal and inalienable right and an integral part of fundamental human development, and strive to ensure that they are respected, protected and observed.

Several points about these formulations are worth noting. First, the importance of the language of rights. Repeated references to them might indicate a broad international consensus on human rights and freedoms and attest to the moral and political force of the idea of human rights or at least of its rhetoric. In recent decades the idea of respect for human rights seems to have become a driving force in international and regional policies and conduct, as in the intervention of the United Nations in the restoration of rights and democracy in Bosnia and Herzegovina, Cambodia, East Timor, Haiti and Nicaragua; or in the more specific regional mediations and interventions by the Organization for Security and Cooperation in Europe.

Extensive references to democracy and human rights in the Declaration are evidence of the desire, if perhaps not necessarily the feasibility, of using human rights as a framework for sustainable development and solving other ailments of humankind. All of this enthusiasm and commitment to human rights must be taken with some caution, for the international human rights movement has been distinguished more by rhetoric than practice.

Human rights are understood differently in different places, and the apparent consensus on rights conceals profound differences on and even conflicts over, values and goals. Second, the frequent invocation of rights in the different contexts in the Declaration attests to the enlarged scope of the concept and content of human rights. Rights have travelled a long distance from their origins in the emerging liberal economic orders of Europe and the United States since the seventeenth century, when the focus was on civil and political rights as the means to restrict the power of the government and enhance that of economic entrepreneurs.

Their philosophical foundations have broadened, fed by various political and intellectual traditions. A large and diverse number of groups and interests have advanced their claims in the language of rights. The first additions to the classical liberal category of rights were economic, social and cultural rights. Since then specialized instruments have dealt with the claims and rights of vulnerable groups, such as women, children, refugees, migrants, indigenous peoples and people with disabilities. More broadly, but also ambiguously, there is the right to development, and notions of the preservation of the environment are being woven into the regime of rights. There is now a rich menu of rights, perhaps too rich as some complain, and the rights do not appear to be seamless. The regime of rights guarantees democracy and participation, and the accommodation of diversity.

A fundamental assumption of contemporary human rights is social justice, and thus the alleviation of poverty, which is a primary concern of the Declaration. Social justice has also promoted the idea of equity as between men and women, between groups, and between generations. There is a considerable widening of the range of entitlements of citizens and others, transforming people from supplicants into citizens.

The broadening of human rights has focused attention on the state not merely as facilitator but also as provider. The logic of social, economic and cultural rights is positive obligations of the state, necessitating an active role, to ensure basic needs of people, and thus their dignity. It is not surprising that these developments in the concept and scope of human rights have produced controversy. Behind the seeming consensus on the formulations in the Declaration on rights and democracy lurk several disagreements. How far the apparent disagreements reflect genuine differences of values is hard to say, for there is considerable hypocrisy and posturing in the position of governments.

Human rights have become one of the frameworks for international relations, and the debates about them have become highly politicized.

Having said that, it is possible to identify differences in approaches to human rights, and to their contents. These differences have been a major obstacle to a genuine consensus and the feasibility of consistent and effective international action to promote and protect human rights. The challenge to human rights of the Declaration is to achieve coherence of rights, founded on common values and understandings as to their purpose.

There are considerable advantages in using the human rights framework for social development. Despite the controversies that have prevented unified action on human rights, they seem to attract broad international support and few governments publicly condemn their values.

The language of rights has the capacity to evoke a response and to provide moral and legal justification for certain forms of action. The ideology of and claims based on, human rights have become increasingly effective ways to pressure governments and the international community. The regime of rights provides a basis for international or regional action and justifies the imposition of sanctions and, in extreme cases, humanitarian intervention.

Human rights standards can also compensate for the weakness of international political institutions and machinery. In contradistinction to the growth of the idea and substance of rights in national systems where they followed the establishment of the apparatus of the state in the international system rights have developed with remarkable speed and are well ahead of the development of political institutions. However, that does not mean there is not sufficient authority or mechanism for their international enforcement.

The framework of rights is feasible because rights are now being defined in detailed terms and there are numerous decisions of courts and other tribunals that have elaborated the parameters of rights and their implications. They are no longer abstract formulations. Moreover, the regime of rights is now complex and multilayered, dealing with different kinds of claims and interests.

It speaks to a variety of concerns, and provides doctrines as well as mechanisms for striking a balance between different claims. Rights are a way to mobilize and empower the disadvantaged, and in many parts of the world this is their principal function. The language of rights makes people conscious of both their oppression and the possibility of change Rights have been extraordinarily effective as a basis of networking in and across states and have demonstrated the possibility of international solidarity, particularly for women and indigenous peoples.

Many nongovernmental organizations justify their existence by the need to promote rights and it is the regime of rights that has enabled them to perform their promotional and investigative role, which has generally proved more effective than internal state mechanisms for accountability. It would be fair to say that the human rights regime has sustained civil society in its confrontation with the state. Even more fundamentally, the regime of rights is crucial because it speaks in the language of entitlements.

Poverty is not just a matter of a deprived economic situation; it is defined and sustained, on the part of the poor, by a sense of helplessness and dependence, and by a lack of opportunities, self-confidence and self-respect. It is increasingly being recognized that poverty can only be eradicated if the poor are given a greater share in decisions about programmes of poverty alleviation and their implementation. The language of rights makes it clear that the poor are not the subject of charity or benevolence, but are entitled to a decent standard of living and that civil and political rights are the vehicles for their participation and empowerment.

The effectiveness of the rights regime is, however, diminished by the fact that not all of them have been integrated into the international economic or financial systems, which are market oriented and primarily protect the interests of capitalists. Many types of rights are not favoured by the capitalist system. Historically only those rights have been upheld that support the interests of the dominant classes thus civil and political rights were propounded by a bourgeoisie coming into power.

Today's economic and social rights speak to the claims of the oppressed and the powerless, and the chances of their fulfilment are slim. Developments in human rights have been at the level of rhetoric and to some extent the establishment of institutions, but they have not led to the redistribution of resources or to building the economic base that favours economic justice.

Although norms of the human rights regime represent a serious challenge to the international market system, and an alternative vision, the material forces of the international market system are more powerful than the moral claims and rhetoric of human rights.One further point needs to be made to establish the context for a rights oriented strategy: it concerns.globalization..

The Declaration correctly identifies the contradictory nature of globalization, on one hand opening up possibilities of increased economic growth, and on the other foreclosing options central to the Copenhagen aspirations, such as those of income redistribution, alleviation of poverty, employment opportunities and equity. It states that.the global transformations of the world economy are profoundly changing the parameters of social development in all countries.

The challenge is how to manage these processes and threats so as to enhance their benefits and mitigate their negative effects upon people. There are grave doubts as to whether this challenge can be met successfully. The inherent tendency of economic globalization is to diminish democracy and to privilege marketoriented rights, reducing the importance and feasibility of social and solidarity rights.

It is impossible to discuss the salience of the human rights strategy for the Copenhagen social development envisioned in Copenhagen without taking on board the impact of globalization and the redistributions of power that it has produced.

DEVELOPMENT OF TECHNOLOGY

Developing countries have, relatively poor scientific and technological capacities at their disposal. The promotion of science and technology in these countries thus requires strong international communications and a pooling of the existing scientific knowledge and technological potential, in line with the developmental needs of developing countries.

The main issue connected with the utilisation of science and technology as a pool to speed up the development of the developing countries is, therefore, the transfer of technology and, in this respect, the choice of technology. Technology being a system consisting of hardware, software and orgware, the transfer of technology must be viewed as a complex process, involving a range of economic, financial, legal and sociological factors. In this connection, local inputs—primarily knowledge and information on technologies, trained cadres, legal and other regulations, etc.—are needed. The process of selection of technologies calls for an analysis and assessment not only of the economic impact, but also of the social impact. While must be kept in mind is that while technology itself is natural, the application of technology can have considerable social effects, since, through technology, a system of domination and exploitation, as well as a set of social norms and ethics may be transferred. A social impact analysis should be a constituent part of any transfer of technology arrangement. This analysis should specifically consider the impact of technology on women family and community life and other social and cultural values of the new environment to which the technology will be transferred.

Women are involved in science and technology through the structural transformations that occur with the transfer of technology and scientific and technological development, and as participants in research and technological activities; and experiencing the impact of the technologies on their everyday lives. In all cases, their involvement should be much stronger than it is at present. It is also very important that women understand scientific and technological innovations, because this enables them to influence the general social attitudes towards technological change through the existing non-formal education.

The radical changes in the organisational pattern and activities of the society, associated with rapid scientific and technological change in the overall organisation, which are presently being experienced in the developed countries, may also dramatically affect all developing countries, and lead to either a more dynamic and humane development or to an ever higher degree of dependency and exploitation. The problem of the marginal position of some members of society, and of women specifically, cannot be solved unless the elements of these new technologies can be built into development strategies in accordance with the concept of integral development.

Furthermore, the latest so-called frontier and transdisciplinary technologies can be used in different ways and at different levels. Their use can serve to accontuate the productive role of women, because such technologies are applicable to a number of areas which are of relevance to the betters quality of life and to the integration of women in development, i.e. food production, clean water supply, improved housing conditions, use of alternative energy sources, in the services education etc. Such technologies also stimulate the growth of employment, as they offer a variety of employment combinations.

However, it should be kept in mind that it is economic and political considerations, rather than social and cultural ones, which determine the availability and terms and conditions for the access of developing countries to new technologies and which are important for national development. Women's access to technological development thus also depends on the global relations between the technology owners and users and those who try to secure access to new technology and to processes of industrialisation. This implies that major efforts should be made to maximise the utilisation of the existing knowledge in developing countries and to lessen the technological dependence on developed countries.

Women have traditionally gained knowledge and experience (e.g., in agricultural production, energy utilisation, running the household, manufacturing objects for everyday use, home medicine etc.,) which have not been, exploited from the developmental point of view. The application of new scientific and technological devices and knowledge may lighten household drudgery in urban and rural areas, providing better water, energy and other community facilities. This would release energies which women might be encouraged to direct forwards active and useful participation in other economic and social areas, and in the overall technological transformation of the society.

A greater involvement of women in scientific and technological development would therefore require:

- popularisation of scientific and technological knowledge and skills in order to enable their further development, by mass media, through changes in school programmes, and through all participatory and community development activities (especially in agriculture but also in other areas, e.g., household activities, health, education, housing, etc.).
- an increase of the level of scientific and technological self reliance by developing national scientific and technological potentials, maximisation of the possibilities for technical proporation among developing countries and the introduction of selective transfer of technology systems.
- changes in the traditional attitudes towards women by enabling them to fully participate in scientific and technological development by stimulating their involvement in various forms of education and training.
- establishment of linkages between the existing traditional technologies and know-how and the new technologies. The involvement of women in the strengthening of these links could provide a firm basis for self-reliance and ensure a certain continuity in the development of authentic and original approaches, thus avoiding imitative modernisation, and developing participatory research as well as relating scientific and technological development to the specific needs of the country.
- establishment and strengthening of cooperation among developing countries in the areas of information on scientific and technological knowledge and devices transfer of technology and exchange of experience on application of science and technology in development, joint research, etc.

SKILLS AND SERVICES

The term services or tertiary sector encompasses a wide range of activities. Therefore, the analysis of the role of women in the services sector covers the generally complex problem of services classification and data, the identification of the manpower problem in general, and women's hidden economic role in particular, and the relationship between the services sector and the overall economy of the country. Over the last decades this sector's contribution to GDP increased substantially, not only in developed market economies but also in developing countries, where this upward trend was evident even in the least developed countries. By 1980, the services sector accounted for the largest share of GDP in both developed market economies (56.9 per cent) as well as in developing countries (44.3 per cent). In developing countries the services sector expanded at a past faster rate than the GDP in the period 1973-80, implying that the general slowdown of their economies during these periods affected the services sector less severely than other major economic sectors. However, the expansion of the services sector in developing countries, particularly in least developed countries, is probably due to quite different economic causes and could the attributed to the marginalisation of the labour force in agriculture and industry. The development of services is partly due to major changes in agriculture and industry, and partly to their heterogenous production and consumption characteristics.

The role of women in the tertiary sector is very difficult to determine. However, the distribution of the female labour force may serve as an indicator. In 1980, 66.3 per cent of the total female labour force in developing countries was employed in agriculture, 16.3 per cent in industry and 17.4 per cent in services. This is very different from the situation in developed countries, where the shares are 13.7 per cent for agriculture, 29.0 per cent for industry and 57.3 per cent for services.

In developing countries the share of females in the total labour force, by economic sectors, was highest in agriculture (36.4 per cent, even with universed figures) and much lower in the services sector (26.9 per cent) and industry (26.5 per cent).

There are considerable disparities between developing countries in the different regions—disparities between Latin America on the one hand and Asia and Africa on the other. In Asia the main feature is the relatively high share of women in the total labour force in industry (28.8 per cent) and the lower share in services (23.2 per cent). In Latin America the low share of women in the total agricultural labour force (9.3 per cent) is in sharp contrast to the situation in the other two regions. In this region female employment in the services sector is as high as 38.3 per cent. In Africa women account for 31.6 per cent of labour in services, while their share in industry is only 19.7 per cent. (UNIDO, 1984). In relation to the integration of women in development some partial issues arising in the service sector have been studied. These include trade (women being active internal trade, mostly in the petty trade of the informal sector); transport (links between rural and urban areas, developed and underdeveloped regions, formal and informal sectors); banking (mainly in connection with the problems of access to credit); tourism (increased opportunities for productive employment, provision of lodging, catering, etc., could discourage some negative forms of tourism).

Many of the service activities in which women are employed do not require formal technical qualifications. Other activities such as health (especially nursing) and education (especially teaching) do require professional qualifications, but these are in many cases considered an extension of the essentially female role which has its origin in the household—the mother care offered to the family. Thus women's contribution in this sector has not really been adequately recognised.

Much of the productive activity of women in the services sector remains invisible because of its mainly traditional and informal nature in developing countries. Some thought should be devoted to the services which this sector could provide to meet the needs of households in this countries, that is, what the services sector should produce for the household and its members.

In view of the importance of the role of women in this sector and of the significance of the services sector for the improvement of the status of women in developing countries, it is suggested that:

- attention be paid to the analysis of the functioning, growth and development of the services sector (both public and private) in all developing countries, especially as regards the interlinkages among this and all other sectors;
- services classification and data collection should be made more transparent and accessible.
- the position of women in this sector should be viewed as developmental and integrative of other activities, which means that the new developmental trends observed in this sector must be closely linked to overall development and the advancement of women;
- women's hidden economic role in the services should be further studied and analysed;
- cooperation among developing countries in this sector, which is scattered over different areas and usually invisible being traditional and informal;
- could be pursued with a view to the development of self-reliant schemes. Cooperation among developing countries in this sector could contribute

to exchange of experiences, to development of self-reliant schemes and linkages between micro and macro levels of implementation. This may be an avenue for the promotion of new approaches to the development of the services sector.

CREATING AWARENESS

Education is a double-edged instrument: it can contribute to and be an ally of structural changes in society by training people in required skills—old, newly emerging and anticipated. It is also a value-generating process—influencing the behaviour, norms and cultural attitudes of people, particularly younger ones. From the beginning of the movement for the equality of women in recent history, great emphasis was placed on education as the major instrument for the elimination of gender inequality. Developing countries have viewed education as an instrument to stimulate development in all fields, and to reduce their dependence on external advisers. The basic problems were to promote a rapid expansion of development and cultural structures to meet the manpower requirements of development and cultural progress in general. Scarcity of resources and the shifting priorities of development have constrained the balanced pursuit of these aims. One of the objectives which had a low priority in the allocation of efforts and resources was the elimination of gender inequality.

Illiteracy still remains a major problem in most developing countries and women constitute a large proportion of the illiterates. A bout 60 per cent of the approximately.800 million adult illiterates in developing countries today are women. Although the proportion of illiterates in the total adult population has decreased, the results are still unsatisfactory. The absolute number of illiterates in these countries is still increasing. Gender differences persist among illiterates, especially because the lower enrolment ratios for girls at the elementary level increase the number of illiterate women. The gender gap among illiterates is increasing In developing countries. In 1960 the share of women among illiterates was 57.9 per cent. This increased to 59.5 per cent in 1970.

Trends in the process of equalising the access of men and women to different levels of the educational system, as measured through enrolment ratios, show some interesting results. Over two decades (1960-80) the gender gap in enrolment ratios for the age groups 6—11 and 12— 17 has remained virtually constant in developing countries, although there is overall improvement in entrolment for both sexes. At the higher level of education, the gap is much narrower, in contrast to developed countries, where the gender gap exists mainly at the higher level. At this level the gender gap has shrunk in the developed countries during the last decade, and it has slightly widened in the group of developing countries. (Sicherl, 1984).

The persistence of these gaps prevents the equalisation of educational opportunities with consequent effects on employment, skill acquisition and participatory opportunities in all fields. The widening of the gap in higher education is a matter of serious concern, because this sector is the training ground for entry into many areas important development, *e.g.*, science and technology, communication industries utilising high level technology, professions such as law, medicine, etc. It is also the training ground for most managerial and decision-making occupations. The participation of women in decision-making positions, which is already limited, could shrink still further if this gap were to expand.

In addition to resource constraints, educational progress in developing countries has been impeded by many other problems. Lack of harmony with productive and other developmental activities, which is often a consequence of borrowed models of educational systems, imposed the need to reform and adapt educational systems and institutions, to turn increasingly to the informal aspects of education (vocational training, on the job-training, etc.), and to introduce mass media and other modern devices as useful means of spreading educational programmes and contents in an effort to reach as many social groups as possible. Developing countries have been experiencing great problems in education, reflected in poor material basis and functional difficulties, in sometimes alarming drop-out levels (especially in Sub-Saharan Africa and South Asia), in the fact that a substantial proportion of children are unable to read and write even after going to primary school for four or five years, etc.

Women are still mostly employed in traditional and informal sectors where there has been a lower level of technological and information support. This further compounds their educational handicaps. However, women with education have entered many new areas of occupation where their participation was virtually non-existent before. This process of occupational diversification through education has been accelerated during the Decade in many developing countries.

The enable women to participate actively in all spheres of economic and social life, vocational and professional training must be further developed. In this respect, the training of trainers is of primary importance, as is the introduction of management training for women. Apart from the conventional types of training (seminars, workshops, export group meetings training through doing, etc.), the non-conventional types are often also suitable. Of special relevance are also the new participatory types of training, which include learner-centred methods developed in the framework of non-formal education in which trainers are facilitators, to elicit productive response and interaction-and local social and cultural forms that can be built upon for effective training. These include-decision making patterns, social groupings and communications networks.

Culture

The major lacunae in educational development are in the areas of cultural change and promotion of social values which support and reflect the goals of development. Cultural transformations are taking place in developing countries, but in many cases through processes over which the people and even the governments have little control. New values and aspirations are often promoted, directly or indirectly, for profit maximisation-by forces inside or outside the country. Changes in consumption patterns and role models are stimulated by mass media, commercial interests and a process of borrowing or emulation of life styles from developed countries. In many countries such changes have contributed to a widening of the gap between the elites and the masses of the people between the rural and urban populations, between the rich and the poor. This presents a challenge to the educational system, which must correct the trend if it is to promote the goals of participatory development, and collective self-reliance, eliminate the dependency on external support and contribute to comprehensive integrated development.

While there is evidence that the process of unplanned cultural change helps to promote illusory images which are far removed from the social realities of developing countries, cultural reaction, which tries to counter these influences by looking only to the past, may also have a negative impact on development. In their efforts to preserve their cultural identities developing countries have sought to reaffirm their attachment to their cultural heritage. While pride in this heritage can contribute to the spirit and the value of self-reliance, this process may also lead to distortions-to a withdrawal from present-day problems and realities to a glamorisation of the past, to the imposition of the culture of dominant groups on other culturally diverse groups and to a strengthening of some of the forces and institutions that oppose the goals of comprehensive, participatory development of all peoples, classes and groups. Such trends have often inhibited the equality of women and attempts to enhance their role in development.

In view of the crucial importance of culture values in the dynamics of development, it will be essential to enhance the role of the women and to promote new cultural values that take into account existing social realities and support the efforts to build a different future. Integral development, which subsumes equal participation in development *i.e.,* in production and decision making will enhance the role of culture in the development context. Women will no longer be viewed as marginal producers (or providers of an auxiliary workforce), but rather as equal partners in the promotion of development.

Educational institutions will have to play an active role in the promotion of the development of such new cultural values. Hitherto, their contribution has been inadequate. Structurally pedagogically and philosophically, educational institutions will have to play a far more active role in the development of a new cultural context that can contribute to the realisation of the goals of comprehensive development—human and material. This also requires that they internalise the concern for the equality of women and the enhancement of their role-in their curricula, pedagogic methods, organisation and research agendas.

A strategic interrelationship between education and cultural and socio-economic development which integrates concern for the emancipation of women would have to be characterised by respect for the specific cultural features of a particular environment and clearly define the cultural and developmental function of education in social transformation and support the process of educational reform.

In this connection, the promotion of new knowledge about women and new perceptions of the role of women in development could be viewed as an instrument for educational and cultural development with a view to:

- strengthening and extension of training activities so as to embrace all relevant problems, such as: improvement of professional skills, education for family life and responsibilities, training for community organisation and management, decision waking etc.;
- equal participation of the local population, and particularly of women, in devising, deciding upon and implementing development programmes; this can be achieved by clearly defining the developmental interests of all groups of the population;
- promotion of integral and interdisciplinary links among developing countries in the field of cultural transformation and education and especially in professional and vocational training as well as in all forms of non- conventional training, to ensure availability of cadres capable of handling the new technology.
- enhancement of the collective self-reliance of nonaligned and other developing countries in culture and education by intensifying their communication in these fields, especially as regards the methodologies for educational reform which incorporates the advancement of women as one of its concerns.

Mass Media

This section focuses on the possibilities which the media offer provided they are used judiciously to reflect the contribution which women are making to the nation's development efforts. Communication media have been a powerful social influence, both as instruments of change and for maintaining *status quo.* In the last decade, an impressive amount of literature on the portrayal of women in the media has been produced.

These studies have expressed concern about the stereotyped and negative images of women which are being projected through the media without any cognizance of the new and expanded roles of women in society. Communication media are a powerful tool for the creation of an alternative and positive image of women and could promote new attitudes and strategies for action directed towards the achievement of the goal of equality for women. It is imperative to democratises the control over the communication media and to make them an instrument for the creation of an awareness of women's needs and problems.

Mass media, especially the audiovisual media, play an important role by influencing the consumption patterns and life-styles, and usually promote commercial interests (often of external producers), thus creating pressures to distort trade and industrial policies.

They also contribute to the distortion of cultural development, promoting imported values which militate against comprehensive integrated development and the principle of collective self-reliance. There has been a recent trend among media professionals in developing countries towards greater realism in their portrayal of social problems. Realism, however, must be used to inspire people to struggle for change. A search for new options in human relationships, the reshaping of social institutions, political and economic structures and cultural values, would go a long way towards integrating women into the world of the media, and enable the media to play a more positive role in integrated development.

In the past, there has been a one-way flow of information from the developed to the developing countries, and from government to the people. The goals of self-reliance and participatory development, which are being actively pursued by the non-aligned countries, involve a shift from excessive reliance of the developing countries on foreign resources towards a mobilisation of their indigenous resources, which would make these countries less vulnerable to external pressures and develop their own potential for growth. The new information and communication technology, the micro-chip revolution, has considerably magnified the power of the media. Satellite communication has exposed millions of people to new information. The strengthening of the autonomous capacities of the individual countries and improvement of the organisational framework and media content will depend on the socio-political context of each country.

Women are today an important factor in the strategy of self-reliance and the media could do much to create public awareness of the role of women and their potentials. There are a number of steps which the media could take at various levels to strengthen the role of women as equal partners in development:

- a democratisation of the structures and control of the communication media could contribute to the representation and participation of women in the media at the decision—making levels;
- more women should be involved in media training programmes; communication and advertising policies involving participation by women could be developed;
- media content could be improved through coordinated efforts for increased interaction between non-governmental organisations in formulating guidelines for monitoring programmes;
- listeners and viewers from consumer groups or NGO action groups, etc., could be effectively utilised to create an awareness of women's issues and to evolve common strategies for the promotion of more positive approaches to women's issues;
- various international seminars, conferences and expert group meetings, which have already covered a wide range of issues connected with women and the communication media indicate the need for further in depth studies, research training for women in communication technology, the organisational framework, including the development of a code of ethics with regard to the presentation of women in media and using traditional folk media to encourage participation of women.
- horizontal communication and cooperation among developing countries in this field could be strengthened in order to create an awareness of issues of common concern, identifying solutions to common problems and areas of cooperation.

MODERN CHANGES IN RELIGION

The process of modernization in India, well under way during the British colonial period (1757-1947), has brought with it major changes in the organizational forms of all religions. The missionary societies that came with the British in the early nineteenth century imported, along with modern concepts of print media and propaganda, an ideology of intellectual competition and religious conversion. Instead of the customary interpretation of rituals and texts along received sectarian lines, Indian religious leaders began devising intellectual syntheses that could encompass the varied beliefs and practices of their traditions within a framework that could withstand Christian arguments.

One of the most important reactions was the Arya Samaj (Arya Society), founded in 1875 by Swami Dayananda (1824-83), which went back to the Vedas as the ultimate revealed source of truth and attempted to purge Hinduism of more recent accretions that had no basis in the scriptures. Originally active in Punjab, this small society still works to purify Hindu rituals, converts tribal people, and runs centers throughout India. Other responses include the Ramakrishna order of renunciants established by Swami Vivekananda (1863-1902), which set forth a unifying philosophy that followed the Vedanta teacher Shankara and other teachers by accepting all paths as ultimately leading toward union with the undifferentiated *brahman*. One of the primary goals of the Ramakrishna movement has been to educate Hindus about their own scriptures; the movement also runs book stores and study centers in all major cities. Both of these paths are directly modeled on the institutional and intellectual forms used by European missionaries and religious leaders.

During the 1930s and 1940s, again responding to institutional models from Europe, the more activist Rashtriya Swayamsevak Sangh (RSS—National Volunteer Organisation) emerged to protect Hinduism. The RSS had been founded in 1925 by Keshav Baliram Hedgewar (1889-1944), a native of Maharashtra who was concerned that Hinduism was in danger of extinction from its external foes and needed a strong, militant force of devotees to protect it. Members believe that the Indian nation is the divine mother to whom the citizen devotes mind and body through *karma-yoga*, or disciplined service.

Training consists of daily early morning meetings at which the saffron, white, and green Indian flag and the swallow-tailed, red-ocher RSS banner are raised as rows of members salute silently. There are then group drills in gymnastic exercises, sports, discussions of patriotic themes from a primarily Hindu viewpoint, group singing of nationalist songs, and a final assembly with saluting. Throughout India in the early 1990s, there were cells (*shakha*) of fifty to 100 members from all walks of life (the RSS rejects class differences) who were devoted to the nation. Although it has attracted hundreds of thousands of members from all over India, the RSS has never projected itself as a political party, always remaining a national club that is ready to send its members to trouble spots for the defense of the nation and the national culture, embodied in Hinduism. The Jana Sangh, established in 1951, was the RSS's political arm until it joined the Janata Party in 1977 and its membership split away in 1980 to form the BJP.

Another activist organization is the Vishwa Hindu Parishad (VHP—World Hindu Council), founded in 1964. The VHP runs schools, medical centers, hostels, orphanages, and mass movements to support Hinduism wherever it is perceived as threatened. This ultraconservative organization played a role in the extensive agitation for the demolition of a mosque in Ayodhya, leading to the destruction of the structure during a huge demonstration in 1992. As a result of the VHP's complicity in the affair, the Ministry of Home Affairs imposed a two-year ban on the Vishwa Hindu Parishad under the Unlawful

Activities Act. When the ban expired in December 1994, the government reimposed it for two additional years.

The spread of Hindu "communal" (that is, religious) sentiment parallels a similar rise in religious chauvinism and "fundamentalist" ideologies among religious minorities, including Muslims and Sikhs. Against this background of agitation, the periodic outbreak of communal riots in urban areas throughout India contributes to an atmosphere of religious tension that has been a hallmark of the national political scene during the twentieth century.

Hindu-Muslim riots, especially in North India, reached a peak during the partition of India in 1947 and periodically escalated in urban areas in the early 1990s. This strife typically involves low-income groups from both communities in struggles over land, jobs, or local resources that coalesced around a religious focus after seemingly trivial incidents polarized the two communities. In practice, although members of other religious communities are the victims of violence, rioters are rarely motivated by religious instructors, although fundamentalist agitators are often implicated.

The situation in North India became complicated during the 1980s by Sikh terrorism connected with the crisis in Punjab, the widespread anti-Sikh riots after Prime Minister Indira Gandhi's assassination in November 1984 by her Sikh bodyguards, and a series of terrorist or counterterrorist actions lasting into the 1990s. In all of these cases, many observers believe that religion has appeared as a cover for political and economic struggles.

The perception that one's religion is in danger receives periodic reinforcement from the phenomenon of public mass religious conversion that receives coverage from the news media. Many of these events feature groups of Scheduled Caste members who attempt to escape social disabilities through conversion to alternative religions, usually Islam, Buddhism, or Christianity. These occasions attract the attention of fundamentalist organizations from all sides and heighten public consciousness of religious divisions. The most conspicuous movement of this sort occurred during the 1950s during the mass conversions of Mahars to Buddhism. In the early 1980s, the primary example was the conversion of Dalits to Islam in Meenakshipuram, Tamil Nadu, an event that resulted in considerable discussion in the media and an escalation of agitation in South India. Meanwhile, conversions to Christianity among tribal groups continue, with growing opposition from Hindu revivalist organizations.

Alongside the more publicized violent outbreaks, there have been major nonviolent changes, as new sectarian movements continue to grow and as established movements change. For example, the Radhasoami Satsang movement of North India, which includes adherents in Punjab and Uttar Pradesh, encompasses yogic ideas on the relationship between humans and the universe, the *bhakti* saint tradition including select Sikh influences, and the veneration of the enlightened guru. The dominant tendency of these new religions, following the example of the great teachers of the past that was reiterated by Mahatma Gandhi and most modern gurus, remains nonviolence to all living beings and acceptance of the remarkable diversity of Indian religion.

CRUCIAL DEVELOPMENT ISSUES

The still largely unresolved problems of the interconnections between economic and social development and the increasing concern for the distributional and human dimensions of development indicate the need to pay more attention to all aspects of social development. The issues of health, social security, population trends and family planning, housing urbanisation and the environment, are linked with the general problem of the level of socio-economic development of a country its resource base and social policies.

HEALTH DELIVERY SYSTEMS

Millions of people in developing countries are trapped in poverty, malnutrition, hunger and disease, although there are regional variations in living conditions. It is estimated that acute forms of potential energy malnutrition affect 35 per cent school children in Africa, 16 per cent in Asia and 4 per cent in of Latin America.

Similarly, it is estimated that two-thirds pregnant women in the developing world suffer from nutritional anaemia. High maternal and infant mortality rates are closely linked with inadequate maternal and child health care services, lack of proper sanitation and a safe drinking water supply. By the end of the last decade, only 42 per cent of households in developing countries had access to a potable water supply and over three quarters of the population lacked access to sanitary facilities.

A disaggregation of social indicators by regions reveals that not only is there a very great gap between the developed and developing countries but also that there is great diversity among the developing regions.

The average life expectancy in Sub-Saharan Africa is 47.4 years while it is 63.9 years in some Asian Countries. Similarly, infant mortality is highest in Sub-Saharan Africa (127.1 per thousand live births), while it is 56.2 in South East Asia. In the South Asian region the mortality differentials by sex indicate higher infant mortality among females and empirical data also show sex-based health and nutrition related behaviour. In the health care sub-systems, there are interesting variations: Latin America—with the highest per capita GDP—has 7.5 physicians and 11.7 nurses per 10,000 population, followed by some countries in South East Asia, where despite low GDP per capita the averages are 5.4 physicians and 5.2 nurses per 10,000 population.

Most developing countries are faced with the problem of a decline or slowing down of the growth rate of production, rising unemployment, growing deficits in balance of payments and inflation. All these adversely affect the availability of resources for social services, *i.e.,* health, education and social security.

Despite the methodological weaknesses of the existing social indicators and an absence of data on access to and distributional characteristics of the social development infrastructure, the trends indicate that results differ sharply also within regions and that social improvements definitely do not come automatically as a by-product of economic growth. In many cases health resources are disproportionately concentrated in big cities, at the expense of primary health care for the masses in rural areas. Problems requiring careful study include disparities in increase and living standards, and the care available to different social groups, inadequate planning and management of health development, problems of inter and intra-sectoral coordination, administrative decentralisation and involvement of the people in the planning, programming and implementation of health care programmes.

Very few developing countries have systems of social security. Even where such systems exist, a large part of the population in the informal sector—a substantial proportion of which are women—is not covered by the existing systems of mater benefits, health insurance, old age benefits, etc.

In some countries voluntary and philanthropic organisations supplement state action. However, their work is often uncoordinated and not adequate to deal with the increasing, demands of urbanisation and poverty. The development of social protection is linked to changes in the development strategies and orientation directed towards the satisfaction of basic minimum needs, the reduction and elimination of poverty, promotion of employment opportunities and improvement of the working conditions of labour.

The global strategy of *Health for All by 2000* adopted by the Thirty Fourth World Health Assembly in 1981, which emphasises basic health protection, the primary health care approach and organisation of an effective health care and health information system, identified priorities for health cooperation and drew up an Action Programme, stressing the need for a review of a number of policy orientations in the areas of primary health care, health information and monitoring system, community involvement in health programmes, prevention of infectious diseases, development of national services of health care and health education, production, distribution and consumption of drugs and protection of the human environment.

On the basis of the Medium-Term Programme for Technical Cooperation among Developing Countries for Health for All (1984-89) and in view of the calls for an acceleration of the development of national health care capabilities and the establishment of local points for TCDC in the area of health some priority activities may be identified:

- introduction of effective health surveillance systems at the national level, of health indicators for target setting and formulation of national priorities and plans of action, and of appropriate Systems for assessing strengths and weaknesses of national health programmes;
- linking of health policies and 'programmes with economic development and those facilities which can directly reduce women's drudgery and work burden and directly improve their health situation, *i.e.*, provision of adequate housing, water supply, sanitation, health regulations at the work-place, and health protection of women, particularly those working in the informal sector of the economy who are not covered by social protection policies;
- integration of maternal and child health care with family planning services and accelerated development of national capacities through development of health institutions and infrastructures and increase of the number of health experts and particularly health workers;
- involvement of women's organisations in primary health care activities and their representation on national and local health councils;
- promotion of health education and indigenous system of health care;
- involvement of woman's organisations in primary health care activities and their representation on national and local health councils;
- promotion of health education and indigenous systems of health care;
- introduction of ECDC/TCTC programmes for the promotion of industries which are important for the development of health care systems. The developing countries could evolve suitable mechanisms for cooperation in training and development of human resources, collaborative research, joint programming, exchange of information and references, and exploring the application of low-cost technologies for water supply and waste disposal.

Demographic Factors

It is becoming increasingly obvious that population policies should be implemented parallel with better health care and general socio-economic development as population issues touch on very fundamental human values.

As the Mexico Conference on Population in 1984 stressed, population strategies cannot be limited to the analysis of population trends, since there is a dynamic interrelationship between these and socio-economic transformations. Hence, what is required is a set of coordinated strategies and activities for the promotion of economic development of the quality of life, human rights and in particular the fundamental right to individual choice.

The status of women and the advancement of their role in development remains a critical element in the achievement of these objectives. The persisting inequalities between men and women—which are evident in the higher incidence of poverty, unemployment and illiteracy among women—the limited range of employment categories offered to women, and the uneven sharing of borne and family responsibilities make it difficult for women to participate actively in the socio-economic development of the country. Population policies should be viewed as an integral part of overall socio-economic development.

There is sufficient evidence to show that it is lower income groups with a low level of literacy, low and insecure income and low health and nutritional levels which have larger families. This is points to a need for planning policies which have a more integrated approach. Rapid population growth will affect the efforts of countries to achieve food security and to reduce pressure on the natural resources; also, its effects on urbanisation and on land and capital will exacerbate inequalities.

Many governments have launched subsidised family planning programmes. However, incentives are offered to encourage people to reduce family size. Experience has shown that a clinical approach which threatens social values, beliefs and customs does not succeed and is actually a disincentive. To break through the vicious circle of poverty, high fertility and mortality calls for a more careful and humane public policy with a judicious balance between individual choice and dignity and promotion of a sense of responsibility among parents to ensure a better future for all children. This could be further stimulated and promoted through various forms of technical assistance at various levels as well as enriched through mutual exchange of information and experience among developing countries.

Coping with Over Population: Women in the Cities

The rapid growth of cities in developing countries has created serious problems, since a large proportion of urban migrant workers are living in temporary hutments and settlements without adequate basic amenities. The growth of cities and the steep rise in rural-urban migration is a manifestation of imbalances in the location and expansion of productive activity. Women are particularly affected, as many of their activities are connected with their homes and bad housing and hygiene conditions are detrimental to both their own and their families health. The growth of cities has also created ecological problems. The growing demands of expanding cities have put undue pressure on natural resources, destroying the harmony between human beings and nature, and has led to a degradation of productive resources like water, land and forests. With increasing pressure on the land, overgrasing and deforestation, severe environmental damage has followed.

The expansion of agriculture by clearing large tracts of forest has caused desertification due to severe soil erosion, a problem which is extremely serious in Sub-Saharan Africa (Sahel), north-western Asia and the Middle East. Forests are crucial to the ecological life of many developing countries and deforestation has created serious problems, as the consumption of forest resources has exceeded replacement possibilities through natural growth. This has affected millions of rural households and the role of women in these households, as well as the nutritional level of the families. The human costs of malnutrition, famine and disruption in the lives of people seeking employment are a matter of serious concern.

Environmental issues conceiving the environment in its broadest social context are most relevant for women. The increasing marginalisation of certain sections of the population, growing poverty and deprivation of the masses, decreasing food production, the energy crisis and human environmental degradation in many developing countries are all symptoms of a pattern of growth and resource utilisation which is geared to existing power structures and prevents a large section of the population from satisfying its basic needs. The multidimensional problems facing developing countries are interconnected, but often these connection are not understood by those who formulate sectoral policies. In the long run, social development policies will have to be closely integrated with economic development policies and a strong commitment to the improvement of the quality of life. The methods and instruments of analysis and planning of socio-economic development should therefore take adequate account of environmental constraint.

DEVELOPMENT THROUGH ENTERPRISE

One of the important factors in the development programmes and plans of developing countries is the growth and expansion of public enterprises and the public sector. Initially, public enterprises operated principally in the infrastructure and the public utilities, but their range of activity has now considerably expanded. Being part of the broader stream of the public sector in developing countries, public enterprises are important instruments of national and collective self-reliance and are oriented towards increasing the countries autonomy in using and developing their natural and human resources in order to increase the well-being of the population as a whole.

One of the responsibilities of public enterprises is the promotion of the integration of women into the developmental process and of a conscious policy directed towards the advancement of women. The responsibilities of public enterprises in this regard, however, differ in accordance with their scope and nature, their mandate and function, their scope and coverage of national planning and the legislative framework. But, by and large, they cover a wide range of commercial and; or non-commercial functions of great importance in everyday life. Practical experience in the operation of public interprises in developing countries has shown that they generate progressive social change in these countries, including positive moves towards involving women in the main streams of development. However, the public sector in general and the public enterprises in particular are still not strong enough to constitute a major or even a very important factor in involving women in the transformation of their socio-economic position and are thus not making a sufficient response to this complex task. Within the framework of the national development programmes, the public enterprise in general, and each specific enterprise in particular should be provided with guidelines indicating the special steps expected from the enterprise for the promotion of the role of women in developing countries, which might include the following:

- More emphasis on clarity of aims and objectives, a regular review of the current status of women, including job profiles for the improvement of the position of women in training programmes, social welfare measures relating to child bearing and child rearing, provision of creches and the allocation of specific responsibilities to appropriate national institutions;
- preparation of concrete action plans which should include both short-term and long-term strategies in the area of manpower planning, recruitment systems promotional opportunities, incentives, training and women's representation at the management level. These strategies should also envisage a regular procedure and criteria for the evaluation of the performance of public enterprises in terms of the fulfilment of economic and social objectives;
- identification of areas of activity in which women are currently not represented but can be recruited. The human resources development plans should include a specific component on the employment of women;
- efforts should be made to involve more women in on going training courses, particularly management training, as well as to develop the curricula of these courses with an emphasis on the role and responsibilities of public enterprises in the advancement of women;
- in view of the need to involve more women at higher levels of management, special training programmes for the induction of women at these levels of enterprise management could be stimulated and developed as a short-term measure;
- Fuller involvement of women workers and men workers alike in decision-making processes as well as in forms of management at all

levels of enterprise organisation, which is seen as an essential means of their advancement, parallel with the improvement of public enterprises' management patterns and efficiency;

- public enterprises should exploit their opportunities of generating employment in down-stream activities with which they are related. This is of particular significance in the case of sub-contracting to public sector ancillaries. Some cases of sub-contracting to women's cooperatives and to regional development corporations which stimulate small business could also promote both employment and entrepreneurship among women. However steps must be taken to ensure that such practices are not deterimental to the position of women or to the overall regional development;
- an agreed system of performance evaluation arising from the predetermined corporate plans should identify the evaluation criteria for each social objective including the objective of advancing the status of women. Whenever possible, an attempt should be made to quantify the criteria;
- the existing or/and newly created mechanisms at the national level responsible for scrutinising the policies and practice of public enterprises and evaluating their operations and contributions towards the socio-economic objectives of development could advise governments on the formulation of policies through which public enterprises could act as model employers and real promoters of the status of women, and could also undertake regular evaluation and monitoring of these efforts of public enterprises.

In view of the need to implement the socio-economic objectives of development and the advancement of women, due consideration should be given to the role of private enterprises. Governments should seek appropriate ways and means to ensure that public and private enterprises share the responsibilities for the improvement of the status of women. Some suggestions in this connections might be, for example:

- private enterprises are established in developing countries under various systems of public licensing which include certain provisions for the enforcement of laws and these could be used for regulating the working conditions of women;
- similarly, credit/banking agencies which give loans to private enterprises for equity and working capital could give specific incentives for the promotion of the advancement of women;
- it may expected that the linkages between the public and private enterprises could promote the realisation of some of these ideas.

THE CHANGING NATURE OF JAJMANI SYSTEM

The Jajmani system in the three villages is basically the same and fits into the following description by Kolenda: The Jajmani system is a system of distribution in Indian Villages whereby high-caste land-owning families called 'Jajmans' are provided services and products by various lower castes such as carpenters, potters, blacksmiths, water-carriers, sweepers, and laundrymen. Purely ritual services may be provided by Brahmin priests and various sectarian castes, and almost all serving castes have ceremonial and ritual duties at their Jajman's births, marriages, funerals and at some of the religious festivals. Important in the latter duties is the lower castes capacity to absorb pollution by handling clothing and other things defiled by birth or death pollution, gathering up banquet dishes after the feasts and administering various bodily attentions to the new mother, bride or groom (1963:11)

In Krishna District, the Jajmani system is termed as 'Mirasi Paddhati'. The Jajmans are called 'Aasaamis' and Kamins 'Panivallu'. In the three villages under study the upper caste Brahmins, Kshatriyas, Kammas and Kapus constitute the Jajmans. They are largely land-lords, big and small, even though every Jajman need not be a cultivator. A cultivator takes secular as well as religious services from all types of Kamins; only rarely he may dispense with the services of some groups. The Kamins belong to six caste groups: (1) Vedic Brahmin (purohit); (2) Wadla (carpenter); (3) Kummari (potter); (4) Chakali (washerman); (5) Mangali (barber); and (6) Madiga (cobbler). The Brahmin, 'however, is not included in the category of "Panivallu"*. Except in the case of Madigas, the local caste names of the Kamins denote their traditional calling or occupation. Traditionally the Madigas are leather-workers and they are known as such. Not all Vedic Brahmins are priests. In the semi-developed village (in which only the Brahmins are working as priests) the poor Brahmin families with or without land are working as priests. In the other two villages, the Brahmins are not working as priests; they are either land-lords or engaged in other vocations.

While no one from the traditionally Jajmani castes has turned a Kamin, the families of Kamin castes use the services of other Kamin castes and as such a given Kamin could also be a Jajman. The Brahmin could be a Jajman as a land-lord, and a Kamin as a priest. So is the case with other Kamins. All the above mentioned Kamin caste groups are present both in the developed and less-developed villages, whereas in the semi-developed village, the Kummari and Wadla caste groups are absent. But here, 10 families of Madigas (9 Christian and 1 Hindu) have taken to carpentry and blacksmithy and cater to the needs of the villagers. In terms of Gould's usage (1964) this may be termed as 'functional interchangeability'. This practice of functional interchangeability is reported to have been in existence for the last 40 or 50 years in this village and has been for some time limited only to carpentry and blacksmithy work and not to others. All occupations are followed strictly in accordance with the tradition. Indication of village interdependence and extension of the Kamin's services beyond one's own village is also seen when in absence of Kummaris in the semideveloped village, residents of that village obtain pots from the Kummaris of a nearby village.

In all the three villages the Kamins are attached to the Jajmans hereditarily as per the permanent allotment decided at the time of partition among the sons of a given Kamin. There is no periodical reallotment as reported by Bronger (1975), Raju (1979) and Benson (1976) in respect of Telangana villages. Among the families of Kamins, the women from Brahmin, Wadla, Kummari, Mangali and Madiga castes do not render any regular Jajmani services. They work occasionally during some festivals and religious functions and receive some gifts in return. It is the washer-women who bear the major brunt of the job of washing everyday while the men work during rituals.

The functioning of the Jajmani system also reveals the fact that the ex-untouchable Madigas were not served by the higher Kamin castes. In the three villages under study the Mangalis and Chakalis have recently started rendering services to the Madigas but in a modified form without totally violating the traditional principle of purity-pollution.

Dube (1955), Berreman (1962), Gould (1964) and Benson (1976) mentioned four types of payments to the Kamins. They are: (1) Semi-annual grain payments to a specialist engaged on a permanent basis; (2) Payments of cash or grain on a piece-work basis to a specialist permanently engaged; (3) Payments of cash, grain or both on a piece-work basis to any specialists; and (4) Exchange of services particularly among artisans. In the three villages under study all but the last practice are in existence.

It means that the service castes do not have a fixed mode of exchange; they make payments to one another in accordance with the nature and magnitude of services and the payments made are adjusted against the payments received. The payments for the ritual and non-ritual services are made periodically according to the tradition during the time of harvest and only some payments are made either in kind or in cash during or after the particular work or function is carried out. By and large, the mode and extent of payment are governed by custom though the status of the family and the amount of labour put in are duly considered and payments are accordingly adjusted. There is nothing like a written code as mentioned by Wiser (1936) and Lewis (1956) in connection with their studies in north Indian villages. The amount of payment either in kind or cash is on the increase over a period of time as a consequence of the growing cost of living. The extent of increase is again locally settled in an informal manner roughly taking the market value of grain into consideration.

PAYMENTS TO WADLA KAMIN

Jajmani annual payments are made on the basis of the number of ploughs used by the Jajman for cultivation each year. For each plough, there is a fixed payment in kind made during harvest. The amount paid also varies between the villages. While in the developed village, three-fourths (75 Kilograms) of a bag of paddy is paid for each plough, in the other two villages only half a bag of paddy is paid. However, a bundle of crop yielding about ten kilograms of paddy is also allowed in these two villages. This variation in payments in the villages is attributed to the variation in the intensity of cultivation in the villages and other factors.

In the developed village the carpenters are the upper caste Wadlas who follow their traditional occupation of carpentry together with blacksmithy. But in the other two villages, the carpentry work *is* done by the Madigas. Since the Wadla carpenter is also useful for certain other non-agricultural purposes, he is paid more than the Madiga carpenter whose services are not utilised on ritual occasions.

Further, the developed village, being situated on the road-side is subject to various kinds of outside influences. These are reflected in higher payments to the Kamins. In the interior villages the Kamins are more traditional and less demanding. Today, in all the villages agriculture and other occupations are slowly getting mechanised but naturally the road-side village is more mechanised than the others.

The big and medium ryots have started using engines for lifting water for irrigation, reducing the amount of work to be done by the carpenter for preparing and repairing the traditional water-lifting device, locally called *Mota.* But the carpenters engage themselves in other kinds of work such as preparation of wooden material for house construction and making household furniture. There is more such work in the developed village than in others and is done on daily cash- wage basis. The slowly increasing use of tractors is also reducing the traditional work of carpenters in the villages and consequently the farmers have started cutting the payments made to Kamins. In view of the growing need for men with new skills in modern technology, skilled technicians are finding a place in the three villages, more so in the developed village followed by the semi-developed village.

Payments to Madiga Kamin

Madiga is another Kamin whose services are essential to all agriculturists. According to traditional practice, payments to the Madiga were also made on the basis of the number of ploughs the Jajman used for cultivation every year. The Madiga removed dead cattle, tanned the hides and prepared leather goods such as *chappals* and pipes for lifting water from the wells. Some amount of grain (one-fourth bag)was also being paid towards preparation of chappals and water-lifting pipes.

But now the Madiga is paid annually, item-wise, a fixed amount of grain for the supply and repair of a particular item of leather used for cultivation. Since the rich and medium farmers have taken to lift-irrigation with the aid of engines, the use of leather pipes and consequently the work of Madigas got minimised.

About two decades ago, a little bit of the standing crop used to be left out for the Madigas who in turn used to protect the harvest till the grain was threshed and taken home. But now this practice has totally disappeared in the three villages. In the developed village, the dead cattle are now sold to the nearby leather factory, whereas this new practice has not yet been fully adopted in the other two villages, one of the reasons being lack of communication and transport facilities between these two villages and the leather factory. The Kamin Madiga continues to have the responsibility of setting up the funeral pyre whenever there is a death in the village.

Payments to Chakali Kamin

The traditional practice, among agriculturists and non-agriculturists, of using the services of Chakalis for washing and other ritual services generally continues in all three villages. In fact greater use of Chakalis during rituals is reported in the developed village than in the other villages.

This is because the Jajmans of Kamma caste in the developed village are more affluent and can afford to pay more and enjoy the facility of more services from the Chakali. This is indicative of a strange relationship between increasing economic status and the desire to use Kamins more for ritual services through increasing adoption of Sanskritised practices, notwithstanding the decline in the purity-pollution aspect.

Otherwise, the normal mode of the Chakali's services continues to be the same in all three villages. It is largely the Chakali women who continue the hereditary practice of doing the everyday laundry work while their menfolk take to any other occupation which suits their skills, abilities and convenience. Hence, more men from the Chakali caste seem to be moving into other occupations.

Payment is made (for the daily sevice of washing of clothes) according to the number of adult members in each family. If there are more children, due consideration is given to the fact while making payments. For ritual services, traditional payments are made but since the rich can afford it they take more services and pay more than the minimum required. Payments for day-to-day laundry work are mainly in kind (grain + food), and payments for ritual services are mainly in cash and partly in kind (grain + food + clothes).

In the developed village, laundries have come up on the main roads and are open throughout the day and any one, irrespective of his caste, can enter the shop and have the clothes washed. Under the traditional Jajmani system, ex-untouchables were denied the services of the Chakali but the Chakalis have now started washing the clothes of ex-untouchables though they do not collect the soiled clothes from their houses as is done in the case of other Jajmans. Once the clothes are handed over to him by the ex-untouchable, the Chakali directly goes to the laundry place, washes clothes, and then takes a bath signifying the act of purification.

The customary carriage of couples in palanquins is gradually ceasing to be a part of the celebration of marriage among all caste groups, and this would mean that the Chakalis are giving up the traditional job of palanquin-bearing.

Payments to Mangali Kamin

It is a matter of prestige for the elderly rich to have their hair cut in their houses and the Mangali Kamins continue to perform this service. Though some youths use razors or visit the roadside saloons for their haircuts, this traditional work of the Mangalis has not significantly reduced. Mangali services are still used in rituals.

The richer the Jajman, the greater the use made of the services of the Mangali for rituals and ceremonial occasions. Payments for traditional services are based on the number of adults in each family. Some Mangalis also run modern saloons on the road-side, thus adding to their income.

Naturally, there are more saloons in the developed village than in the interior villages. While under the traditional Jajmani system the Mangali visits the houses of Jajmans only in the forenoon to cut hair or shave, this work is done through the day in the saloons on cash payment. Since the women-folk of the Mangalis are free throughout the day and many men are free in the afternoon, the Mangalis are now taking to tenant cultivation in larger numbers.

Under the traditional Jajmani system, the Mangalis did not serve ex-untouchables, who either had barbers of their own caste or borrowed implements from the Mangalis to cut their own hair or have a shave. This discriminating practice is, however, gradually disappearing in all the three villages and more and more ex-untouchables have started visiting saloons where service is rendered irrespective of caste.

In a way, thus, the practice of untouchability is disappearing and the Mangalis as well as the Chakalis are rendering services to the ex-untouchables but in a modified form to console themselves that they still have a higher status in the village caste hierarchy. This explains the change in role-setting and the consequent change in role performance in the context of modernisation (Rao, M.S.A., 1977:295).

Payments to Kummari Kamin

Traditionally, the Kummari is a supplier of earthen utensils and a cook for the non-Dwija upper castes. Today, however, with aluminium utensils replacing earthen ones for cooking and storage purposes among all castes, the Kummari has lost much of his importance. The rich prefer brass or stainless steel. The Brahmins, traditionally, did not use earthen utensils for daily cooking and, even during ceremonies, used it minimally.

This was because it was believed that an earthen utensil used or touched by a non-Brahmin got polluted and, unlike metal utensils, could not be scrubbed for use again. However, earthen utensils are still used during certain ceremonies and festivals and this gives some work to the Kummari.

With the increasing change in the styles of performing marriages and other ceremonies and the preparation of new items of food, the culinary services of the Kummari continue to be used only by the poor or those who still prefer the traditional items of food.

This change is surprisingly evident in all the villages. The Kummaris as Kamins are thus becoming more and more insignificant and, naturally, the payments made to them on the basis of the number of utensils supplied each year is getting reduced in all the villages. Piece-rate payments are now increasingly preferred by the Kamins as well as the Jajmans. The Kummaris have also begun to take to other occupations since intensive use of land for agriculture has made it difficult to find mud for pot-making and firewood for baking the pots.

Payments to Brahmin Kamins

As household priests. Brahmins are Kamins. Traditionally, learned, and rich priests visited only Brahmins and other Dwijas (Kshatriyas and Vysyas) and the less learned served the peasant castes as well. Lower castes did not get the benefit of the Brahmin's services.

Today this situation is gradually changing and in all three villages those who can afford to make payments hire the services of the Brahmin priest The very low castes are still less Sanskritised and perform the festivals involving local nonSanskritised deities with non-Brahmin priests.

The ex-untouchables have their own priests. The more learned the Brahmin priest, the more is his attachment to the upper castes and accordingly the more are his earnings. Hence, in the developed village the two Brahmins who serve the poor are poorer than the Brahmin priests who serve the rich. There are no

Brahmin priests in the other two villages but they are served by some Brahmins from neighbouring villages. The Brahmin Kamin is not paid annually as are other Kamins.

He receives payment partly in kind and largely in cash at the time of each ceremony and the payments received by him are more than those received by other Kamins who render manual services. Normally the incomes of the priests increase during marriage seasons, but there is no guarantee that every year a marriage ceremony will be performed in the house of each Jajman.

Caste Panchayats among Kamins

Traditionally, the Kamin castes, other than the Brahmins, had their own caste panchayats which looked after the distribution of Jajmans among members of that caste. The panchayats adjudicated on specific cases brought to them either by the Jajmans or the Kamins. But these days the caste panchayats seem to function rarely, as complaints rarely reach them.

Normally, either the Kamin goes on strike or the Jajman refuses the services of the Kamin but, after a few days, they patch up their differences and reach an understanding. If the case becomes very serious, it is taken to the traditional village Panchayat for settlement.

The caste panchayat may lend a helping hand in this process. In the overall changing situation, neither the Kamin nor the Jajman seems to care much for the continuation of the relationship.

Once either of them decides to discontinue the relationship, a substitute Kamin is selected by the Jajman. This is indicative of the weakening Jajmani relationship. The instances of Kamins changing their traditional occupations and severing their relationship with the Jajmans are on the increase. When a traditional relationship breaks up, the first chance of serving a Jajman is given to the brothers of the erstwhile Kamin and only then to other relatives in accordance with the principle of genealogy and the traditional allotment of Jajmans.

Socio-economic Background of Kamins

Kamins largely depend upon Jajmani work but they also desire to own some land for better economic and social security. In the three villages tinder study, out of a total of 188 households of Kamins of all castes as many as 61 (32.4 per cent) possess land ranging from less than an acre to ten acres.

Contrary to expectation, more Kummaris own land, followed by Brahmins, Chakalis, Mangalis, Wadlas and Madigas. Of course, if the total amount of land owned by all the families in each Kamin caste is taken into consideration, Brahmins come first, followed, by Mangalis, Chakalis, Kummaris, Madigas and Wadlas.

Many non-Brahmin Kamin caste families do not own land and the Wadlas are the weakest in this respect. The job of Wadlas is such that it does not allow them time to supervise of take to agriculture.

The Brahmins, in line with the overall trend in the region, are losing land because of land reforms as also because of sale as a consequence of their migration to towns. Despite the talk of distribution of land to ex-untouchables, the Madigas continue to be without any land. It is, however, heartening to note that the Mangalis followed by the Chakalis continue to acquire more and more land.

In the three villages all the Kamins, barring Brahmins, have very little housing space. Today, the Madigas are in a better position in this respect because in every village the government has taken up the programme of distributing house-sites to Madiga and Mala ex-untouchables.

The non-Brahmin Kamin houses are largely thatched mud houses, while those of a majority of the Brahmins are pucca tiled houses though some are getting dilapidated for want of proper maintenance. A majority of the peasant Jajman castes in these three villages are rich and many own modern or pucca houses.

In terms of literacy, the Brahmins are far better off than the other Kamins, the least literate group being the Hindu Madigas. At any rate, barring Brahmins (100 per cent) and Kummaris (70 per cent), the literacy rate is less than 50 per cent among the Kamin castes.

The literacy rate among the Kamins varies between 52.1 per cent in the semi-developed village and 32.6 per cent in the less-developed village. The slightly higher percentage of literacy among the Kamins in the semi-developed village than in the developed village may be attributable to the higher literacy rate among the Christian Madigas in the former village.

Occupational Mobility among Kamins

To understand the special nature of occupational mobility among Kamins, who are followers of age-old, traditional occupations, a processual analysis of the pattern and extent of such mobility is helpful. In the three villages put together, 156 or 61 per cent of the 257 earning members of the Kamin castes now depend on occupations other than their traditional caste occupations as the primary source of livelihood.

Further, the greatest number of such earners belong to the Kummari caste, followed by the Brahmin, Madiga and Chakali castes. Only 31 per cent of the Wadla and Madiga carpenters have taken to occupations other than carpentry as the primary source of livelihood. Similarly, only 29 per cent of Mangalis follow occupations other than hair-cutting as their main occupations.

Putting all castes together, deviations are found in larger numbers in the developed village followed by the semi-developed and the less developed villages. However, the figures have to be interpreted cautiously. Almost all such earners from among the Brahmins and Madigas have ceased to follow their caste occupations.

A great majority of Kummaris and quite a good majority of the Chakalis still follow their caste occupations as secondary sources of livelihood. The given differential pattern of occupational mobility away from the traditional occupations explains the fact that no more do the Jajmans depend on the Kummaris and Madiga cobblers for their household utensils and agricultural goods respectively, because substitutes are available in the market.

However, many Kummaris still continue pottery as a secondary occupation because, despite a decline in the demand for earthen utensils, they continue to monopolise the occupation and all family members can finish the job together during slack seasons and thus serve their own and the villagers' needs. Many Brahmins have taken to other occupations as the primary ones because of their inclination to migrate to urban areas and settle in modern occupations.

In a village only a limited number of Brahmin priests can earn enough for livelihood provided they are prepared to visit Jajmans belonging to all castes; but, today, they seem to feel that continuing in the traditional occupation is degrading to their status and hence they are looking for other kinds of occupation.

The case of Chakalis is somewhat peculiar. The women are involved in the caste occupation of washing clothes everyday while the men have taken to other occupations and perform traditional services only occasionally. This explains why a greater percentage of Chakali households still follow their traditional occupation as a secondary source of income.

The lesser percentage of deviation from the traditional occupations among the Wadlas and Mangalis explains two different aspects of the problem. First, because of technological change the demand for traditional carpentry work is on the decline in the sphere of agriculture and, as a result, the bonds between them and the Jajmans are getting weaker.

Even though small peasants depend on the Wadlas, the relationship is not purely Jajmani in character. Yet, the Wadlas are in their traditional occupation in large numbers because their services are in demand in other fields such as house construction and preparation of furniture.

This is true also in the case of the Madiga carpenters in the semi-developed village who have been in carpentry for a long time. In the case of Mangalis, it has been found that they still hold a monopoly over their traditional occupation and as such there is a demand for them. Those who have time, have taken to secondary occupations, agriculture being preferred to others. In the developed village the Mangalis are going in for management of saloons on the road-side and this is becoming common among the educated youth.

On the whole, almost 40 per cent of earners from all the Kamin castes still follow caste occupations as primary ones. Others follow them as a secondary source. This shows an increasing trend of change in occupations. This change is gradual in that first they take to other occupations as secondary occupations and then, if they find them remunerative, they take to them as primary ones while continuing the caste occupations as secondary ones.

This is either because of the feeling that the skill acquired should be used or that the traditional occupation still has not become such a bad source of earning as to be abandoned altogether.

This behaviour is obviously rational and pragmatic in the given circumstances and opportunity structures. Another fact is that notwithstanding this differential pattern of change, the Kamin occupations continue to be the monopoly of the concerned castes without any perceptible breakdown.

While a person may be willing to take to agriculture or business or use his own traditional caste-occupational skill on a commercial basis, he is not prepared to do the job which is still considered to be either the legitimate right of the other caste and/or derogatory to his status. This behaviour is clearly visible among the castes such as the Brahmins Chakalis, Kummaris, Mangalis and Madiga cobblers.

Given the nature of economy and the social values of the village, this is understandable. However, there is no taboo as such for other castes to enter into occupations such as carpentry. There has been a slight change in recent times in the playing of marriage-music, the traditional monopoly of Mangalis in the three villages. In the semi-developed village, Chakalis have taken to the job of playing band-music since it is believed that there is no element of purity-pollution in band-playing. Carpentry and band-playing are thus treated on the same footing.

As for the intergenerational occupational mobility among the 257 earners, the sons of Kummaris top the list of deviants from their parental occupations with slight alterations in the ranking of the Brahmin, Madiga and Chakali caste in the three villages.

The carpenters fall in the fifth rank, and the Madigas in the sixth rank of deviants. An analysis of the pattern of occupational mobility among different age groups reveals that the deviation from caste occupation was more, in all the three villages, among those aged 30 or less than among the other age groups. However, in the developed village the variation was greater in the 31-50 years age-group, while in other villages it was greater in the age group of below 30 years.

This shows that in the developed village, people in the 31-50 age-group had exploited the opportunities for occupational change available to them when they were young, while in the other two villages which are developing only now it is the youth of today who are taking advantage of the opportunities that have become available in recent times. Hence, the more developed the village, the greater is the deviation from caste occupation. The chi-square test analysis highlights this. This variation is not, however, clear with regard to inter-generational mobility, possibly because while the variations are real they are not high enough to be confirmed through the chi-square test.

DEVELOPMENT THROUGH TECHNOLOGY

In view of the importance of industrialisation, the pattern of industrialisation adopted in developing countries is most relevant. Differences in the socio-economic environment of individual developing countries resulted in various industrialisation strategies.

However, regardless of the different industrialisation policies and practices of the individual developing countries, they have a common desire to generate national product, promote employment and secure the most dynamic possible modernisation, so as to secure a greater degree of technological and financial independence from the developed countries. The level and the features of the industrialisation of developing countries are usually determined by the individual country's resources, both material and human, and by its past experience of development.

The great dependence of the industrialisation processes in developing countries or developed countries, on technology transfer, capital investment, export markets, etc., has resulted in a high degree of exploitation and in unbalanced industrial structures which are highly sensitive to international economic fluctuations.

Thus, the introduction of new industries and changes. In the industrial structure of a developing country may profoundly and rapidly influence the overall economic structure. Such influences may bring about unexpected or unplanned changes unplanned and social life.

Developing countries often find it difficult to fully control the structural changes in their industries and thus avoid industrial instability and exploitation of the workforce. This may to some extent be possible for those countries which have large internal markets, strong public sectors, or were able to control investments in industrial development through generation of sufficient internal funds.

The industrialisation processes in developing countries have also been affected by transnational corporation from the developed countries, which often see industrial development in developing countries as a means of transferring obsolete and unclean technologies, or as a means of increasing profits through redeployment of labour-intensive industries. This has particularly affected the position of women, since their employment in the industrial sector has greatly increased, without, however, securing legally recognised working conditions, protection, remuneration, etc.

The share of women in industrial employment in developing countries rose from 21 per cent in 1960 to 26.5 per cent in 1980. About two thirds of the net increase in the female industrial workforce (the number of women employed in industry in the world increased by 104 per cent in the last two decades) took place in developing countries mainly in Asia. In contrast to Africa and Latin America, Asia has a higher share of the female than of the male world industrial labour force.

However, for an appropriate assessment of the improvements in the field as analysts of the qualitative aspects of such employment is needed.

Women are usually engaged in labour-intensive industries with low productivity (e.g. processing industries—textile, food, leather, etc.). Their wages are influenced by their poor bargining position, and they have no influence at all on working, conditions. Thus, for instance, although the working hours in manufacturing have generally tended to decline, in some developing countries working hours have tended to rise.

The treatment of the female labour force is to a large extent a reflection of women's low status on the labour market (reserve labour army), lack of proper education and training low or non-existent organisation, the lack of or non-implementation of protective legislation (particularly in export-oriented industries) and their generally unfavourable social position.

The recent upward trend in women's employment in developing countries is not very significant in relation to the absolute size of the female population or workforce in these countries. Moreover, although this increase is in some of the most modern industries in the world, it does not appear to have made a substantial difference to women status, since it has done little to break the isolation and discrimination of women in the industrial workforce.

The extension of the practice of subcontracting of home workers for certain stages of industrial production processes may have considerable counter-productive consequences, for women's formal employment. Such organisational changes may sometimes lead to a circumvention of legal protective measures for labour, a deterioration of working conditions, lower wages within and outside industry, greater exploitation of women's and children's labour, diminishing union activity and, in the long run, also to increased formal unemployment of both men and women.

While the short-term positive effects of income generation cannot be discounted, the negative effects of channelling or restricting women's employment to the informal sector make it considerably more difficult and could lead to a higher degree of isolation, exploitation and inequality of women, by excluding them from the mainstream of socio-economic activity. It is unlikely that the position of women in the industries of developing countries can be changed without changes in the models of industrial development and organisation of industrial production.

Therefore, formulation and implementation of national industrialisation policies based on the needs and interests of all strata of the population, as well as on an evaluation of domestic potentials continue to be priority tasks confronting developing countries.

The existing potentials of developing countries are certainly conducive to positive changes. Balanced development planning and policies which aim at maximum utilisation of national resources and at an expansion of domestic demand are also the proper framework for the advancement of the role of women in this sector of the economic and for promotion within overall development.

To improve women's position in industry, a number of measures would have to be incorporated in the industrial policies of developing countries:

- changes in education, which would enable women to improve their position in industrial employment, and to acquire transferable skills through various forms of vocational and informal training;
- legal arrangements covering all aspects of industrialisation, from investment codes to regulations, which would provide for better general treatment of labour in industry. In this connection, there should be regulatory measures in free exporting zones to ensure that social costs are also covered. However, it must be recognised that collective action by the developing countries is needed for the successful legislation and implementation of such measures;
- extention of employment opportunities in accordance with human resources development policies;
- adoption of technologies which ensure stability of employment and professional progress to women workers;
- establishment of overall social control and of schemes for genuine workers' participation in management and decision making;
- elaboration of criteria for determining the size of enterprises in various industrial branches and the ways of organising them; promotion of small and medium-size enterprises in developing countries; establishment of industrial cooperatives;

- selection, development and transfer of technology and know-how as well as training of personnel;
- strengthening of self-reliance in industrial policy through industrial cooperation among developing countries, exchange of information and experience through ECDC/TCDC programmes and projects.

This would improve the bargaining position of developing countries *vis-a-vis* developed ones, particularly in case of transfer of technology or foreign investment, in enforcement of national legal mechanisms for the protection of the industrial labour force, including women workers. All this calls for urgent action among developing countries in the field of industrialisation.

Bibliography

Abbasayulu, Y. B.: *Scheduled Caste Elite,* Hyderabad, Osmania University, 1978.

Ainapur, L. S.: *Dynamics of Caste Relations in Rural India,* Jaipur, Rawat Publications, 1986.

Ankit Prasad: *Social Welfare and Social Action : YMCA at Work,* Mittal, Delhi, 2005.

Bandopadhyay Arun : *Tribes, Forest and Social Formation in Indian History,* Manohar, Delhi, 2004.

Bandura, A.: *Social Learning and Personality Development,* New York, Holt, Rinehart, and Winston, 1963.

Bhatt, Anil: *Caste, Class and Politics: An Emperical Profile of Social Stratification in Modern India,* Delhi, Manhohar Book Service, 1975.

Brass, P. : *Ethnic Groups and the State,* Totowa, Barnes and Noble, 1985.

Brussa, L.: *Survey on Prostitution, Migration and Traffic in Women: History and Current Situation,* Strasbourg, Council of Europe, 1991.

Carsten, F. L. : *The Rise of Fascism,* London, Methuen and Co., 1967.

Clough, John E.: *Social Christianity in the Orient. The story of a man, a mission and a movement,* New York, The Macmillan Company, 1914.

Cohan, B. N.: *The Changing Status of a Depressed Class,* Chicago, The University of Chicago Press, 1955.

Damon, William: *Social and Personality Development: Infancy through Adolescence,* New York, Norton, 1983.

Devi A. Sailaja : *Socio Economic Conditions of Tribes,* Sonali, Delhi, 2005.

Dietrich, Gabriele: *Dalit Movements and Women's Movement,* Horizons India Books, New Delhi, 1992.

Dube, S.C.: *Indian Village,* London: Routledge & Kegan Paul, 1955.

Dumont, Louis: *Homo hierarchicus. The caste system and its implications,* Chicago, University of Chicago Press, 1980.

Epstein, T. Scarlett: *Economic development and social change in South India,* Manchester, Manchester university Press, 1962.

Farquhar, J.N.: *Modern Religious Movements in India,* Munshiram, New Delhi, 1967.

Farquhar, J.N.: *Modern Religious Movements in India,* Munshiram, New Delhi, 1967.

Gorhe, Neelam: *Social Development and Dalit Women,* Gyan Pub. House, New Delhi, 1995.

Hajira Kumar : *Social Work, Social Development and Sustainable Development,* Regency, Delhi, 1997.

Jaya Chakravarty: *Media and Women's Development*, Sarup, Delhi, 2007.

Kenneth, R.: *Social, Emotional, and Personality Development*, New York, Wiley, 1998.

Kosambi, D. D. : *The Culture and Civilisation of Ancient India in Historical Outline*, London, Routledge and Kegan Paul, 1956.

Kumar, Hajira : *Social Work, Social Development and Sustainable Development*, Regency, Delhi, 1997.

Maheshwari, Shriram: *Rural Development in India: A Public Policy Approach*, New Delhi, Sage, 1995.

Mallik, Suneila: *Social Integration of the Scheduled Castes*, New Delhi, Abhinav, 1979.

Marriott, McK: *Structure and Change in Indian Society*, Chicago, Aldine, 1968.

Misra Pramod : *Ecology, Culture and Health : A Primitive Tribe*, Serials Pub, Delhi, 2004.

Mitchiner, John E.: *Traditions of the seven Rsis*, Delhi, Motilal Banarsidas 1982.

Oppert, Gustav: *The original inhabitants of Bharatavarsa or India*, Westminster, Constable, 1893.

Patel, Arjun: *Dalits in Modern India*, New Delhi, Vistaar, 1999.

Patwardhan, Sunanda: *Change Among India's Harijans: Maharashtra a Case Study*, New Delhi, Orient Longmans, 1973.

Rao, M. S. A.: *Social Movement and Social Transformation: A Study of Backward Class Movement*, New Delhi, Macmillian Press, 1978.

Robb, Peter: *Dalit Movements and the Meanings of Labour in India*, New Delhi, Oxford University Press, 1993.

Sarkar, J.: *Caste, Occupation and Change*, Delhi, B. R. Publishing Co., 1984.

Satyanarayana, K.: *A study of the history and culture of India*, New Delhi, People's Publishing House, 1983.

Seidman, Steven: *Liberalism and the Origins of European Social Theory*, Berkeley, University of California Press, 1983.

Shah, G.: *Social Movements in India: A Review of Literature*, New Delhi, Sage, 1990.

Sharma, K. L.: *Caste, Class and Social Movements*, Rawat Publications, Jaipur, 1986.

Silverberg, James: *Social Mobility in the Caste System in India*, Mouton Publishers, The Hague, 1968.

Throsby, David, *Economics and Culture*, Cambridge University Press, 2001.

Weber, M.: *The Theory of Social and Economic Organizations*, New York, Oxford University Press, 1947.

Whitehead, Henry: *The village gods of India*. Calcutta, Association Press, 1921.

Index

❑❑❑